CALVIN'S
CALVINISM

CALVIN'S CALVINISM

God's Eternal Predestination and Secret Providence
together with
A Brief Reply
and
Reply to the Slanderous Reports

by John Calvin

translated from the Latin by Henry Cole

SECOND EDITION
edited by Russell J. Dykstra

Reformed Free Publishing Association
Jenison, Michigan

© 2009 "Historical Introduction to
*God's Eternal Predestination and
Secret Providence*" and "Historical
Introduction to *A Brief Reply* and
Reply to the Slanderous Reports,"
by Russell J. Dykstra

1856, *Calvin's Calvinism* published in England
by the translator, Henry Cole

1927, *Calvin's Calvinism* of 1856 reprinted by the
Sovereign Grace Union, London, England,
as SGU Publication No. 150

1987, reprinted by the Reformed Free Publishing
Association, Grand Rapids, Michigan, as a first edition

2009, second edition published by the Reformed
Free Publishing Association, Jenison, Michigan,
with added historical introductions written by
Russell J. Dykstra, editor

Reformed Free Publishing Association
1894 Georgetown Center Drive
Jenison MI 49428-7137 USA

Phone:	616-457-5970
Fax:	616-457-5980
Website:	www.rfpa.org
Email:	mail@rfpa.org

ISBN 978-0-916206-88-8
LCCN 2008930494

Nay but, O man, who art thou
that repliest against God?
Shall the thing formed say to him that formed it,
Why hast thou made me thus?

— THE APOSTLE PAUL

Paul, comparing man with God, as he here does,
shows that the counsel of God in electing and reprobating men
is without doubt more profound and more deeply concealed
than the human mind can penetrate.
Therefore, O man, consider . . . who and what thou art,
and concede more to God
than the measure and compass of thine own nature . . .
But when you hear of a mystery that surpasses all human understanding,
you may immediately conclude that all solutions of men
derived from common natural judgment,
which might avail in a profane court of justice,
are frivolous and vain.

—JOHN CALVIN

Let us, then, understand the calling whereby they become elected
—not those who are elected because they have believed,
but who are elected that they may believe.
For the Lord himself also sufficiently explains this calling
when he says, "Ye have not chosen me, but I have chosen you."

— AUGUSTINE, BISHOP OF HIPPO

CONTENTS

PART TWO

EDITOR'S PREFACE

"*Calvin's Calvinism*—This definitive title is prefixed to the present publication advisedly and purposely, as embodying in its expression the nature of the original works of the immortal Genevese Reformer, and also the object of the present translation. The originals are Calvin's testimony and real mind concerning the doctrines of God's electing, predestinating and sovereign grace; while his own exposition and expression of his faith therein satisfactorily evince and beautifully manifest the spirit in which he held and taught those divine and sublime doctrines."

So begins the "Translator's Preface" of Reverend Henry Cole to the first English edition of these works of Calvin, printed in 1856. Cole rightly identifies their significance in that "they are the only productions of Calvin which he devoted expressly, exclusively and purposely, to the exposition and defence of the sublime doctrines of electing, predestinating and persevering grace."

In 1987 the Reformed Free Publishing Association (RFPA) published an edition of *Calvin's Calvinism* identical to the Sovereign Grace Union's British edition, except for the addition of an index of scriptural texts cited. Faced with the need to reprint this book, the RFPA decided to retypeset it and to make some minor changes in spelling, punctuation, paragraph length, insertion of headings, and such like. More scriptural references were noted in the body of the works, and the index expanded accordingly.

However, two changes in the book are worthy of note. The first change involves the main treatise on God's sovereign predestination and secret providence. The original English edition divided the main treatise into two parts according to subject matter—the first part on predestination, and the second on providence. Since Calvin wrote both parts as one treatise, this edition puts the two parts back together. Second, because knowledge of the historical setting of a writing is helpful for a full understanding of it, the RFPA added brief historical introductions to the documents that make up this volume.

As Henry Cole noted already many years ago, one can find "many different shades, phases, kinds and degrees of Calvinism." Scholars today go so far as to claim that John Calvin would not endorse the Calvinism set forth in the Canons of Dordrecht. At best, such "Calvinists" pay lip service to Calvin's theology of God's absolute sovereignty. Many reject it outright. This volume demonstrates that a true follower of Calvin will wholeheartedly maintain the sovereignty of God both in double predestination and in providence.

Part One

Historical Introduction to
God's Eternal Predestination and Secret Providence

J ohn Calvin wrote this treatise on the related doctrines of eternal predestination and the providence of God during his second stay in Geneva. It is the fruit of many years of study and presents Calvin's mature convictions on the doctrine of predestination. The immediate occasion was the Genevan pastors' battle with Jerome Bolsec over these doctrines. The treatise was published in January of 1552, shortly after the Genevan city council expelled Bolsec from Geneva for promoting heresy. Although this was from the pen of Calvin, it had the united support of the Genevan pastors. For this reason this work also has the name *Consensus Genevensis*, or the "Consent of the Pastors of the Church in Geneva." Calvin dedicated the treatise to the rulers of Geneva because they had stood for the vitally important truth of predestination.

As Calvin indicates, the treatise answers objections to sovereign, double predestination as well as to the sovereignty of God in providence. Calvin takes specific aim at the errors promoted by three men, one of whom he deliberately left unnamed.

Albert Pighius is the first identified enemy of the truth whom Calvin refutes in this work. Pighius, who hailed from Kampen, the Netherlands, was a Roman Catholic theologian with some high connections. He studied under the fellow Dutchman who would later be elected pope (Adrian VI, 1552–1553, a vigorous opponent of Luther). Pighius followed Adrian to Rome. Two subsequent popes (Clement VII and Paul III) commissioned Pighius to represent the papacy on various tasks.

Pighius attacked Luther and especially Calvin on the doctrine of the bondage of the will. In 1542 Pighius wrote a work of ten "books," or chapters, entitled *Ten Books on Human Free Choice and Divine Grace*. The first six books are a defense of the position that fallen man has a free will. The last four books attacked sovereign predestination and included the doctrine of God's sovereignty in providence. Calvin answered the first six books in 1543 in the work *Defense of the Sound and Orthodox Doctrine of the Bondage and Liberation of Human Choice against the Misrepresentations of Albert Pighius of Kampen*.[1]

Calvin intended to write a refutation of the last four books of Pighius on providence and predestination, but Pighius died unexpectedly, and Calvin dropped his plans to write more. As he explains in the opening paragraph of his treatise, he does not wish to "insult a dead dog."

God providentially determined, however, that the issue of predestination would not die out without a solid treatment from the pen of John Calvin. Various others strove to lift up the heretical banner of Pighius, one of whom was a certain Georgius of Sicily. Little is known about this man other than what Calvin mentions in the treatise itself. Georgius was a Roman Catholic monk whose books attacking predestination caused a stir in Italy. Thus, in spite of his disparagement of the abilities of Georgius and his arguments, Calvin felt compelled to devote some of this treatise to refuting this man's arguments.

It was, however, a controversy stirred up by an unnamed foe, that some nine years after Pighius died became the immediate occasion for publishing this treatise. Calvin refused even to identify the man. His name was Jerome Bolsec. A native of Paris, Bolsec had once joined the contemplative order of Carmelite monks, but he forsook it and left the church of Rome about 1545. He married and

---

1. Baker Books in Grand Rapids, Michigan, published a translation of this work in 1996 with the title *The Bondage and Liberation of the Will*. This treatise of Calvin is highly recommended.

established himself as a physician. In this capacity he came to Geneva in 1550. However, he began to express disagreement publicly with the doctrine of predestination. *The Register of the Company of Pastors of Geneva* records that in May of 1551 the pastors "summoned into their presence M. Jerome Bolsec, a physician, who held certain mistaken opinions concerning free will and predestination, and sternly reprimanded him, adducing passages of Scripture. Jerome, however, showed himself most obstinate until the passage from Ezekiel was read to him."[2] Subsequent events would reveal that Bolsec was not at all changed in his convictions. Five months later he stood up in a public, weekday meeting in which the pastor, Saint-Andre, had expounded John 8:47 ("He that is of God heareth God's words") and "began once again to put forward his false propositions concerning election and reprobation."[3]

Bolsec's propositions were not minor errors, striking as they did at the heart of salvation by sovereign grace. He insisted that election and reprobation were not decrees from eternity. Bolsec maintained that election and reprobation were simply decrees of God based on whether or not the people would believe or reject the gospel. He charged that those who taught eternal predestination made God to be a tyrant and an idol. In addition, this doctrine, he declared, made God the author of sin. He went so far as to insist that certain passages of Scripture had been corrupted by translators in order to support sovereign predestination!

Calvin had, unknown to Bolsec, come into the aforementioned public meeting. He stood up, refuted Bolsec, and ably demonstrated the truth of sovereign predestination. Bolsec was unmoved. For his public defamation of the pastors and his blasphemy, Bolsec was arrested, to be tried before the city council.

---

2. *The Register of the Company of Pastors of Geneva in the Time of Calvin*, ed. and trans. Philip E. Hughes (Grand Rapids: Wm. B Eerdmans, 1966), 132. The particular passage in Ezekiel is not identified.

3. *Register*, 137. Additional details of his teaching and trial are found on pages 137–184.

In the ensuing trial, Bolsec was equivocal and evasive, but unrepentant. He boldly claimed the protection of the city of Berne. He demanded that letters be written to the pastors in other cities and promised to abide with their verdict. In fact, letters were sent to the other Swiss churches, such as Basel, Zurich, and Berne, containing Bolsec's written answers to the pastors' questions. The Genevan pastors' cover letter demonstrates the right concern they had for all the churches, as they wrote (after summarizing the charges), "Now we desire that our church should be rid of this pestilent person, but in such a way that he does not become injurious to our neighbors."[4]

The replies from the other churches were disappointingly weak. While affirming their belief in predestination, with emphasis on election, the other Swiss pastors urged moderation and a measure of tolerance. The view generally held was that this doctrine was so profound and mysterious that Bolsec ought not to be condemned as a heretic. Only the letter from Neuchatel, written by the stalwart Farel, expressed wholehearted agreement with the predestination taught by Calvin and urged Geneva "to condemn the impious and sacrilegious Jerome."[5]

The outcome of the trial was that the city council banished Jerome Bolsec from Geneva on December 23, 1551, under penalty of being whipped if he returned. Bolsec left for the region of Berne, where he openly reviled Calvin as a heretic and an antichrist. He did all in his power to turn the sentiment of the preachers and the government of Berne against Calvin, with no little success. He would later return to the Roman Catholic Church. From those safe confines, he wrote vile and slanderous "biographies," first of Calvin and subsequently of Beza. Opposition—sometimes violent—to the doctrines of predestination and providence remained in Geneva even after the expulsion of Bolsec. Continued controversy induced

---

4. Letter dated January 1552, in *Selected Works of John Calvin: Tracts and Letters*, ed. Jules Bonnet, trans. David Constable, vol. 5 (Grand Rapids: Baker Book House, 1983), 331–334.

5. *Register*, 183.

Calvin to publish this treatise shortly after Bolsec was condemned. Calvin informed Bullinger in a private letter, "The dishonesty of that worthless wretch [Bolsec]...induced me to publish...what remained of my reply to Pighius on *Predestination*."[6]

In the introductory "Consent of the Pastors," Calvin declares his intent not to print so much as the *name* of Bolsec. He writes,

> Satan, the father of all strifes, has subtlely introduced, by means of a certain worthless person, a wide-spreading error and has attempted to root out our doctrine, which is drawn from the pure word of God, and to shake the faith of the people. But since this hungry hunter after vainglory wishes to gain notoriety out of the very flames of the temple of God, lest he should catch that reward of his unholy audacity for which he has laid his nets, let his name be buried under our silence, while we leave it purposely unmentioned.

Calvin adds, later, that it is not necessary to refute this "person," since he draws on Pighius and Georgius for his errors anyway. Besides, Calvin reasons, the refutation of Bolsec has already been made in the proper place and time, before the council. Calvin determined to answer Pighius and Georgius because they had written books on the issue, which books ought to be answered in print.

Calvin suffered immensely in consequence of this bold stand for the truth of sovereign, double predestination. A close friend in Geneva, who employed Bolsec as his family physician, forsook Calvin and left Geneva. There were ministers in Swiss churches outside of Geneva who publicly reproached Calvin in speeches and sermons, rejecting his teaching on predestination. Still others, closer friends like Bullinger and Melanchthon, made it known that they did not agree with the handling of Bolsec. At best, these ministers failed to recognize the central importance of predestination in the body of truth; at worst, they doubted the truth of predesti-

---

6. Letter dated January 1552 in *Selected Works*, 331–334.

nation. And in Geneva the false charges of Bolsec were echoed in the homes and taverns: "Calvin makes God the author of sin!" Vile and noxious reproaches were heaped upon him. More than five years after the publishing of this treatise, Calvin wrote in his preface to the Psalms that he had experienced much of what the psalmist wrote in his affliction. "The trial of these five years," he said, "was grievous and hard to bear; but I experienced not less excruciating pain from the malignity of those who ceased not to assail myself and my ministry with their envenomed calumnies."[7] And, "because I affirm and maintain that the world is managed and governed by the secret providence of God, a multitude of presumptuous men rise up against me, and allege that I represent God as the author of sin."[8]

In the face of such opposition, Calvin did not yield; rather, he more clearly set forth these truths of God's sovereignty. God kept him faithful. Calvin exhorted and admonished his friends. He rebuked his enemies. He taught the people in Geneva. And in this treatise, he continues to teach us.

RUSSELL J. DYKSTRA
Professor of New Testament and Church History
Theological School of the Protestant Reformed Churches
Grandville, Michigan, USA

---

7. A *calumny* is a deliberate misrepresentation maliciously calculated to damage another's reputation. It is also a deliberate misrepresentation of someone's doctrine in order to blacken it and to turn people away from believing and confessing it. Calvin later writes that "your malicious purpose is to root out every doctrine of that holy religion that the sacred oracles of God reveal and teach."

8. John Calvin, *Commentary on the Book of Psalms*, trans. James Anderson, vol. 1 (Grand Rapids: Wm. B. Eerdmans Publishing Company, 1949), xlv–xlvi.

The Consent of the Pastors of the Church in Geneva

The pastors of the church of Christ in Geneva pray that God would grant to those most excellent men, their supreme lords, and to the Syndics and Senate of Geneva, a just and holy administration of the State and all happy prosperity and success.

The same motive which impelled us to write this book, most excellent sirs, constrained us also to dedicate it to you that it might go forth under your name and auspices. The free election of God, by which he adopts unto himself whom he will out of the lost generation of men, has hitherto been publicly declared by us in this city with all reverence, sobriety, and sincerity and has been peacefully received by the people. But now Satan, the father of all strifes, has subtlely introduced, by means of a certain worthless person, a widespreading error and has attempted to root out our doctrine, which is drawn from the pure word of God, and to shake the faith of the people. But since this hungry hunter after vainglory wishes to gain notoriety out of the very flames of the temple of God, lest he should catch that reward of his unholy audacity for which he has laid his nets, let his name be buried under our silence, while we leave it purposely unmentioned.[9]

Since the trouble that this vain mortal endeavored to cause us reaches unto you also, it is just that you should partake of the blessed fruit that God brings out of it. And as we have ever found you strenuous and hearty defenders of our holy cause, we have felt

---

9. As pointed out in the "Historical Introduction" to the treatise, the reference is almost certainly to Jerome Bolsec.

it to be our duty to testify our gratitude with all our ability. The performance of this our duty will also plainly testify what that doctrine is that you have protected by your favor and authority. Although it becomes neither the rulers of the state nor the ministers of Christ to be too anxious about rumors and tumults and although all insidious revilings (which are generally lost by degrees in the noise they make) should be despised with fortitude and an exalted mind, both by rulers and ministers of Christ, it is of the utmost importance that the great reality of the matter should ever be kept in the hands and (as engraven on public tablets) before the eyes of all so that the plain statement of it may condemn and stop the false tongues of the foolish, the vain, or the wicked, and at the same time repress the frivolous whispers of the people in general.

There was spread abroad in many places a rumor that this vain person was severely bound in prison, whereas he was perfectly free and openly flying about the city every day. And with what malignity some virulent ones imagined and stated that we wished him to be put to death, you are yourselves our best witnesses. To refute such calumnies until they shall have vanished by contempt and tranquil magnanimity is the becoming duty of gravity and prudence.

However, lest some unstable ones should be moved, serious care must be taken to set forth plainly before all the real state of the case and cause at issue. This is no less expedient than a solemn duty on our part, for iniquity, unless it be resolutely met, makes its creeping way, says Paul, "like a canker" [2 Tim. 2:17]. This defense, which we offer to all the godly, will we hope be a strong and effectual remedy to those who are healable and will serve also as a wholesome antidote to the sound and the whole. And the subject itself is one to which the children of God should devote their most studious attention, that they become not ignorant of their heavenly birth and origin. For some fools, because the gospel is called "the power of God unto salvation to everyone that believeth" [Rom. 1:16], would blot out under this pretext the election of God; whereas it ought to have entered into the minds of such to think from whence faith comes. Scripture everywhere proclaims aloud that God gives to his Son those who were ever his, that he calls those whom he has chosen, that those whom he has adopted for sons he begets by his Spirit, and that the men believe whom he has taught within and to whom his "arm is revealed" [Isa. 53:1]. Therefore, whoever shall hold faith to be the earnest and pledge of adoption will assuredly confess that faith flows from divine election as its eternal source. And yet the knowledge of salvation is not to be sought from the secret counsel of God. Life is set before us in Christ, who not only makes himself known in the gospel, but also presents himself for our enjoyment. Into this mirror let the eye of our faith ever fixedly look. Let it not desire to penetrate where access to its sight is not given.

Since this is the right way, let the children of God walk therein, lest by winging their flight higher than is lawful, they plunge themselves deeper into a labyrinth than they would wish to find themselves. But as there is none other gate into the kingdom of heaven than faith in Christ, as contained in the promises of the gospel openly set before us, so it must be the greatest ignorance not to acknowledge that the eyes of our minds are opened by God, for he chose us unto faith in Christ before we were conceived in the womb. Yet, that the object of this impure and abandoned one was not only to blot out all knowledge of God's election from the minds of men, but also to overturn his power is clearly manifest from those mad dreams of his that you possess in your public records, written with his own hand, wherein he asserts that faith does not depend on election, but that election stands in faith, and that none remain in blindness on account of the inborn corruption of nature, seeing that all men are rightly enlightened of God and that we do a great injustice to God when we declare that those are passed by of him whom he deigns not to illumine by his Spirit.

This worthless being also maintains that all men, generally and equally, are "drawn" of God [John 6:44]; that there is no difference, except where resistance begins it; and that when God promises to make "hearts of flesh" [Ezek. 11:19] out of "hearts of stone" [Ezek. 36:26], nothing else is meant than his making us capable of receiving the grace of God, and this capability, or the being made capable, extends without distinction to the whole human race, whereas Scripture most clearly affirms that this is the peculiar privilege of the church of God.

As to the providence of God by which the world is ruled, all the godly ought ever to confess and hold fast that there is no reason that men should make God a sharer in their sins or in any way involve him with themselves in a participation of their fault. Scripture teaches that the reprobate are also instruments of the wrath of God, by some of whom he instructs the faithful unto patience and on others of whom, as his enemies, he inflicts the punishments they deserve, but this profane trifler contends that no act of God is just, but what lies as a plain reason before our eyes. Thus doing away with all difference between remote and proximate and immediate causes, he will not allow the severe afflictions laid on Job to be considered the work of God lest he should be made equally guilty with the devil and the Chaldean and Sabean plunderers.

Passing by this fellow in silence, the reason we enter into the battle with the other two—Albertus Pighius and Georgius the Sicilian—is, as we will explain, twofold. This ignorant pettifogger could bring forth nothing but what he obtained from these two sources, and so would make what was bad in them worse and worse. To contend with him, therefore, would have been a contest cold and profitless. Let our readers be content with one proof. With what cavils Pighius and Georgius would darken the first chapter of Paul to the Ephesians has been shown in its proper place. They indeed were ignorant and disgusting, but the folly of this worthless being is fouler still, for he blushed not to babble his nonsense in your Senate and venerable assembly, and not only this, but he dared to defend with pertinacity what he had thus blattered in folly. He maintained that Paul was not speaking in Ephesians 1 concerning the common salvation of the godly, but showing only that he and his fellow laborers were elected to the apostolic office. To disprove so futile a figment would be but a moment's work, seeing it is still fresh in your memories. If any are willing to put themselves under such a teacher as this, they must be content to learn a miserable theology indeed, which would deprive nearly all men of a confidence in eternal life, for, according to it, the apostles alone could be partakers of divine adoption, could alone be reconciled to Christ, could alone be blessed, and could alone be joined to the company of the saints. But the place and time for the refutation of the vain figment in question was where and when it occurred. To refute so insipid an animal by a published book would not perhaps be so desirable and agreeable, for you are not ignorant how conceited he is, nor need it be a matter of wonder that a man who could throw off his monk's cowl and immediately transform himself into a physician should be a person of such consummate audacity. But to nauseate many by pleasing him with an answer of folly "according to his folly" [Prov. 26:5] would be somewhat foreign to my usual moderation. Further, since those two characters are known and professed enemies of the gospel, and one of them in attacking Calvin by name has proclaimed war with us and this church, it has seemed much better that the poison of the impious doctrine that has been spread abroad in their published books should be purged away altogether, than that their absurdities should be further propagated, which would better remain buried out of knowledge. Moreover, it would be utterly tiresome to wear out the ears of men, already fatigued and tormented with such superfluous contentions.

Noble and excellent sirs, may God grant that, as you have hitherto done with the highest praise, you may go on unto the end to defend, by your unwearied faith and authority, the pure doctrine of the gospel of Christ, which is attacked on every side by the angry violence of the world; and that you may never cease to receive under your protecting care all the godly who flee to your protection so that your city may ever be a sanctuary devoted to God and a faithful asylum for the members of Christ, remaining immovable amid these horrid tumults. Thus shall you ever find God to be an everlasting guardian of your safety, for whatever dwelling place of man is dedicated to him shall abide safe under his power and shall never fall.

JOHN CALVIN
January 1, 1552

God's Eternal Predestination and Secret Providence

Calvin's Opponents and Their Theses

Nine years have now elapsed since Albertus Pighius the Campanian, a man of evidently frenzied audacity, attempted at the same time and in the same book to establish the free will of man and to subvert the secret counsel of God by which he chooses some to salvation and appoints others to eternal destruction. But as he attacked me by name, that through my side he might stab holy and sound doctrine, I have deemed it necessary to curb the sacrilegious madness of the man. At that time, however, being distracted by various engagements, I could not embrace in one short space of time the discussion of both subjects, but having published my thoughts upon the former, I promised to consider, when an opportunity should be given, the doctrine of predestination. Shortly after my book on free will appeared, Pighius died. That I might not insult a dead dog, I turned my attention to other serious matters. From that time until now I have always found plenty to do. Moreover, as I had already copiously treated of this great point of doctrine, had set it forth clearly, and confirmed it by solid testimonies of Scripture, this new labor upon it did not seem so absolutely necessary, but it might safely be suffered to rest for a time.

Since at the present day certain maddened and exulting spirits strive with all their might, after the example of Pighius, to destroy all that is contained in the Scriptures concerning the free election of the godly and the eternal judgment of the reprobate, I have considered it my duty to prevent this contagion from spreading farther by collecting and summarily refuting those frivolous objections by which such men delude themselves and others. Among these characters, there started forth in Italy a certain one, Georgius, a Sicilian, an ignorant man indeed and more worthy of contempt than public notice in any form were it not that a notoriety, obtained by fraud and imposture, has given him considerable power to do mischief. For when he was a monk, he remained unknown in his cell until Lucius Abbas, one of the Tridentine fathers, raised him on high by a lying commendation, hoping that he himself should be able, from the shoulders of his favorite, to take a flight into heaven itself. This abandoned fellow, having mendaciously given it out that Christ had appeared to him and appointed him an interpreter of the whole Scripture, persuaded many, without much trouble, to believe with a stupid, shameless, and more than vain folly what he had thus published. And that he might push the drama to the last act, he so trumpeted forth his insane visions that he rendered his ignorant adherents, already fast bound by prejudice, perfectly astonished. And certain it is that the greater part of men in our day are worthy of just such prophets. For the hearts of most of them, hardened and rendered obstinate by wickedness, will receive no healing; while the ears of others are ever itching with the insatiable desire of depraved speculations. There are, perhaps, others who are exceptions and whom we might mention willingly and becomingly, but we will leave them unmentioned, resolving to make all our readers see and understand how frivolous and worthless are the objections of all the enemies of the truth.

I propose now to enter into the sacred battle with Pighius and George the Sicilian, a pair of unclean beasts, by no means badly matched. Though I confess that in some things they differ, yet in hatching enormities of error, in adulterating Scripture with wicked and reveling audacity, in a proud contempt of the truth, in froward impudence, and in brazen loquacity, the most perfect likeness and sameness will be found to exist between them, except that Pighius, by inflating the muddy bombast of his magniloquence, carries himself with greater boast and pomp, while the other fellow borrows the boots by which he elevates himself from his invented revelation. And though both of them at their commencement agree in their attempt to overthrow predestination, yet they afterwards differ in the figments that they advance. An invention of them both is that it lies in each one's own liberty whether or not he will become a partaker of the grace of adoption, that it does not depend on the counsel and decree of God who are elect and who are reprobate, but that each man determines for himself by his own will the one state or the other, and that some believe the gospel while others remain in unbelief does not arise from the free election of God nor from his secret counsel, but from the will of each individual.

Pighius explains his mind on the great matter before us thus: God by his immutable counsel created all men to salvation without distinction, but as he foresaw the fall of Adam, in order that his election might nevertheless remain firm and unaltered, he applied a remedy that might therefore be common to all, which remedy was his confirmation of the election of the whole human race in Christ, so that no one can perish but he who, by his own obstinacy, blots his name out of the book of life. And his view of the other side of the great question is that as God foresaw that some would determinately remain unto the last in malice and a contempt of divine grace, he by his foreknowledge reprobated such unless they should repent. This, with Pighius, is the origin of reprobation, by which he makes it out that the wicked deprive themselves of the benefit of universal election, irrespectively and independently of the counsel and will of God altogether. Moreover, Pighius declares that all those who hold and teach that certain persons are positively and absolutely chosen to salvation, while others are as absolutely appointed to destruction, think unworthily of God and impute to him a severity utterly foreign to his justice and his goodness. And our human reasoner condemns the sentiments of Augustine, mentioning him by name.

In order to show, as he thinks, that the foreknowledge of God detracts nothing from the freedom of our own will, our impostor betakes himself to that cunning device of Nicolaus of Cusa, who would make us believe that God did not foresee in their future aspect and reality those things that were known to him from all eternity, but viewed them, as it were, in a then-present light. And here, moreover, he elevates his brow in a manner peculiar to himself, as if he had discovered some deeply hidden thing, whereas this subterfuge of his is in the mouth of every schoolboy. But as he still finds himself truth-bound by the leg, he struggles to escape by introducing a twofold foreknowledge of God. He asserts that God formed the design of creating man to life before he foreknew his fall, and that therefore in the mind of God the thought of man's salvation preceded the foreknowledge of his death. As he rolls out these sentiments in a muddy torrent of words, he thinks that he thereby so befloods the senses of his readers that they can perceive nothing distinctly and clearly. I hope, however, by my brevity, to dispel presently the darkness of this man's loquacity.

It is the figment of Georgius that no man whatever, neither one nor another, is predestinated to salvation, but that God preappointed a time in which he would save the whole world. In his attempt to prove this, he wrests certain passages of Paul, such as this: "Even the mystery which hath been hid from ages and from generations, but now is made manifest to his saints" [Col. 1:26]. Having twisted this passage of the apostle to his purpose, Georgius slips away in security, thinking himself victorious, as if no testimony of Scripture plainly declares that some are chosen of God to salvation, while others are passed by. In a word, in the matter of election, this man considers nothing but the time of the New Testament.

Calvin's Theses

What my mind on this momentous subject is, my *Institutes* furnish a full and abundant testimony, even if I would now add nothing more. I entreat my readers carefully to bear in memory the admonition that I there offer: This great subject is not, as many imagine, a mere thorny and noisy disputation, nor a speculation that wearies the minds of men without any profit, but a solid discussion eminently adapted to the service of the godly, because it builds us up soundly in the faith, trains us to humility, and lifts us up into an admiration of the unbounded goodness of God toward us while it elevates us to praise this goodness in our highest strains. For there is not a more effectual means of building up faith than our giving open ears to the election of God, which the Holy Spirit seals upon our hearts while we hear, showing us that it stands in the eternal and immutable goodwill of God toward us, and that, therefore, it cannot be moved or altered by any storms of the world, by any assaults of Satan, by any changes, or by any fluctuations or weaknesses of the flesh. For our salvation is sure to us when we find the cause of it in the breast of God. Thus when we lay hold of life in Christ, made manifest to our faith, the same faith being still our leader and guide, our sight is permitted to penetrate much farther and to see from what source that life proceeded. Our confidence of salvation is rooted in Christ and rests on the promises of the gospel. But it is no weak prop to our confidence when we are brought to believe in Christ, to hear that all was originally given to us of God, and that we were as much ordained to faith in Christ before the foundation of the world as we were chosen to the inheritance of eternal life in Christ.

Hence arises the impregnable and insubvertible security of the saints. The Father, who gave us to the Son as his peculiar treasure, is stronger than all who oppose us, and he will not suffer us to be plucked out of his hand. What a cause for humility, then, in the saints of God when they see such a difference of condition made in those who are by nature all alike. Wherever the sons of God turn their eyes, they behold such wonderful instances of blindness, ignorance and insensibility as fill them with horror; while in the midst of such darkness, they have received divine illumination and know it and feel it to be so. How, say they, is it that some, under the clear light, continue in darkness and blindness? Who makes this difference? One thing they know by experience, that is, whereas their eyes were also once closed, they are now opened. Another thing is also certain: Those who willingly remain ignorant of any difference between them and others have never learned to render unto God the glory due to him for making that difference.

No one doubts that humility lies at the bottom of all true religion and is the mother of all virtues. But how shall he be humble who will not hear of the original sin and misery from which he has been delivered? And who, by extending the saving mercy of God to all without difference, lessens, as much as in him lies, the glory of that mercy? Those most certainly are the farthest from glorifying the grace of God according to its greatness who declare that it is indeed common to all men, but that it rests effectually in them because they have embraced it by faith. The cause of faith itself, however, they would keep buried all the time out of sight, which is this: The children of God who are chosen to be sons are afterwards blessed with the spirit of adoption. Now what kind of gratitude is that in me if, being endowed with so preeminent a benefit, I consider myself no greater a debtor than he who has not received one hundredth part of it? Therefore, if to praise the goodness of God worthily it is necessary to bear in mind how much we are indebted to him, those are malignant towards him and rob him of his glory who reject and will not endure the doctrine of eternal election, which being buried out of sight, one-half of the grace of God must of necessity vanish with it.

Let those roar at us who will. We will ever brighten forth with all our power of language the doctrine that we hold concerning the free election of God, since it is only by it that the faithful can understand how great that goodness of God is that effectually called them to salvation. I merely give the great doctrine of election a slight touch here lest anyone, by avoiding a subject so necessary for him to know, should afterwards feel what loss his neglect has caused him. I will, by and by, in its proper place, enter into the divine matter with appropriate fullness. Now if we are not really ashamed of the gospel, we must of necessity acknowledge what is therein openly declared: God by his eternal goodwill (for which there was no other cause than his own purpose) appointed those whom he pleased unto salvation, rejecting all the rest, and those whom he blessed with this free adoption to be his sons, he illumines by his Holy Spirit so that they may receive the life that is offered[10] to them in Christ; while others, continuing of their own will in unbelief, are left destitute of the light of faith in total darkness.

Supporting Evidence from the Apostle Paul

Against this unsearchable judgment of God many insolent dogs rise up and bark. Some of them, indeed, hesitate not to attack God openly, asking why, foreseeing the fall of Adam, he did not better order the affairs of men. To curb such spirits as these, no better means need be sought than those which Paul sets before us. He supposes this question to be put forth by an ungodly person: How can God be just in showing mercy to whom he will and hardening whom he will? Such audacity in men the apostle considers unworthy of a reply. He does nothing but remind them of their order and position in God's creation: "Who art thou, O man, that repliest against God?" [Rom. 9:20]. Profane men, indeed, vainly babble that the apostle covered the absurdity of the matter with silence for want of an answer. But the case is far otherwise.

The apostle in this appeal adopts an axiom, or universal acknowledgment, which not only ought to be held fast by all godly minds, but also deeply engraven in the breast of common sense: The inscrutable judgment of God is deeper than can be penetrated by man. And what man, I ask you, would not be ashamed to compress all the causes of the works of God within the confined measure of his individual intellect? Yet on this hinge turns the whole question: Is there no justice of God but that which is conceived of

---

10. Offered: from *offerre*, which means "to present, to exhibit or set forth." This explanation of the word *offer* as used by Calvin has been supplied by Henry Atherton, the secretary of Sovereign Grace Union that reprinted Henry Cole's translation, *Calvin's Calvinism*, in 1927.

by us? If we should throw this into the form of one question—
whether it is lawful to measure the power of God by our natural
sense—there is not a man who would not immediately reply that
all the senses of all men combined in one individual must faint under an attempt to comprehend the immeasurable power of God;
and yet as soon as a reason cannot immediately be seen for certain
works of God, men somehow or other are immediately prepared to
appoint a day for entering into judgment with him. What, therefore, can be more opportune or appropriate than the apostle's appeal that those who would thus raise themselves above the heavens
in their reasonings utterly forget who and what they are?

Suppose God, ceding his own right, should offer himself as
ready to render a reason for his works? When the matter comes to
his secret counsels, which the angels adore with trembling, who
would not be utterly bereft of his senses before such glorious splendor? Marvelous indeed is the madness of man who would more
audaciously set himself above God than stand on equal ground
with any pagan judge! It is intolerable to you, and hateful, that the
power and works of God should exceed the capacity of your own
mind, and yet you will grant to an equal the enjoyment of his own
mind and judgment. Will you, with such madness as this, dare to
make mention of the adorable God? What do you really think of
God's glorious name? Will you assert that the apostle is devoid of
all reason because he does not drag God from his throne and set
him before you to be questioned and examined?

Let us, however, be fully assured that the apostle, in the first
place, here curbs with becoming gravity the licentious madness of
these men, who think nothing of attacking openly the justice of
God; and that, in the next place, the apostle gives to the worshipers
of God a more useful counsel of moderation than if he had taught
them to soar on eagles' wings above the forbidden clouds. For that
soberness of mind, which regulated by the fear of God keeps itself
within the bounds of comprehension prescribed by him, is far better than all human wisdom. Let proud men revile this sobriety if
they will, calling it ignorance. But let this sober mindedness ever

hold fast that which is the height of all true wisdom, so that by holding the will of God to be the highest rule of righteousness, we ascribe to him his own proper and peculiar glory.

But Pighius and his fellows are not hereby satisfied. For, pretending a great concern for the honor of God, they bark at us as imputing to him a cruelty utterly foreign to his nature. Pighius denies that he has any contest with God. What cause, or whose cause is it, then, that Paul maintains? After he had adopted the above axiom—that God hardens whom he will and has mercy on whom he will—he subjoins the supposed taunt of a wicked reasoner: "Why doth he yet find fault? For who hath resisted his will?" [Rom. 9:19]. He meets such blasphemy as this by simply setting against it the power of God. If those clothe God with the garment of a tyrant who refer the hardening of men even to his eternal counsel, we most certainly are not the originators of this doctrine. If they do God an injury who set his will above all other causes, Paul taught this doctrine long before us. Let these enemies of God, then, dispute the matter with the apostle. For I maintain nothing in the present discussion but what I declare is taught by him. About these barking dogs, however, I would not be very anxious. I am the rather moved with an anxiety about some otherwise good men who, while they fear lest they should ascribe to God anything unworthy of his goodness, really seem to be horror-struck at that which he declares, by the apostle, concerning himself.

We are holding fast all the while a godly purpose of vindicating the justice of God from all calumny. And the modesty of these timid ones would be worthy of all praise if it were not the offspring of moroseness, inflated with a certain secret pride. For such men speak according to their own natural sense and understanding. But why do they fear to concede to the power of God what is beyond the power of their own mind to comprehend, lest his justice should be endangered? Why, I ask, is this? It is because they presume to subject the tribunal of God to their own judgment. Now Paul shows us that it is an act of intolerable pride in any man to assume to himself the judgment of his brother, because there is one judge by whom we all stand or fall, and to whom every knee must bow [Rom. 14:10]. What madness is it, then, for a man to raise his crest against this only judge himself and to presume to measure his infinite power by natural sense!

They, therefore, who allege as an excuse that modesty prevents them from subscribing to the apostle Paul's testimony must of necessity, in the first place, confess that whatever praise they give to the justice of God is restricted to the bounds of their own natural comprehension. And in the next place, if agreeing in reality with us, they choose rather to suppress this part of the great doctrine lest they should give rein to the insolence of the wicked, such caution is quite preposterous. As if the honor of God could be protected by our lies! God himself not only rejects such protection as this, but also declares in the Book of Job that it is hateful to him. Let such defenders take care lest by affecting greater caution than the Lord prescribes in his word, they become guilty of twofold madness and folly.

The moderation and caution that these men recommend are, indeed, beneficial in repressing the blasphemies of the impious. But if such persons persuade themselves that they shall be able by their words to put the bridle on rebels against God and his truth, their hope and expectation are ridiculous. The apostle Paul, after having dwelt upon the secret counsels of God as far as was needful, puts forth his hand, as it were, to forbid us to go farther. Restless spirits, however, will kick and butt, and with unsettled levity, leap over the barrier placed before them. How think you, then, that such will stop at the nod of this or that sober mind that would set still narrower bounds to their headlong course? You may as well attempt to hold with a cobweb a fierce-spirited horse that has burst the bars and prances in his strength. But you will say, In a matter so difficult and deep as this, nothing is better than to think moderately. Who denies it? But we must, at the same time, examine what kind and degree of moderation it is lest we should be drawn into the principle of the Papists, who to keep their disciples obedient to them, make them like mute and brute beasts.

But shall it be called Christian simplicity to consider as hurtful the knowledge of those things that God sets before us? But, say our opponents, this subject is one of which we may remain ignorant without loss or harm, as if our heavenly teacher were not the best judge of what is expedient for us to know and to what extent we ought to know it. Therefore, that we may not struggle amid the waves nor be borne about in the air, unfixed and uncertain, nor by getting our foot too deep be drowned in the gulf below, let us so give ourselves to God to be ruled by him and taught by him that, contented with his word alone, we may never desire to know more than we find therein. No, not even if the power to do so were given to us. This teachableness, in which every godly man will ever hold all the powers of his mind under the authority of the word of God, is the true and only rule of wisdom.

Wherever and however far he who is "the way" [John 14:6] thus leads us with his outstretched hand, whose Spirit spoke by the apostles and the prophets, we may most safely follow. And remaining ignorant of all those things which are not learned in the school of God far excels all the penetration of human intellect. Therefore, Christ requires of his sheep that they should not only hold their ears open to his voice, but also keep them shut against the voice of strangers. Nor can it ever be but that the vain winds of error from every side must blow through a soul devoid of sound doctrine. Moreover, I can with all truth confess that I never should have spoken or written on this subject unless the word of God in my own soul had led the way. All godly readers will indeed gather this from my former writings, and especially from my *Institutes*. But this present refutation of my enemies, who oppose themselves to me, will perhaps afford my friends some new light upon the matter.

Supporting Evidence from Augustine

Since the authority of the ancient church is, with much hatred, cast in my teeth, it will perhaps be worth our while to consider at the commencement how unjustly the truth of Christ is smothered under this enmity, the ground of which is in one sense false, and in another frivolous. This accusation, however, such as it is, I would rather wipe off with the words of Augustine than with my own; for the Pelagians of old annoyed him with the same accusation, saying that he had all other writers of the church against him. In his reply he remarks that before the heresy of Pelagius, the fathers of the primitive church did not deliver their opinions so deeply and accurately upon predestination, which reply, indeed, is the truth. And he adds,

> What need is there for us to search the works of those writers who, before the heresy of Pelagius arose, found no necessity for devoting themselves to this question, so difficult of solution? Had such necessity arisen, and had they been compelled to reply to the enemies of predestination, they would doubtless have done so.

This remark of Augustine is a prudent and a wise one. For if the enemies of the grace of God had not worried Augustine himself, he never would have devoted so much labor, as he himself confesses, to the discussion of God's election.

Hence in reference to his book *Of the Blessing of Perseverance*, he pointedly says,

> This predestination of the saints is certain and manifest, which necessity afterwards compelled me to defend more diligently and laboriously when I was discussing the subject in opposition to a certain new sect. For I have learned that every separate heresy introduces into the church its peculiar questions that call for a more diligent defense of the Holy Scripture than if no such necessity of defense had arisen. For what was it that compelled me to defend, in that work of mine, with greater copiousness and fuller explanation those passages of the Scriptures in which predestination is set before us? What, but the starting up of the Pelagians, who say

that the grace of God is given to us according as we render ourselves deserving of it.

Augustine had, moreover, just before denied that any prejudice against his books could be justly entertained because of their want of the authority of the ancient church. "No one," says he, "can surely be so unjust, or so invidious, as not to allow me to gain some instruction and profit for myself from this important subject." And he afterwards contends that it could be gathered from the testimonies of some of the ancient fathers that their sentiments and teaching were the same as his own. Not to mention other authorities to which he refers, it is a more than satisfactory one that he cites from Ambrose: "Whom Christ has mercy on, he calls." Again, "When he will, he makes out of careless ones devoted ones." And again, "But God calls whom he condescends to call; and whom he will, he makes religious." Who does not see that the sum of the whole divine matter is comprehended in these few words? Ambrose here assigns the reason or cause that all men do not come to Christ to obtain salvation is that God does not effectually touch their hearts. The holy man declares that the conversion of a sinner proceeds from the free election of God and that the reason he calls some, while others are left reprobate, lies solely in his own will. Ambrose neither hesitates nor dissembles here. Now who that is endowed with the most common judgment does not perceive that the state of the whole question is contained in, and defined by, these three summaries?

In a word, Augustine is so wholly with me that if I wished to write a confession of my faith, I could do so with all fullness and satisfaction to myself out of his writings. But that I may not on the present occasion be too prolix, I will be content with three or four instances of his testimony, from which it will be manifest that he does not differ from me one pin's point. And it would be more manifest still how fully and solidly he agrees with me in every particular if the whole line of his confession could be cited. In his book *Concerning the Predestination of the Saints*, he has these words:

Lest anyone should say, My faith, my righteousness (or anything of the kind) distinguishes me from others, meeting all
such thoughts, the great teacher of the Gentiles asks, "What
hast thou that thou hast not received?" [1 Cor. 4:7], as if the
apostle had said, From whom indeed couldst thou receive it
but from him who separates thee from every other, to whom
he has not given what he has given to thee?

Augustine then adds:

Faith, therefore, from its beginning to its perfection, is the
gift of God. And that this gift is bestowed on some and not
on others, who will deny but he who would fight against the
most manifest testimonies of Scripture? But why faith is not
given to all ought not to concern the believer, who knows
that all men by the sin of one came into most just condemnation. But why God delivers one from this condemnation
and not another belongs to his inscrutable judgments, and
"his ways are past finding out" [Rom. 11:33]. And if it be investigated and inquired how it is that each receiver of faith
is deemed of God worthy to receive such a gift, there are not
wanting those who will say, It is by their human will. But we
say that it is by grace or divine predestination.

The holy father then makes these beautiful and striking observations:

Indeed the Savior of the world himself, the adorable Son
of God, is the brightest luminary of divine grace and eternal
predestination, not only with respect to his divine nature as
the Son of God, but especially also in reference to his human nature as "man." For in what way, I ask you, did "the man
Christ Jesus" [1 Tim. 2:5], as man, merit so great a glory as
that, being taken into union with the divine person of the
Son by the word of the coeternal Father, he should become

the "only begotten Son of God"? What good word or work preceded in this glorious case? What good thing did "the man" perform? What act of faith did he exercise? What prayer did he offer up that he should be exalted to such pre-eminent dignity?

Now here, perhaps, some profane and insolent being may be inclined to say, "Why was it not I that was predestinated to this excellent greatness?" If we should reply in the solemn appeal of the apostle, "Nay, but who art thou, O man, that repliest against God?" [Rom. 9:20], and if such a one should not even then restrain his daring spirit, but should give more rein to his blasphemy and say, "Why do you utter to me the caution, 'Who art thou, O man...?' Am I not a man as he was, concerning whom thou speakest? Why, then, am I not now what he is? He, forsooth, is what he is, and as great as he is, by grace. Why, then, is the grace different where the nature is the same? For most assuredly there is no acceptance of persons with God."

Now I would solemnly ask, What Christian man, what madman, would thus reason, speak, or think? Let, then, our glorious head himself, the fountain of all grace, be an ever-shining luminary of eternal predestination and a divine example of its sovereign nature. And from him let the stream of electing grace flow through all his members, "according to the measure of the gift in each" [Eph. 4:7]. This, then, is the eternal predestination of the saints, which shone with such surpassing splendor in the Saint of saints.

And as he alone was predestinated, as man, to be our head, so many of us are also predestinated to be his members.

Now, that no one might attribute it to faith that one is preferred above another, Augustine testifies that men are not chosen *because* they believe, but *that they might believe*. In like manner, when writing to Sextus, he says,

As to the great deep—why one man believes and another does not, why God delivers one man and not another—let him who can, search into that profound abyss; but let him beware of the awful precipice.

Again, in another place he says,

Who created the reprobate but God? And why? Because he willed it. Why did he will it?—"Who are thou, O man, that repliest against God?" [Rom. 9:20].

And again, elsewhere, after he had proved that God is moved by no merits of men to make them obedient to his commands but that he renders unto them good for evil, and that for his own sake and not for theirs, he adds,

If anyone should ask why God makes some men his sheep and not others, the apostle, dreading this question, exclaims, "O the depth of the riches both of the wisdom and knowledge of God! how unsearchable are his judgments, and his ways past finding out!" [Rom. 11:33].

And as Augustine, tracing the beginning or origin of election to the free and gratuitous will of God, places reprobation in his mere will likewise, so he teaches that the security of our salvation stands in that will also, and in nothing else. For writing to Paulinus, he affirms that those who do not persevere unto the end belong not to the calling of God, which is always effectual and without any repentance in him.

In another work, Augustine maintains more fully that perseverance is freely bestowed on the elect, from which they can never fall away:

Thus when Christ prayed for Peter that his faith might not fail [Luke 22:32], what else did he ask of God but that there might be with or in Peter's faith a fully free, fully courageous, fully victorious, fully persevering will or determination? And he had just before said, "The foundation of God standeth sure, having this seal, The Lord knoweth them that are his" [2 Tim. 2:19]. The faith of such, which works by love, either fails not at all, or if there be any in whom it does partially fail, it is renewed and restored before this life is ended. That iniquity which had interrupted it is done away, and the faith still perseveres unto the end. But those who are not designed of God to persevere—if they fall from the Christian faith, and the end of life finds them in that state thus fallen—such, doubtless, could not have been of this number of God's elect, even while they were, to all appearance, living well and righteously. For such were never separated from the general mass of perdition by the foreknowledge and predestination of God, and therefore were never "called according to his purpose" [Rom. 8:28].

So that no one might be disturbed in mind because those sometimes fall away who had been considered the sons of God, Augustine meets such perplexed ones thus:

Let no one think that those ever fall away who are the subjects of predestination, who are the called according to God's purpose, and who are truly the children of promise. Those who live godly in appearance are, indeed, called by men the children of God; but because they are destined sometime or other to live ungodly and to die in that ungodliness, God does not call them his children in his foreknowledge. Those who are ordained unto life are understood, by Scripture, to be given unto Christ. They are predestinated and called, according to God's purpose. Not one of them ever perishes. And on this account no such one, though changed from good to bad for a time, ever ends his life so, because he is for that end ordained of God and for that end given unto Christ that he might not perish, but have eternal life.

A little afterwards the same Augustine says,

> Those who, by the all-foreseeing appointment of God, are foreknown, predestinated, called, justified and glorified [Rom. 8:30] are the children of God, not only before they are regenerated, but before they are born of woman; and such can never perish.

He then assigns the reason:

> Because God works all things together for the good of such; and he so makes all things thus to work together for their good that if some of them go out of the way, and even exceed all bounds, he makes even this to work for their good and profit [Rom. 8:28]; for they return to him more humble and more teachable than before.

And if the matter be carried higher, and a question be moved concerning the first creation of man, Augustine meets that question thus:

> We most wholesomely confess what we most rightly believe, that God, the Lord of all things who created all things "very good," foreknew that evil would arise out of this good; and he also knew that it was more to the glory of his omnipotent goodness to bring good out of evil than not to permit evil to be at all. And he so ordained the lives of angels and of men that he might first show in them what free will could do, and then afterwards show what the free gift of his grace and the judgment of his justice could do.

In his *Manual* to Laurentinus,[11] Augustine more freely and fully explains whatever of doubt might yet remain.

---

11. This *Manual* is Augustine's *The Enchiridion*, a manual or handbook of Christian doctrine.

When Christ shall appear to judge the world at the last day, that shall be seen in the clearest light of knowledge that the faith of the godly now holds fast, though not yet made manifest to their comprehension; how sure, how immutable, how all-efficacious is the will of God; how many things he could do, or has power to do, that he wills not to do (but he wills nothing that he has not power to do); and how true is what the psalmist sings: "The Lord hath done in heaven whatsoever pleased him" [Ps. 115:3].

This, however, is not true if he willed some things and did them not. Nothing, therefore, is done but that which the Omnipotent willed to be done, either by permitting it to be done or by doing it himself. Nor is a doubt to be entertained that God does righteously in permitting all those things to be done that are done evilly. For he does not permit this but by righteous judgment. Although, therefore, those things that are evil, insofar as they are evil, are not good, yet it is good that there should not only be good things, but evil things also. For unless there were this good that evil things also existed, those evil things would not be permitted by the great and good omnipotent God to exist at all. For he, without doubt, can as easily refuse to permit to be done what he does not will to be done as he can do what he wills to be done. Unless we fully believe this, the very beginning of our faith, by which we profess to believe in God Almighty, is periled.

Augustine then adds this:

These are the mighty works of the Lord, shining with perfection in every instance of his will; and so perfect in wisdom that when the angelic and human nature had sinned—that is, had done not what God willed but what each nature itself willed—it came to pass that by this same will of the creature, God, though in one sense unwilling, yet accomplished what he willed righteously and with the height of all wisdom, overruling the evils done, to the damnation of those whom he had justly predestinated to punishment, and to the salvation of those whom he had mercifully predestinated to grace. Therefore, as far as these natures themselves were concerned, they did what they did contrary to the will of God, but as far as the omnipotence of God is concerned, they acted according to his will; nor could they have acted contrary to it. Hence by their very acting contrary to the will of God, the will of God concerning them was done. So mighty, therefore, are the works of God, so gloriously and exquisitely perfect in every instance of his will, that by a marvelous and ineffable plan of operation peculiar to himself as the "all-wise God," that cannot be done without his will, which is even contrary to his will because it could not be done without his permitting it to be done. This permission is evidently not contrary to his will, but according to his will.

I have gladly extracted these few things out of many like them in the writings of Augustine so that my readers may clearly see with what a very modest face it is that Pighius represents him as differing from me and makes use of him to support his own errors. I shall, indeed, hereafter occasionally refer to the testimonies of this same holy man in the course of this discussion.

The Witness of Scripture

I will now enter upon the more express subject and object of the present undertaking, which are to prove that nothing has been taught by me concerning this important doctrine but that which God clearly teaches us all in the sacred oracles, the sum of which is this: The salvation of believers depends on the eternal election of God, for which no cause or reason can be rendered but his own gratuitous good pleasure.

Most plain and eloquent on this point are the words of the apostle Paul in the first chapter of his Epistle to the Ephesians: "Blessed be the God and Father of our Lord Jesus Christ, who hath blessed us with all spiritual blessings in heavenly places in Christ, according as he hath chosen us in him before the foundation of the world" [vv. 3, 4]. Now I hear the babble of Pighius: "The whole human race was chosen in Christ, so that whoever should take hold of him by faith should obtain salvation." In this absurd invention of his there are two most gross blunders, which may be immediately refuted by the words of Paul.

First, there is, most certainly and evidently, an inseparable connection between the elect and the reprobate, so that the election of which the apostle speaks cannot be maintained unless we confess that God separated from all others certain persons whom it pleased him thus to separate. This act of God is expressed by the term *predestinating*, which the apostle afterwards twice repeats [vv. 5, 11]. Moreover, he calls those "chosen," or elected, who are engrafted by faith into the body of Christ, and that this blessing is by no means common to all men is openly manifest. The apostle, therefore, by the "chosen," evidently means those whom Christ condescends to call after they have been given to him by the Father. But to make faith the cause of election is altogether absurd and utterly at variance with the words of the apostle. As Augustine wisely observes,

> Paul does not declare that the children of God were "chosen" because he foreknew they would believe, but in order that they might believe. Nor does the apostle call them "chosen" because God had foreseen that they would be holy and without spot, but in order that they might be made such.

Again Augustine says,

> God did not choose us because we believed, but in order that we might believe, lest we should appear to have first chosen him. Paul loudly declares that our very beginning to be holy is the fruit and effect of election. They act most preposterously, therefore, who put election after faith.

He further observes,

> When Paul lays down, as the sole cause of election, that
> good pleasure of God which he had in himself, he excludes
> all other causes.

Augustine, therefore, rightly admonishes us ever to go back to
that first great cause of election, lest we should be inclined to boast
of the good pleasure of our own wills.

Paul then proceeds to declare that "God abounded toward us in
all wisdom and prudence, according to the riches of his grace, having made known unto us the mystery of his will, according to his
good pleasure which he hath purposed in himself" [vv. 7–9]. Readers, you hear in these words the grace of illumination, flowing like
a river from the fountain of the eternal counsel that before had been
hidden. Far, very far, is this removed from the idea that God had
any respect to our faith in choosing us, which faith could not possibly have existed except that God had then appointed it for us by
the free grace of his adoption of us. And Paul further confirms all
this by declaring that God was moved by no external cause—by no
cause out of himself—in the choice of us, but that he himself, in
himself, was the cause and the author of choosing his people, not
yet created or born, as those on whom he would afterwards confer
faith "according to the purpose of him who worketh all things after
the counsel of his own will" [v. 11].

Who does not see that the eternal purpose of God is set here
in diametrical opposition to our purpose and will?

This passage also was deeply weighed by Augustine, who in his
interpretation of it observes that "God so works out all things that
he works also in us the very willingness by which we believe."

It is thus, I think, clearly brought out and proved who they are
whom God calls by the gospel to the hope of salvation, whom he
engrafts into the body of Christ, and whom he makes heirs of eternal life; they are those whom he had adopted unto himself by his
eternal and secret counsel to be his sons; and that he was so far from

being moved by any faith in them to come, thus to adopt them; that this, his election, is the cause and the beginning of all faith in them; and that, therefore, election is, in order, before faith.

Equally plain and manifest is the eighth chapter of the apostle's Epistle to the Romans. For after Paul had said that all things work together for good, or are a help, to the faithful who love God, so that men might not trace the source of their happiness to themselves or suppose that by their first loving God they had merited such goodness at his hands, the apostle, by way of correcting every error of that kind, immediately adds, "...who are the called according to his purpose" [v. 28]. Whereby we see that Paul is anxious to secure to God all the originating glory, for the apostle shows that God by his calling causes men to love him who of themselves could do nothing but hate him. For if you thoroughly examine the whole human race, what inclination to love God will you find in anyone by nature? Indeed, Paul declares, "The whole carnal mind [all the senses of the flesh] is enmity against God" [v. 7].

If all men are by nature enemies of God and his adversaries, it is quite evident that it is by his calling alone that some are separated from the rest and caused to lay aside their hatred and brought to love him. Moreover, no doubt can exist that the apostle means the effectual calling by which God regenerates those whom he had before adopted unto himself to be his sons. For the apostle does not simply say, "who are the called" (for this is sometimes applicable to the reprobate whom God calls or invites promiscuously with his own children to repentance and faith), but he says in all fullness of explanation, "...who are the called according to his purpose" [v. 28], which purpose must, from its very nature and effect, be firm and ratifying.

To explain this text as applying to the purpose of man is, as Augustine argues, absurd in the extreme. Indeed, the context banishes every scruple, as if to render the intrusion of an interpreter wholly unnecessary. For the apostle immediately adds, "...whom he did predestinate [or definitely appoint], them he also called; and whom he called, them he also justified" [v. 30]. Here it is evident that the apostle is speaking of a certain number whom God destined for himself as a peculiar property and treasure, for although God calls very many—by many means and especially by the external ministry of men—he justifies and at last glorifies no one except him whom he had ordained unto eternal life. The calling of God, therefore, is a certain special calling, which so seals and ratifies his eternal election as to manifest openly what was before hidden in God concerning each one who is so called.

I know well the cavils of many: When Paul affirms that those were predestinated whom God foreknew, he means that each one was chosen in respect of his future faith when he should believe. But I do not concede to those what they falsely imagine: We are to understand that God foresaw something in them that would move him to confer upon them his favor and grace. For it is evident that the elect of God were foreknown when and because they were freely chosen. Hence the same apostle elsewhere teaches that God knows those who are his because he has them marked, as it were, and holds them as numbered on his roll [2 Tim. 2:19].

Nor does Augustine omit even this important point: By the term *foreknowledge* we are to understand the counsel of God by which he predestinates his own unto salvation. That it was foreknown of God who should be heirs of eternal life, no one will deny. The only question that can possibly arise is whether God foreknew what he would do in them or what they would be in themselves. It is a piece of futile cunning to lay hold on the term *foreknowledge* and so to use it as to pin the eternal election of God upon the merits of men, which election the apostle everywhere ascribes alone to the purpose of God.

Peter also salutes the church as "elect according to the foreknowledge of God" [1 Pet. 1:2]. Did he do this believing that some virtue in them foreseen of God gained them his favor? No. Peter is not comparing men with men to make some of them better or more worthy than others, but he is placing on high, above all other causes, that decree which God determined in himself, as if he had said that those to whom he wrote were now numbered among the children of God because they were chosen or elected of him before they were born. On this same principle he afterwards teaches that Christ was "verily ... foreordained before the foundation of the world" [v. 20] to be the Savior who should wash away by his blood the sins of the world. By this, that apostle doubtless means that the expiation of sin, completed by Christ, was preordained by the eternal counsel of God. Nor can that be otherwise explained which we find in the sermon of Peter recorded by Luke in the Acts of the Apostles: Christ was delivered to death "by the determinate counsel and foreknowledge of God" [Acts 2:23]. Peter here joins *foreknowledge* to *counsel* in order that we may learn that Christ was not hurried away to death by chance or by the mere violent assault of men, but because the all-good and all-wise God, who knows all things, had thus purposely decreed it.

Indeed, one passage of the apostle Paul ought to suffice for the end of all controversy among those who have a sound mind. He says, "God hath not cast away his people which he foreknew" [Rom. 11:2]. And what that foreknowledge was, he shortly after explains where he says that "a remnant according to the election of grace" was saved [v. 5]. And again, that Israel did not obtain by works that which they sought after, but that "the election" did obtain it [v. 7]. What in the former passage he called *foreknowledge*, he afterwards defines to be *election*, and that gratuitous and free.

The fiction of Pighius is puerile and absurd when he interprets grace to be God's goodness in inviting all men to salvation, although all were lost in Adam. For Paul most clearly separates the foreknown from those on whom God deigned not to look in mercy. And the same is expressed, without any obscurity, in the memorable words of Christ: "All that the Father giveth me shall come unto me; and him that cometh unto me I will in no wise cast out" [John 6:37].

Here we have three things, briefly indeed, but most perspicuously expressed. First, all who come to Christ were before given unto him by the Father. Second, those who were thus given unto him were delivered, as it were, from the hand of the Father into the hand of the Son that they might be truly his. Third, Christ is the sure keeper of all those whom the Father delivered over to his faithful custody and care, for the very end that he might not suffer one of them to perish. If a question is raised as to the beginning of faith, Christ here gives the answer when he says that those who believe, therefore, believe because they were given unto him by the Father.

The unbelief of the scribes was a great obstacle to the ignorant multitude, because the scribes always persuaded the multitude that no doctrine was worthy of belief except that which was received under their sanction. However, Christ declares aloud that the light by which we are guided into the way of salvation is the gift of God. And if anyone be inclined to turn his back upon the truth that all those whom the Father chose in Christ were given unto him, it nevertheless remains fixed and a fact that this gift was not only antecedent to faith, but also the cause and origin of it.

In the remaining part of this sentence of Christ, "... shall come unto me," there is a more marvelous weight still. For he not only declares that none ever come to him except those to whom the hand of God is stretched out, but he also asserts that all who were given unto him by the Father are, without exception, brought to believe in him. And this he still more fully confirms in the context of his divine discourse: "No one," says he, "can come unto me, except my Father draw him" [v. 44].

Pighius will confess that there is need of illumination to bring unto Christ those who were adversaries to God; at the same time he holds fast the fiction that grace is offered equally to all, but that it is ultimately rendered effectual by the will of man, just as each one is willing to receive it.

Christ, however, testifies that the meaning of his words is very different from this. For he adds immediately afterwards, "There are some among you who believe not ... Therefore said I unto you, that no man can come unto me except it were given unto him of my Father" [vv. 64, 65]. You see here that Christ excludes those who "believe not" from the number of those who are "drawn." Now Christ would have uttered all this in vain and out of place if faith were not

a special gift of God. But that is the clearest of all which he con-
clusively adds in continuation of his discourse. After having cited
the prophecy of Isaiah, "All thy children shall be taught of the Lord"
[Isa. 54:13], he subjoins, by way of interpretation, "Every one therefore that hath heard, and hath learned of the Father, cometh unto
me" [John 6:45]. Herein he shows that the prophecy of Isaiah is
then fulfilled when God, by his Spirit, speaks to his children and
disciples within, in order that he may deliver them into the hands
and possession of Christ. Isaiah defines this to be the manner in
which God renews and increases his church: by teaching his children from above—"And they shall be all taught of God." The
prophet, therefore, is recording a peculiar favor of God, of which
none are deemed worthy except his own children. Christ also declares by this his doctrine that those are effectually drawn to him
whose minds and hearts God "compels."

Augustine says,

> Thus does God teach those within who are "the called ac-
> cording to his purpose," at the same time giving them to
> know what they ought to do and giving them the power to
> do what they know. He, therefore, who knows what he ought
> to do and does it not, has not yet learned of God according
> to grace, but according to the law only; not according to the
> spirit, but only according to the letter.

Again, a little afterwards, Augustine says, "If as the truth says,
'Everyone that hath learned cometh,' he who does not come most
certainly has not learned."

At length the holy father arrives at this conclusion:

> It does not follow that he who can come, therefore does
> come. The sacred matter is not perfected unless he is willing
> to come, and does come. Now everyone that has learned of
> the Father has not only the power to come, but also does
> come.

Here, therefore, we have the forward movement of the power, the affection of the will, and the effect of the act.

I do not thus cite Augustine as a witness on this occasion so that I may fight my enemies under cover of his authority, but I cannot find words more appropriate than his wherewith to express the mind of Christ in the evangelist. If there be any not yet quieted, Augustine thus discusses the matter more fully elsewhere:

> What does Christ mean when he says, "Everyone that hath learned of the Father cometh unto me" [John 6:45]? What is it but as if he had said, "There is no one who heareth and learneth of the Father that cometh not unto me." For if everyone who has heard and learned of the Father comes [unto Christ], most certainly whoever comes not unto him has never heard or learned. For if he had heard and learned he would certainly come. This school of God is very far removed from all carnal sense and understanding. In it the Father teaches and is heard, so that those who hear and learn may come to the Son.

A little further on, Augustine observes,

> This grace, which is secretly communicated to the hearts of men, is received by no heart that is hardened. Indeed, it is given for the very end that the hardness of the heart may be first taken away. When, therefore, the Father is heard within, he takes away the "stony heart" and gives "a heart of flesh" [Ezek. 11:19; Ezek. 36:26]. For it is thus that he makes his own the children of promise and vessels of mercy that he had before prepared unto glory. If it be asked why he does not thus teach all men so that they may come to Christ, the answer is, because those whom he does teach, he teaches *in mercy*, but those whom he does not teach, *in judgment* he teaches them not. For "he hath mercy on whom he will have mercy, and whom he will he hardeneth" [Rom. 9:18].

However, the sum of this sacred matter may be compressed into a smaller compass still. Christ does not say that those are drawn by the Father who have a flexible heart given them to render them able to come to him, but rather that those who do come to him are they whom God by his Spirit touches within, and who, under the efficacy of that touch, actually come. That this privilege is not given to all promiscuously is a fact that universal experience makes manifest, even to the blind.

And next, when Christ declares that he will by no means cast out one of those who do come to him—indeed, that the life of all such is hidden and kept in security in himself until he shall raise them up at the last day—who does not see that the final perseverance of the saints (as it is commonly termed) is in like manner ascribed to the election of God? It may be, and has been, that some fall from the faith, but those who are given to Christ by the Father are, as Christ himself declares, placed beyond the peril of destruction. In the same manner also, when in another place Christ said that some of the Jews did not believe because they were not of his sheep [John 10:26], he places, as it were, the sheep themselves in a sure haven of safety. "They shall never perish, neither shall anyone pluck them out of my hand. My Father who gave them me is greater than all, and none is able to pluck them out of my Father's hand" [vv. 28, 29]. Pighius surely would not dare to rest the safe state of the salvation of these sheep on their present faith. Yet he will suspend it all upon the free will of man!

Nor are we to consider it a point for ambiguous discussion when Christ here sets himself alone as a sufficient protection against all the machinations of Satan, and when he declares that we shall be safe even unto the end because it is his will to save us. That there might remain no doubt upon the subject in anyone's mind, as to the persons whom he does undertake in his faithfulness to protect and preserve, he calls our attention a second time to the gift of the Father, declaring both the gift of the Father and the teaching of the Father. Nor should we pass, without special notice, Christ's making the Father greater than all adversaries that can possibly oppose his people. Our Lord does this so that our confidence in the security of our salvation might be as great as our reverence for the power of God. For our security and God's omnipotence are equal, the former not being less than the latter. Therefore, amidst all the violent assaults, all the various dangers, all the mighty storms, and all the shakings, convulsions and agitations with which we have to contend, the continuance and perpetuity of our standing lie in this: God, by the omnipotent power of his arm, will constantly defend what he has decreed in himself concerning our salvation. If anyone of us looks into himself, what can he do but tremble? For all things shake to their center around us, and there is nothing more weak and tottering than ourselves. But our heavenly Father suffers not one of those whom he gave to his Son to perish, so great is his power, so certain is our confidence, and so great our glorying. And his omnipotence is such that he stands the invincible vindicator of his own gift.

Hence Augustine advisedly observes,

If anyone of these should perish, God would be deceived. But not one of them ever does perish, because God never is, or can be, deceived. If anyone of these should perish, God is overcome and outdone by the sin of man. But not one of them ever does perish, because nothing can conquer or outdo God. The elect of God are chosen that they may reign with Christ forever. They are not like Judas, who was chosen to a temporary office only, for which he was naturally fitted.

Again,

Of these, not one perishes, because they are all chosen according to a purpose—not their own purpose, but God's— seeing that there is not conferred upon them such a gift of perseverance by which they may persevere if they will, but a gift by which they cannot but persevere.

Augustine then confirms this by the following excellent argument:

> If in the great weakness of this life (in the midst of which
> weakness there is nevertheless need of mighty power to keep
> down human vanity and pride), men were left to their own
> will whether or not they would persevere, so that under the
> helping power of God (without which they could not per-
> severe at all), they might stand still if they pleased; and if
> God did not work in them that will, man's own will would,
> amid such and so great temptations, sink under its own in-
> firmity. And thus men could not persevere at all, because,
> sinking under their own weaknesses, they would not be will-
> ing to persevere, or being willing, would not have the power.
> A remedy, therefore, is provided for the infirmity of human
> will by its being caused to act unceasingly and inseparably
> under divine grace. Thus the human will, though infirm in
> itself, can neither fail nor be overcome by any infirmity of its
> own.

Now let that memorable passage of Paul [Rom. 9:10–13] come
forth before us. This passage alone should abundantly suffice to put
an end to all controversy among the sober minded and obedient
children of God. And although it is no wonder that the eyeless
monster Pighius should mock with contempt the words of the
apostle, yet I hope I shall bring all readers of a sound mind to abhor such barbarous audacity in profaning Scripture as this monster
evinces. The Jews, priding themselves on the name of *the church*, rejected under this pretext the gospel of Christ because it had been
condemned by the consent of the so-called church. To prevent the
majesty of the gospel from being overshadowed by such shameless
pride, the apostle Paul tears from the faces of these enemies of
Christ the mask, under cover of which they falsely boasted.

It was indeed a very great difficulty and a formidable obstacle in
the way of the weak when they saw the doctrine of Christ rejected

by nearly all these very persons whom God had appointed the heirs of his everlasting covenant. The apostles had all along preached that Jesus was the Messiah of God. But the whole of this nation to whom the Messiah had been promised opposed and rejected him. And why should we wonder when this very day we see thousands totter, fail, and faint, frightened by this very church mask that the Papists hold before their eyes, boasting themselves to be the church?

The apostle, therefore, enters into the battle with the Jews in this manner: He by no means makes the fleshly seed the legitimate children of Abraham, but counts the children of promise alone for the seed [v. 8]. Now he might have counted the seed according to their faith. And that surely would have been consistent when, in reference to the promise, he was stating the difference between the genuine and the spurious offspring; that, indeed, he had done before. But now he ascends higher into the mind of God and declares that those are the children of promise whom God chose before they were born. In proof of this, he cites that promise given by the angel to Abraham:

> At this time will I come, and Sarah shall have a son [as if the apostle had added, "Before Isaac was conceived in the womb, he was chosen of God"]. And not only this, but when Rebecca also had conceived by one [embrace], even by our father Isaac, (for the children being not yet born, neither having done any good or evil, that the purpose of God according to election might stand, not of works, but of him that calleth), it was said unto her, The elder shall serve the younger. As it is written, Jacob have I loved, but Esau have I hated [Rom. 9:9, 10].

Pighius would slide away under the excuse that this is one of the most difficult places of Scripture. And suppose I concede this? I do not thereby acknowledge that his impious barking is to be endured when he boastingly asserts that it is a labyrinth in which no straight way can be found. What? Are we to suppose that the Holy Spirit, speaking by the mouth of the apostle, went out of his way or lost himself so as to lead us aside and beyond what is useful or proper for us to know? It would have been very easy, as I have just said, for the apostle to distinguish the true children of Abraham from the spurious ones by the mark of faith alone. But Paul purposely introduces the question of election, far higher and much farther removed. And (according to his own record of himself) most certainly as the apostle had been carried up into the third heaven and those secrets of God had been revealed to him that are not lawful for a man to utter [2 Cor. 12:2], it must be evident that he well knew how far it was expedient and lawful for him to go in publishing the secret things of the Most High. When, therefore, he purposely carries the question to so great a height and brings it down to so important a point when it might have been settled in so general, brief, and compendious a manner, what godly person will hesitate to lend an attentive and teachable ear to what he testifies? Otherwise, we are to entertain a supposition that this furious, blind monster would restrain by his great moderation the Spirit of God himself, wantoning, in his own opinion, beyond due bounds! Our very modest opponent adds, "This is one of the portions of Scripture that unlearned and unstable persons corrupt to their own destruction" [2 Pet. 3:16]. This is the very fact that, by the plainest proof, Pighius forces us to declare concerning himself, so lawlessly does he twist and pervert the whole context of the apostle Paul. And when he exhorts his readers to hold themselves obedient to the church in the interpretation of all such difficult passages of Scripture, he should have me a seconder of his grave admonition if he would show to his readers as the church, a sheepfold of Christ, and not a stinking sty of swine. For what is Pighius' church but that vortex formed of the congregated mass of all iniquities, and ever filling, but not yet full, of every kind of error?

Pighius' last admonition is that his readers should admit nothing that is inconsistent with the infinite goodness of God, nor anything by which they might be incited to hate God rather than to

love him. Yet he runs full sail directly against God because he pre-
destines some to destruction from their very creation. But suppose
the whole of this doctrine were suppressed, the reprobate would
ever find occasion for hating God and for assailing him with their
impious reasonings and arguments. What real reason they have for
their noisy opposition shall be duly considered when we shall
have fully explained the mind of the apostle. At the present moment, let all those who are willing to be taught in the school of God
hear what the apostle plainly, without any ambiguity, really says and
means.

The apostle places before us the two sons of Isaac who, when
begotten together in the secret and sacred womb of nature, as in a
temple of God, as it were, were nevertheless, while in the womb together, separated by the oracular word of God to an entirely different destiny. Now the apostle assigns the cause of this difference
(which otherwise might have been sought in the merits of the lives
of these two children) to the hidden counsel of God "that the counsel of God might stand" [Rom. 9:11]. We here distinctly learn that
it was determined of God to choose one only of these two children.
Yet Pighius, by a senseless cavil, as by a hog's snout, tries to root up
these words of the apostle with all their positive plainness of meaning. He replies that the election of grace means that Jacob had merited no such thing beforehand. But since the apostle commends this
electing grace of God on the very ground that while the one was
elected, the other was rejected, the vain fiction of Pighius concerning universal grace falls to the ground at once. The apostle does not
simply say that Jacob was appointed heir of life in order that the
election of God might stand, but also that his brother's rejection
meant that the birthright was conferred on Jacob.

I am fully aware of what some other dogs bark out, and of the
murmurings of many ignorant persons that the testimonies of the
apostle that we have cited do not treat of eternal life or of eternal
destruction at all. But if such objectors held the true principles of
theology in any degree, which ought to be well known by all Christian men, they would express their sentiments with a little less con-

fidence and insolence. For the answer of God to Rebecca's complaint was designed to show her that the issue of the struggling that
she felt in her womb would be that the blessing of God and the
covenant of eternal life would rest with the younger. And what did
the struggling itself signify but that both the children could not be
heirs of the covenant at the same time, which covenant had already,
by the secret counsel of God, been decreed for the one?

Objectors allege that this covenant and its decree referred to
Canaan, on which the prophet Malachi dwells [Mal. 1:1–3]. And,
indeed, this objection might be worthy of notice if God had designed merely to fatten the Jews in Canaan as pigs in a sty. But the
mind of the prophet is very different from this. God had promised
that land to Abraham as an outward symbol or figure of a better
inheritance and had given it to Abraham's posterity for a possession, so that God might there collect them together as a peculiar
people unto himself and might there erect a sanctuary of his presence and grace. These great ends and objects are those which the
prophet is revolving in his deep and reflective mind. In a word, the
prophet is holding Canaan to be the sacred habitation of God. And
as Esau was deprived of this habitation, the prophet sacredly gath-
ers that he was hated of God because he had been thus rejected
from the holy and elect family on which the love of God perpetually rests. We also, with the prophet, must carefully consider the
particular nature of that land and the peculiar quality which God
assigns to it, that it might be a certain earnest or pledge of the spiritual covenant into which God entered with the seed of Abraham.
It is in full sacred point, therefore, that the apostle records that the
free election of God fell upon Jacob because, being yet unborn, he
was appointed to enjoy the inheritance while his brother was at the
same time rejected. But Paul is proceeding much farther still in his
sacred argument and maintaining that this inheritance was not obtained by works, nor conferred on Jacob from any respect to works
that he should perform in the future. Nor is even this all. The apostle expressly declares that the brothers were thus separated and this
difference was made between them before either of them had done

anything good or evil. From these facts the apostle solemnly settles it that the difference made between the children was not from any works whatever, but from the will of him who called.

Here Pighius thrusts upon us that rancid distinction of his: Indeed, works performed were not taken into the divine consideration (for no works as yet existed), but the election of God was ratified in the person of Jacob because God foresaw what his faith and obedience would be. And he philosophizes, in a most ingenious way, on the name Israel: Jacob was so named from seeing God so that we may know those to be true Israelites (not who are blind from their own malice and wickedness, but blind only with respect to God), who open their eyes when God presents himself to be seen by them. But is it not a most ridiculous circumstance that while this being is anxious to make others so clear-sighted, he should himself be blinder than a mole? An utterly different etymology is that which is given by Moses. He says that the name Israel was given to Jacob by the angel with whom he wrestled and came off victorious, for Israel signifies "having power with God" or "prevailing over God" [Gen. 32:28].

But whose eyes, I ask, will this mortal be able so to pierce or tear out as to prevent them from seeing his absurdities? Why does Paul so particularly say that the children had done neither good nor evil [Rom. 9:11] unless he might do away with all respect of merit in them? Why unless he might positively affirm that God drew his reasons from no other source than from his own mind and will when he pronounced so different a judgment on the twin brothers? I well know how common an escapeway is this supposed respect of merit, present or future, in the mind of God. But I would first of all ask this question: If Esau and Jacob had been left to the course of their common nature, what greater amount of good works would God have found in Jacob than in Esau? Most decidedly the hardness of a stony heart in both would have rejected salvation when offered. "But" says Pighius, "a flexible heart was given to both of them so that they might be able to embrace the offered grace; the one was willing to do what, by his free will, he could do; the other refused to do it." As if the apostle were testifying that the unwillingness and refusal of Esau were also given of God! And as if God did not promise to cause his Israel to walk in his commandments!

According to the judgment of Pighius, however, John loudly denies that God gives us the "power to become the sons of God" [John 1:12]. Now this crazy fellow is, first of all, utterly out in taking *power* to mean "faculty" or "ability," when it rather signifies "a worthiness of," "right to," or "title to honor." But he betrays more than gross stupidity when he passes over, as with his eyes shut, the *cause* of this power so clearly described by the evangelist, who declares that those become the sons of God who receive Christ; and John asserts directly afterwards that "these are born, not of flesh, nor of blood, but of God" [v. 13]. God therefore deems those worthy of the honor of adoption who believe in his Son, but whom he had before begotten by his Spirit. That is, those whom he had formed for himself to be his sons, he at length openly declares to be such. For if faith makes us the sons of God, the next step of consideration is, where does faith come from? Who gives us faith? It is the fruit of the seed of the Spirit by which God begets again to a newness of life.

Most true is that which Augustine testifies:

> The redeemed are distinguished from the children of perdition by grace alone. These redeemed are ones that the common mass of original corruption would have gathered to the same perdition but for the free grace of God. It follows that the grace of God to be preached is that by which God *makes* men his elect, not that by which he *finds* them to be such.

This the same holy father continually inculcates.

To this may be added that if God foresees anything in his elect for which he separates them from the reprobate, it would have been quite senseless for the apostle to have argued that it was "not of works, but of him that calleth," because God had said, "The elder shall serve the younger" [Rom. 9:11, 12] when the children were not yet born.

Therefore, this vain attempt to solve the difficulty of God's eternal predestination by introducing the idea of his foreseeing works and merits in the future lives of the elect is openly insulting to the apostle Paul and to his divine testimony. Paul concludes that no respect of works existed in God's election of his people, because he preferred Jacob to his brother before they were born and before they had done "either good or evil" [v. 11]. But these opponents of election, to make good their doctrine that those were chosen of God whom some mark of goodness distinguished from the reprobate, would make it appear that God foresaw what disposition there would be in each person to receive or to reject offered grace. And suppose the apostle's expression "not having done either good or evil" be received by these men; yet God, by their doctrine, will still be electing according to works, because his election will depend on future works foreseen by him. But since the apostle takes for a confessed fact what is wholly disbelieved by these excellent theologians—that all men are alike unworthy and the nature of all equally corrupt—he securely concludes that God elected those whom he did elect from his own goodwill and purpose, not because he foresaw that they would be obedient children to him. The apostle, moreover, is deeply considering what the nature of men would be without the election of God. But these men are dreaming of what good God foresaw in man, which good never could have existed unless God had wrought it.

Although these things are in themselves abundantly clear, the context of the apostle leads us much deeper still into this holy matter. It thus proceeds: "What shall we say then? Is there unrighteousness with God?" [v. 14]. Now either this supposed objection is introduced without any reason whatever, or the doctrine of Paul gives no place for works foreseen. For what suspicion of injustice can possibly be conceived where God offers grace equally to all and permits those who become worthy of it to enjoy it? In a word, when these objectors place the cause of election or reprobation in the works of men's future lives, they seem to escape and to solve, quite to their own satisfaction, this very question that Paul supposes them to put in objection. From this it is fully evident that the apostle was not instructed in this new wisdom. For the apostle introduces these men as inappropriately and unreasonably quarrelling with the justice of God. Let us mark the manner in which he repels the objection he supposes to be made: "God forbid! For he saith to Moses, I will have mercy on whom I will have mercy, and I will have compassion on whom I will have compassion" [vv. 14, 15].

Nothing that I see will be more appropriate than my using the words of Augustine in explanation of this passage:

It is marvelous to observe into what gulfs our adversaries precipitate themselves to avoid the nets of truth when they find themselves hemmed in by these mighty straits. They say that God hated one of these children and loved the other, when not yet born, because he foresaw what the works of their future lives would be. What a wonder it is that this acute view of the mind of God in the mighty matter should quite escape the apostle! He saw no such thing, no such easy solution of the difficulty as the view his adversaries intended. His answer implies that the matter was not so brief, so plain, so evidently true, so absolutely clear, as these opponents imagined. For when he had put forth so stupendous a matter for our meditation as this, how could it be rightly said concerning two children not yet born, not having done either good or evil, that God loved the one and hated the other? Paul briefly and solemnly adds, "What shall we say then? Is there unrighteousness with God?" [v. 14]. Now here was the place to introduce the interpretation invented by our adversaries: "because God foresaw their future works." The apostle, however, does nothing of the kind. On the contrary, that no one might dare to boast of the merits of his works, he commends the grace of God alone by the introduction of that all-conclusive word of God to Moses: "For he saith to Moses, I will have mercy on whom I will have mercy, and I will have compassion on whom I will have compassion"

[Rom. 9:15]. Where are merits now? Where are works either past or future, either fulfilled or to be fulfilled, accomplished by the power or strength of free will? Does not the apostle openly declare his mind in commendation of free grace only?

Thus far have I considered the words of Augustine.

Suppose for a moment that the apostle had introduced no such argument as the two sons of Isaac. (And, indeed, if the solution is so plain and satisfactory that God made the difference between the two children from a respect to their future works, why should the apostle have entangled himself deeper and asserted that the cause of the difference rested in the will of God alone?) Yet God, at the first in his conversation with Moses, had claimed to himself the free right of exercising his mercy as, and towards whom, he pleased. And this he did so that no one might dare to prescribe a law for his actions. He then openly declared that he would take out of the whole multitude of the people whom he would and that he would deliver them, and all were alike covenant breakers. He did not say that his choice of them should depend on themselves and that if he should find any worthy of pardon, he would be merciful to such. But he positively declared that he would be the master, lord, and arbiter of his own mercy; that he would spare whom he would spare, as being bound by no necessity to choose either one or another.

The apostle Paul next infers what of necessity follows from the above declaration of God to Moses: "It is not of him that willeth, nor of him that runneth, but of God that sheweth mercy" [Rom. 9:16]. For if the salvation of men depends on the mercy of God alone, and if God saves none but those whom he chose by his own secret good pleasure, there can be absolutely nothing left for men to do, will, or determine in the matter of salvation.

Pighius explains the solemn case thus: Salvation is not due to any endeavor of ours, nor to any works of ours, because God freely calls us to that salvation. Pighius amuses himself with his opinions quite securely, imagining that he can, by one word, easily do away

with the whole doctrine of the apostle at once. Whereas Paul's conclusion is derived thus: Because God elects those whom he saves by
his own absolute good pleasure and not from any difference of
works in their lives from the works and lives of others; therefore, "It
is not of him that willeth, nor of him that runneth, but of God that
sheweth mercy" [v. 16], thus making the whole turn on the mercy of
God alone. But Pighius thinks he has made a clean escape when he
talks about grace being extended to all, whereas it is due to no one.
And when he says that those become partakers of grace whom the
Lord finds well-disposed and obedient to him, Pighius is forced at
last to fall back on this acknowledgment: Both the "willing" and the
"running" do avail something; but since these are not sufficient of
themselves, the palm must, indeed, be given to the mercy of God.

All these absurdities Augustine refutes most admirably:

> If it is said, "It is not of him that willeth, nor of him that
> runneth, but of God that sheweth mercy" because it pro-
> ceeds from both — that is, both from the will of man and the
> mercy of God — this is the same as saying, The will of man
> alone is not sufficient unless the mercy of God be added to
> it; nor is the mercy of God alone sufficient without the ad-
> dition of the will of man. Moreover, if no Christian man
> dares say, It is not of God that shows mercy but of man that
> wills, it evidently follows that we must understand it is not
> of him that wills nor of him that runs, so that the whole
> glory may be ascribed to God, who prepares the will of man,
> when made good, to be aided by him, and who aids it when
> thus prepared.
>
> More absurd still, therefore, is the cunning device of cer-
> tain ones who spin out of these important questions a
> conclusion that there is a kind of concurrence, or halfway
> meeting, between the mercy of God and the endeavors of
> man. As if Paul meant that men can do very little by run-
> ning unless assisted by the grace of God. Whereas the apos-
> tle reduces all other things to nothing so that he may give

empty and whole place to the mercy of God. For whence is the beginning of all right running? Can anyone of himself go to meet God? Can he do it until led and directed by the Holy Spirit?

Here, again, let me adopt the language of Augustine.

There are daily drawn unto Christ those who were his enemies. "No one can come unto me [says Christ], except my Father draw him" [John 6:44]. He does not say "lead him," as if the will of man in some way preceded, for who is drawn that is already willing to go? But he that is chosen of God is drawn in a wonderful way by him who knows how to work in the hearts of men. Not that they may be made to believe against their wills, or unwillingly, but that they may be made willing who before were unwilling. Hence we see that a man's eternal election by God is proved by this subsequent "running"; yet this is so proved that God's mercy alone (which lifts up those who are down, brings back the wandering into the way, raises the dead to life, and calls things into being that are not) has the preeminence.

We have next to consider the remaining parts of the apostle's sentence concerning the reprobate. Of these Paul brings before us Pharaoh as the most signal instance. For God himself thus speaks of him by Moses: "And in very deed, for this cause have I raised thee up, for to show in thee my power" [Ex. 9:16]. This passage the apostle has faithfully rendered, giving as it were word for word, thus: "Even for this same purpose have I raised thee up, that I might show my power in thee" [Rom. 9:17]. The verb used is *hiphil*,[12] derived from the root *amad*, which signifies "to stand." Pharaoh, therefore, is declared to be put forth openly and prominently as one in whom

_____

12. The *hiphil* is the form of the Hebrew verb that expresses cause. Thus, here the verb *to stand* in the *hiphil* means "to cause to stand."

God might make a memorable example of his power. Whence (or from what state or condition) did God receive Pharaoh in order that he might place him in that position? Pighius would have it that God sustained him by his power for a time when deserving of death. Suppose I would permit him to take refuge under such a cover of escape. He is still entangled and held fast in the fact that God, leaving Pharaoh to his own will and inclination, destined him to destruction.

If Pighius be anxious to dwell upon the longsuffering of God, I fully agree with him. This fact nevertheless remains fixed and unaltered: The reprobate are set apart in the purpose of God for the very end that in them God might show forth his power. Also that the longsuffering of God is, in the present instance, far removed from the apostle's mind and argument is evidenced from his immediate inference when he observes, "Whom he will he hardeneth" [v. 18]. He would not have added this unless, under the expression "raised thee up" [v. 17], he had meant to comprehend that purpose of God by which Pharaoh was ordained to magnify, by his obstinacy, the redemption of God's people Israel. For if anyone should say that Pharaoh's being "raised up" signified his being raised from above to the summit of kingly honor, that indeed is some part but not the whole of the matter. For the LXX [Septuagint] Greek interpreters have used the same expression as that by which they render the *hiphil* verb, derived from the radical *kum*, "to arise." Moreover, God is said to "raise up" what he causes by an outstretched arm, as it were, to accomplish the end he has ordained. Scripture here looks, principally, at the beginning, or first cause, of what it is recording to ascribe the whole to God alone. In this same manner God is also said to "raise up" prophets and ministers of salvation so that no man might claim any of these things to himself on the ground of his own industry. Therefore, the meaning of Moses has been faithfully expressed by the term *raised up*, if you will so receive it. Paul himself did not receive the term in any other way. And most certainly the expression *raised up* comprehends, not less distinctly than summarily, what he had touched upon both concerning the elect and the

reprobate, since he is claiming for God the right and the power to
have mercy on whom he will and to harden whom he will, according to his own pleasure and purpose. The apostle therefore maintains that the right of hardening and of showing mercy is in the
power of God alone, and that no law can be imposed on him as a
rule for his works because no law or rule can be thought of better,
greater, or more just than his own will.

But as some formerly would have it that the apostle is here introducing the wicked railing against God, Pighius also flees to this
refuge. And suppose this be granted to him, the knot is by no means
untied then. For, first, the apostle does not ask a question about
nothing. Second, his answer is such that he admits the objection of
the adversaries to be true. What does Pighius get by such shuffling
as this? He only proves by such quibbles that his cause is a bad one.
But who will be found to cede to him what he asks when he thus
violently sunders, on the one hand, things thus immediately connected together, and on the other, binds into one bundle things
manifestly separate and distinct? After the apostle shows that God
had made a distinction between the elect and the reprobate by his
incomprehensible will, he draws in the same context this inference:
"For he hath mercy on whom he will have mercy, and whom he will
he hardeneth" [v. 18]. To which he immediately subjoins, "Thou wilt
say then unto me, Why doth he yet find fault?" [v. 19]. When Paul
thus makes the persons speaking evidently plain and distinct, who
would not rather attend to Paul's own words than to extraneous
comments upon them?

Augustine here also, as in many other instances, most wisely observes:

It signifies but little in whose person you receive that to be
spoken, which the apostle, by his answer, implies to be true.
If the objection had been false, it is not very likely that the
apostle would have been silent if the cause of the adversaries
had been so good, so clear, and so plausible. For if it be false
that God hardens whom he will, this knot, so insolvable by

all human intellect, might have been settled by the apostle in one word.

Pighius, under this view of the matter, pretends that the apostle declined to give a plain and pointed answer because he did not deem impudent persons worthy of being conversed with; they might rather learn to think humbly than proudly to require a reason for the works of God, just as we elsewhere read (says Pighuis) that the Jews who asked Christ by what authority he did his works were repelled by a like question only. But the words of Paul himself stand directly against such a supposition, for he afterwards curbs the insolence of all those who indulge an audacious curiosity in scrutinizing the secrets of God. He maintains, however, while so doing, the fact that the reprobate are vessels of the wrath of God, in whom he shows his power.

Augustine, therefore, reasons far differently from Pighius, and much more accurately, where he argues, "When Paul had supposed the question to be put, 'Why doth he yet find fault?' [v. 19], does he reply, 'That which thou hast said, O man, is false?' No such thing. Paul's answer is, 'Who art thou, O man, that repliest against God?'" [v. 20].

What Augustine says elsewhere is worthy of notice.

Paul does not break off the discourse of the adversaries by a severe reproof when they are contending against God with profane petulance, as if the justice of God required a solemn defense, but he expresses himself in the way that he thinks most expedient. Certain foolish persons consider that the apostle failed in his reply on this occasion, and that having no reason to give, he merely repressed the audacity of the opponents. But the apostle's words have inconceivable weight: "Who art thou, O man?" In such questions as these, the apostle throws a man back into the consideration of what he is and what is the capacity of his mind. This is a mighty reason rendered, in a few words indeed, but in great reality. For

who that understands not this appeal of the apostle can reply to God? And who that understands it can find anything
to reply?

Therefore Augustine says elsewhere,

> If these arguments of Paul have any weight with us as
> men, let us also gravely listen to the apostle when he appeals
> to us, directly afterwards, in those striking words, "Who art
> thou, O man? . . ." For although God did not create the sins
> of men, who but God created men's natures, which are, in
> themselves, undoubtedly good, but from which there were
> destined to proceed evils and sins, according to the pleasure
> of God's will, and, in many persons, such sins as would be
> visited with eternal punishment. If it be asked, Why did
> God create such natures? the reply is, Because he willed to
> create them. Why did he so will? "Who art thou, O man,
> that repliest against God?"
>
> If vain reasoners have anything more to say, behold a rea-
> son is here rendered to man. This reason is sufficient for
> him, and all that is due to him, if indeed he who is disposed
> to contend for the liberty of his own will can receive even
> this while he is himself under the bondage of his own infir-
> mity. But if a depraved desire to quarrel with God still frets
> anyone, let such a one speak and hear as becomes man: "Who
> art thou, O man?" But let him hear and not despise. And if
> anyone be a despiser, let him believe himself to be "hardened
> of God" so that he may despise.
>
> If anyone despise not, let him believe that he is gifted and
> aided of God so that he might not despise. But let the one
> believe that he is hardened according to his desert; the other,
> that he is helped according to grace.

And what the just desert of man is, Augustine had before shown
in these words:

Every sinner is inexcusable, either on account of his original sin and sinful nature or else from the additional act of his own will, whether he knew that he was sinning or knew it not; whether he had a judgment of what is right or had it not. For ignorance itself, in those who will not understand, is undoubtedly sin, and in those who cannot understand, ignorance is the punishment of sin.

Let the testimony of Augustine aid us no farther.

Ponder with me, readers, this momentous matter by itself. Paul, comparing man with God, as he here does, shows that the counsel of God in electing and reprobating men is without doubt more profound and more deeply concealed than the human mind can penetrate. Therefore, O man, consider (as the apostle advises thee) who and what thou art, and concede more to God than the measure and compass of thine own nature.

Suppose we give place for a moment to the philosophizing of Pighius: The condition of all men is equal except in those who deprive themselves of eternal life, although they were elected even as others. What would there be in this view that is obscure or difficult of solution? What would there be that common sense could not receive, that natural judgment could not make clear? But when you hear of a mystery that surpasses all human understanding, you may immediately conclude that all solutions of men derived from common natural judgment, which might avail in a profane court of justice, are frivolous and vain. Here, however, Pighius attempts to meet us with the remark that those who humbly keep their minds in subjection are never repulsed of God or sent away in doubt; therefore those who thus contend against God are the refractory and haughty only, and such contention is found in none others.

To this assertion I will assent without difficulty, on condition that Pighius confesses, on his part, that the apostle condemns of impious pride all who measure the justice of God by their own comprehension. But according to the judgment of Pighius, God must render a plain reason for everything he does in order to obtain the praise of his justice. Whereas our rule of modesty ought to be that where God's reason for his works lies hidden, we should nevertheless believe him to be just.

The son of Sirach is not ashamed to extol God with the praise that, as a potter, he separates and distinguishes vessels according to his will, and that men are also as clay in the hands of God who forms them and renders to them accordingly as he has decreed. For κρίσις,[13] in this passage, if you compare it with what has preceded, cannot signify anything else than the good pleasure of the workman or potter. Nor do we want to seek an interpreter beyond the apostle himself, who under the same figure openly rebukes the audacity of all who require of God a reason for his works. Demands the apostle, Shall the clay say unto the potter, "Why hast thou made me thus?" [Rom. 9:20]. He therefore will truly confine himself to the moderation of the apostle, who, holding the will of God, though hidden, to be the highest justice, gives to him the free power of destroying or saving whom he will. However much, therefore, Pighius may twist himself in twisting the words of the apostle, he cannot make this similitude apply otherwise, in the present instance, than the apostle has applied it when he introduces it to show that God fashions and forms by his own right all men to whatever destiny he pleases and wills.

If this, at first appearance, would seem to anyone out of the way or unintelligible, let him hear a further admonition of the admirable Augustine:

If beasts could speak and should quarrel with their maker because he had not made them men like us, there is not one of us who would not immediately fly into a rage with them. What, then, do we think of ourselves? Who or what are we that we should contend with God for having made each of us what we are? That man is most certainly mad who will not ascribe to God a far greater and higher excellency than

13. κρίσις is a Greek word meaning "separation," "selection," or "judgment."

that which he and the human race possess above the beasts of the earth. What remains, then, but that the sheep of God's flock quietly and peacefully submit themselves unto him?

This would be far more becoming than, after the example of Pighius, making men the potters instead of God and leaving each one to shape out his destiny by his own virtue.

But Pighius says, "What is here obscure is elsewhere made plain. As the furnace proves the vessels of the potter, so does temptation prove the just." This is true. But from this Pighius concludes that if a just man shall be constant in faith and piety, he will be a vessel unto honor, but if he fail, through want of courage and constancy, he will be a vessel unto dishonor. And since, according to Pighius' account, each one by his own will, assisted by divine grace (which is common, he says, to all men and prepared for all men) at length perseveres, he concludes that we are made vessels unto honor by our invincible fortitude.

I will not stop to observe how absurdly Pighius confounds to-gether two entirely different things: the forming of the vessel and the proving of the vessel when formed. I would merely remark that God's proving his own people by various trials and temptations does not at all alter or interfere with his predestination of them by his eternal will and counsel before they were born. Nor does it alter his forming them, from all eternity, such as he willed them to be afterwards in time. Nor does that passage of Paul, where the apostle says, "If a man, therefore, shall purify himself from these, he shall be a vessel unto honor" [2 Tim. 2:21] in any way support these views of Pighius. Paul is not here showing in what way men, extricated and cleansed from their filth, are made vessels unto honor, but how the faithful who are already chosen and called become adapted for the pure uses of God.

Observe what an exact harmony there is between the mind of Pighius and the mind of the apostle. Pighius' words are:

What is here obscure in the apostle, he elsewhere renders quite plain—why and how it is that God makes some ves-

sels to honor and not others. Thus, in order that Jacob might
be a vessel of mercy, his soul had purified itself, on which account he was deservedly made a vessel unto honor. And it
was thus that God, having a respect unto this self-purifica-
tion that he foreknew, loved and chose the patriarch before
he was born.

So Pighius.
Now hear Paul.

He, on the contrary, when exhorting the faithful thus to purify
themselves, in order to lay a foundation for this doctrine, prefaces
it by saying, "The Lord knoweth them that are his" [v. 19]. In the
same way he elsewhere exhorts the people of God to holiness by
arguing, "For we are his workmanship, created unto good works,
which God hath *before ordained* that we should walk in them" [Eph
2:10]. Paul, therefore, who with all soberness of mind glories in being a wise master-builder, lays the foundation of all salvation in the
free grace of God alone.

Pighius, however, begins his building from the earth's plain sur-
face, without any foundation at all. And in the same way, when
handling that passage of Jeremiah,[14] he consumes a multitude of
words to no purpose whatever. The prophet in that passage is not
describing the origin of our formation, but he is asserting and maintaining God's rightful power in breaking to pieces and destroying
vessels already formed and finished. The mind and intent of the
apostle, therefore, in his use of this similitude, are to be carefully
observed and held fast: God, the maker of men, forms out of the
same lump in his hands one vessel, or man, to honor and another
to dishonor, according to his sovereign and absolute will [Rom.
9:21]. For he freely chooses some to life who are not yet born, leav-

---

14. Jeremiah 19:11: "And shalt say unto them, Thus saith the LORD of hosts;
Even so will I break this people and this city, as one breaketh a potter's vessel,
that cannot be made whole again: and they shall bury them in Tophet, till there
be no place to bury."

ing others to their own destruction, which destruction all men by nature equally deserve. When Pighius holds that God's election of grace has no reference to or connection with his hatred of the reprobate, I maintain that reference and connection to be a truth, inasmuch as the just severity of God answers, in equal and common cause, to that free love with which he embraces his elect.

The apostle Paul then arrives at this conclusion: "What if God, willing to show his wrath and to make his power known, endured with much longsuffering the vessels of wrath fitted to destruction, and that he might make known the riches of his glory on the vessels of mercy, which he had afore prepared unto glory?" [vv. 22, 23]. This forms no ground or reason (means the apostle) that anyone should question God or contend with him.

Pighius, as those like him are wont to do, seizes upon the word *longsuffering*. He dwells on that word with a lofty boast bordering on ferocity, as if God hardened not the reprobate[15] otherwise than by parental indulgence, as it were. Pighius says, "God makes men vessels unto dishonor in no other way than by kindly enduring them while they are abusing his longsuffering and treasuring up for themselves wrath against a day of wrath." What, then, becomes of the difference God made between the two brothers before they were born? If we are to believe Pighius, this difference was made because God foresaw what the hardness of Esau's heart would be. How is it, then, that the election of grace is so distinctly manifest in the case of Jacob when Esau stood in the same grade and position with Jacob until he excluded himself from the number of the children and family of Isaac?

This shifting and shuffling of Pighius are so utterly refuted by one very short sentence of the apostle Paul that it is quite needless to go any farther to fetch arguments for refutation. In what sense the Hebrews use the terms *vessels* and *instruments* everyone who has the least acquaintance with Scripture knows. Wherever we hear of instruments, we shall also find God concerned as the author and

---

15. Cole's translation has *elect* for the word *reprobate*, which cannot be what Calvin intended.

overruler of the whole that is done, while his hand directs the whole. And why are men called vessels of wrath but because God shows toward such his righteous severity that he abstains from showing toward others? Why are they made vessels of wrath? Paul tells us: That God might in them "show forth his wrath and make his power known." The apostle says that they were "fitted to destruction" [v. 22]. When and how did this happen but from their first origin and primitive nature, for the nature of the whole human race was corrupted in the person of Adam? Not that the still higher and deeper purpose of God did not precede the whole, but it was from this fountain that the curse of God commenced its operation. From this source began, in effect, the destruction of the human race. Correspondingly, the apostle testifies that God had "afore prepared the vessels of mercy unto glory" [v. 23].

If this being "afore prepared unto glory" is peculiar and special to the elect, it evidently follows that the rest, the non-elect, were equally "fitted to destruction" [v. 22], because being left to their own nature, they were devoted already to certain destruction. That they were "fitted to destruction" by their own wickedness is an idea so silly that it needs no notice. It is indeed true that the reprobate procure to themselves the wrath of God and that they daily hasten the falling of its weight upon their own heads, but it must be confessed by all that the apostle is here treating of that difference made between the elect and the reprobate that proceeds from the secret will and purpose of God alone. Paul says also that the riches of God's grace are made known on the vessels of mercy, while on the contrary, the vessels of wrath rush on to destruction [vv. 22, 23]. Most certainly nothing is heard of Pighius' absurd prating that grace is the same towards all, but that the goodness of God is the more brightly illustrated by his enduring the vessels of wrath while he suffers them to come to their own end. But with respect to God's longsuffering, the solution of its operation is perfectly plain. It is immediately connected with his power. God does not only permit a thing to be done or to continue by his longsuffering, but he also rules and overrules what is done by his almighty power.

On no other grounds than these can that inviolable engagement of God stand where he says, "I the Lord thy God am a jealous God, merciful to a thousand generations, but a severe avenger unto the third and fourth generation" [Ex. 20:6; Num. 14:18]. This compact, I say, cannot stand unless the Lord by his will decrees to whom he will show mercy and whom he will suffer to remain devoted to eternal death. He extends his grace (he declares) even unto a thousand generations. Now I would ask, does God regard the children of the godly according to their own merits when he continues the grace shown to their fathers upon no other ground than his promise to do so? To Abraham, who had deserved no such favor, God freely bound himself in faithfulness, for the patriarch's sake, to be a God to Abraham's posterity. Hence that solemn appeal to God after the patriarch's death: "Remember, Lord, thy servant Abraham" [Deut. 9:27]. Here most certainly is made a choice of men, and a distinction between them, and that not according to the merits of each, but according to the covenant made with their fathers. Not that all the posterity of Abraham, which descends from him according to the flesh, possess this privilege, but the faith and salvation of all those only who, out of the seed of Abraham, are chosen unto eternal life ought to be referred to this promise.

Exactly the same is the nature of the vengeance that God takes even upon the third and fourth generation. As to what some allege—that all who sin are punished from age to age, each one in his day and order—this is a more than frivolous subterfuge. In this manner the Pelagians of old, finding that they could not disentangle themselves from the nets of those testimonies of Scripture that make it evident that all men sinned in Adam, fell a caviling at the truth and hatched the doctrine that all the posterity of Adam sinned by imitation of him, not through a total corruption of nature derived from him.

As godly teachers then attacked the Pelagians, truly maintaining that all were actually condemned on account of the sin and guilt of Adam, from which sin and guilt the grace of Christ alone frees them, it is the same in the present case. So that the antithesis and parallels may agree with and respond to each other, it of necessity follows that God avenges in the persons of the children the sins that he condemned in their fathers. Nor can many other passages of Scripture be otherwise explained where God declares that he recompenses the iniquity of the fathers into the bosom of their children after them [Ex. 20:5; Num. 14:18]. In vain do the opponents bring against us that passage of Ezekiel, "The son shall not bear the iniquity of the father: the soul that sinneth, it shall die" [Ezek. 18:20], because it forms one particular part of God's vengeance on sin when he leaves men void and destitute of his Spirit. Being thus left destitute, each one bears the consequences of his sin. Therefore, the children are said to bear the sins of their forefathers, and not "undeservedly" (as the profane poet would intimate), because they are guilty on the very ground that, being (as the apostle says) the children of wrath, being thus left to their own natural will and inclination, and being from their origin the heirs of eternal death, they can do nothing but augment their own destruction in a perpetual and uninterrupted course.

We may here most opportunely explain the passage of Isaiah that the Holy Ghost has been pleased to repeat with a particular application six times over in the New Testament. The prophet Isaiah is sent forth with a commission of prodigious awfulness, as it at first appears:

> Go, and tell this people, Hear ye indeed, but understand not; and see ye indeed, but perceive not. Make the heart of this people fat, and make their ears heavy, and shut their eyes; lest they see with their eyes, and hear with their ears, and understand with their heart, and convert, and be healed [Isa. 6:9, 10].

The prophet, being here represented as the minister of blindness, arises confessedly from the nature of the office he has to execute and from the effects by which it was certain that it would be followed. Our great question lies in the cause of that blindness. It will also be confessed to be a deserved punishment inflicted on that un-grateful and rebellious people that light to them should become darkness. And there had, moreover, preceded in them a malicious and obstinate unbelief, which fully deserved to be visited with such recompense. But as the prophet testifies that there was a certain se-lect number on whom salvation shone from the preaching of the word of God, the question to be solved is, Did those favored ones, by any virtue of their own, escape the horrible judgment that lay upon the rest, or were they held safe and secure in the hand of God?

And a weightier question still presses itself upon us: How came it to pass that out of that great multitude some repented, while the disease of others remained incurable?

If anyone should weigh this in the balance of human judgment, he would decide that the cause of the difference was in the men themselves. But God will not suffer us to stop here. He declares that all those who do not follow the stream of the common ruin are saved by his grace. Whether or not repentance is his own work ought not to be brought into controversy. Evidently true is what Augustine says: "Those whom the Lord wills to be converted, he converts himself, who not only makes willing ones out of them who were unwilling, but also makes sheep out of wolves and martyrs out of persecutors, transforming them by his all-powerful grace."

If the wickedness of man be still urged as the cause of the dif-ference between the elect and the non-elect, this wickedness might indeed be made to appear more powerful than the grace of God that he shows towards his elect if that solemn truth did not stand in the way of such an argument: "I will have mercy on whom I will have mercy" [Ex. 33:19; Rom. 9:18]. But Paul's interpretation of the pas-sage of Isaiah before us [6:9, 10] leaves no doubt whatever remain-ing, for after he says that the election of God was determined and fixed, he adds, "The rest were blinded" [Rom. 11:7, 8], that it might be fulfilled which was spoken by the prophet.

I grant that this blindness in the Jews was voluntary, and I freely acknowledge their sin therein. But I perceive who they are whom Paul excepts from this blindness; they are those whom it pleased

God to choose out of the rest. Why did he choose some rather than others? Let no one be offended, then, that he still chooses from time to time some and not others; let us, like Paul, except these chosen ones from the general mass of those who are blinded. Let us not ask the reason that God makes the difference, for, as Paul says, "It is not becoming of man to contend with God" [Rom. 9:20].

The same apostle, when speaking elsewhere to the Jews, from whose virulent malice he had so severely suffered, says, "Well spake the Holy Ghost by Esaias the prophet unto our fathers, saying, Go unto this people, and say, Hearing ye shall hear, and shall not understand; and seeing ye shall see, and not perceive" [Acts 28:25, 26]. He charges their sin home upon them, accordingly as they fully deserved. Some persons will erroneously and ignorantly conclude that the cause and beginning of this obduracy in the Jews was their malicious wickedness, just as if there were no deeper and more occult cause of the wickedness itself, namely, the original corruption of nature, and as if they did not remain sunk in this corruption because, being reprobated by the secret counsel of God before they were born, they were left undelivered.

Now let us listen to the evangelist John, who will be no ambiguous interpreter. "But though," says John, "Jesus had done so many miracles before them, yet they believed not on him, that the saying of Esaias the prophet might be fulfilled which he spake, Lord, who hath believed our report? and to whom hath the arm of the Lord been revealed? Therefore, they could not believe, because that Esaias said again, he hath blinded their eyes, and hardened their heart" [John 12:37–40; Isa. 53:1; Isa. 6:9, 10]. Most certainly John does not give us to understand that the Jews were prevented by their sinfulness from believing, for though this be quite true in one sense, yet the cause of their not believing must be traced to a far higher source. The secret and eternal purpose and counsel of God must be viewed as the original cause of their blindness and unbelief. It perplexed, in no small degree, the ignorant and the weak when they heard that there was no place for Christ among the people of God (for the Jews were such). John explains the reason by showing that none believe except those to whom it is given, and that there are few to whom God reveals his arm.

This other prophecy concerning "the arm of the Lord" [Isa. 53:1], the evangelist weaves into his argument to prove the same great truth, and his words have a momentous weight. He says, "*Therefore, they could not believe*" [John 12:39]. Let men torture themselves as long as they will with reasoning that the cause of the difference— why God does not reveal his arm equally to *all*—lies hidden in his own eternal decree. The whole of the evangelist's argument amounts evidently to this: Faith is a special gift, and the wisdom of Christ is too high and too deep to come within the compass of man's understanding. The unbelief of the world, therefore, ought not to astonish us if even the wisest and most acute of men fail to believe. Hence, unless we would evade the plain and confessed meaning of the evangelist that few receive the gospel, we must fully conclude that the cause is the will of God, and that the outward sound of the gospel strikes the ear in vain until God is pleased to touch by it the heart within.

A different occasion for citing this passage of Isaiah [6:9, 10] presents itself to the other three evangelists while they are each recording the life and ministry of our Lord [Matt. 13:10, 11; Mark 4:11, 12; Luke 8:9, 10]. In Matthew, our Savior separates and distinguishes his disciples from the common mass of men. He declares that it was given to them (his disciples) to know the mysteries of the kingdom of heaven, but he spoke to others in parables so that hearing, they might hear and not understand, that the saying of Isaiah might be fulfilled [Isa. 6:9; Matt. 13:11,12].

I am willing to confess that those to whom Christ spoke parabolically were unworthy, in themselves, of greater light. But I would wish to ask: What greater merit in themselves had the apostles in order to be freely admitted into familiarity with Christ, into which familiarity Christ did freely admit them? Here the antithesis is clearly established: Grace was freely conferred on few when it might have been with justice denied equally to all. For shall we say that the apostles procured for themselves, by their own merits, that which the Lord declares was freely "given" to them?

Nor are we to pass by without particular remark that the Savior names the things that he taught them "mysteries" [Matt 13:11]. And most certainly there is nothing in the whole circle of spiritual doctrine that does not far surpass the capacity of man and confound its utmost reach. No explanation by words, therefore, however lucid, will suffice to make the mysteries of the kingdom of God understood unless the Holy Spirit, at the same time, teaches within. But Christ would have his disciples magnify it as a precious pledge of the favor of God toward them that he honored them above the common mass of men in blessing them with the external means of teaching. He was all the while, though, gradually leading them to that high and singular privilege that distinguishes "friends" from "servants," as John has it: "Henceforth I call you not servants, for the servant knoweth not what his lord doeth; but I have called you friends, for all things that I have heard of my Father I have made known unto you" [John 15:15]. These friends are thus taught from above to the very end, that they might understand those things that are beyond all natural comprehension. Hence it was that Christ, on such occasions as these, so frequently uttered that loud appeal, "He that hath ears to hear let him hear" [Matt. 11:15; Matt. 13:9, 43; Mark 4:9, 23; Mark 7:16; Luke 8:8; Luke 14:35]. By this expression Christ not only distinguished attentive from inattentive hearers, but he also implied that all are deaf save those whose ears God is pleased to bore that they may hear, which divine blessing David magnifies in the name of the whole church of God: "Sacrifice and offering thou didst not desire; mine ears hast thou opened" [Ps. 40:6].

I will proceed no farther with discussing the several portions of God's word relative to this divine and deep matter. Let this summary suffice: If we admit the same Spirit of God, who spoke by the apostles, to be an interpreter of the prophet Isaiah, we must also acknowledge that the secret and incomprehensible judgment of God that blinds the greater part of mankind — "that seeing, they may see and not perceive" [Isa. 6:9, 10]—is to be adored while it does so. Here let human reasonings of every kind that can possibly present themselves to our minds cease forever. For if we confine our reflections to men, apart from the grace and eternal purpose of God, the first thing that will strike us is that God gives freely to those who ask him, and that others sink and die under their need, for which they do not seek a remedy. But if we have not in our mind and understanding that which Augustine says—"That the nature of the divine goodness is not only *to open* to those who knock, but also *to cause* them to knock and ask"—unless, I say, we understand this, we shall never know the real need under which we labor.

If we come to *the help*, universal experience proves that all do not comprehend that power of the Holy Spirit by which everything is done that ought to be done. Let no one deceive himself by vain self-flattery. Those who come to Christ were before sons of God in his divine heart, while in themselves they were his enemies. And because they were preordained unto eternal life, they were therefore given unto Christ. Hence the faithful admonition of Augustine:

> Let those who thus come to Christ remember that they are vessels of grace, not of merit, for grace is to them all merit. Nor let us delight in any other knowledge than that which begins and ends in admiration. Let those deride us who will, if God but give his nod of assent from heaven to our stupidity, as men think, and if angels do but applaud it.

The Arguments of Pighius

In summary we will now collect those objections of Pighius that seem to carry with them any kind of color, so that our readers may understand that the weapons with which our antagonist fights are quite as bad as the cause that he alleges for kindling the flame of so mighty a contest. He asserts that the whole question turns on the end to which man was created. And he holds it as a great absurdity to suppose that God expected any return from the creation of man,

for being content in himself alone, he could want no one else or anything else.

I also confess that God has no need of any external aid, prop, or
addition; but I deny the justness of the conclusion that he therefore
had no respect or consideration for himself when he created man for
his own glory. For what does this word of Solomon mean: "The Lord
hath made all things for himself; yea, even the wicked for the day of
evil" [Prov. 16:4]? Therefore, we evince no absurdity when we say
that God, though needing nothing to be added to himself, yet created the race of men for his own glory. The great and essential end
of man's creation ought to be considered, and most deservedly so.

The sophism of Pighius, therefore, is the more ridiculous when
he reasons that God could have no respect for himself in the creation of man, because God is in himself infinitely perfect. It is quite
curious to observe how our opponent wriggles himself out of the net
in which the above word of Solomon entangles him. "God," says
Pighius, "did indeed make all things for himself; not, however, with
any reference to his own glory, but because of the infiniteness of his
goodness." And that this absurd interpretation may not want abundance of weight, he asserts that no commentators agree with me except a few detestable heretics, as he terms them. Now why should I
waste time on the refutation of such futile absurdities as these? The
Hebrew word *lammaanehu* that Solomon uses has the same meaning as the expression "for his own sake." One person, inflated with
his half-Latin gabble, is anxious to explain to us the meaning of the
adverb *propter*; whereas, if he had but one spark of a sound mind, the
context itself would clearly demonstrate to him that "the wicked were
made for the day of evil" only because it was God's will to show forth
in them his glory, just as elsewhere God declares that he raised up
Pharaoh for the very cause that in him he might show forth his
power and name to all the nations of the earth [Ex. 9:16; Rom. 9:17].

To give some color to his absurd error, Pighius introduces the
testimony of Moses, where he appeals to the Jews: "And now, O Israel, what doth the Lord thy God require of thee, but to love him

and to worship him?" [Deut. 10:12]. Which one of my readers is so senseless as not to see at once that we have in Pighius a man destitute of a sound mind, blattering without the least modesty? I am sure there is not such a reader of these pages. What? Does God desire to be worshiped by us more for our sakes than for his own? Is his regard for his own glory so buried out of his sight that he regards us alone? What, then, is to become of all those testimonies of Scripture that make the glory of God to be the highest object and ultimate end of man's salvation? Therefore, let us hold fast this glorious truth: The mind of God in our salvation was such as not to forget himself, but to set his own glory in the first and highest place, and he made the whole world that it might be a stupendous theater whereon to manifest his own glory. Not that he was dissatisfied in himself, or that he had any need to borrow addition from any other sources; but it was his good pleasure so highly to honor his creatures as to impress on them the bright marks of his great glory.

After commencing with so much success, Pighius subjoins another end that God had in the creation of man. Having a respect (he says) to the nature of his own goodness, God wished to create a rational creature capable of receiving that goodness, which he adds could not be done without God's bestowing on that creature freedom of will. This being admitted, Pighius considers all my teaching to fall to the ground at once when I maintain that God decreed a difference between the elect and the reprobate. Man (he argues), being thus made by his free will the arbiter of his future state, had either event—the good or the evil, to be saved or to be lost— in his own hand.

Readers are here to be admonished and exhorted ever to hold God, their maker and creator, in that highest of all honor that is due to him, and never to exercise an insolent or forward eye when considering his purpose in the creation of the human race, but to view him with reverence, soberness, and the pure eye of faith. I know full well that no mention whatever can be made of God's eternal predestination, but immediately numberless unholy and absurd thoughts rush into the mind. Hence many over-modest persons are found who wish that the glorious doctrine of predestination were never named at all, lest occasion should thereby be given to wanton minds to exalt themselves against God. However, passing by all such over-careful speculations and leaving them to others, I consider it unjustifiable in a Christian man thus cautiously to keep back the genuine confession of the truth lest it should be exposed to the grin of the profane. For in the first place, there is nothing more precious to God than his truth. In the next place, he will not have his justice to be protected by our dissimulation. Finally, it needs no such protection. On these points, however, we shall dwell more fully hereafter. I will now briefly reply to Pighius on the point more particularly in question.

Pighius contends that men were so immediately created unto salvation that no counsel of God concerning the contrary event— man's destruction—preceded his creation. As if the Lord did not foresee before man was created what his future condition would be, and as if he did not afore determine what it was his will should be done. Man, that he might be the image of God, was adorned from the first with the light of reason and with rectitude of nature. Therefore, as our opponent would reason, God, being (to speak reverently) blind, foresaw not all events, but waited in doubt and suspense for the issue of those events. Such is Pighius' theological reasoning. Such are the antecedents and consequents of his logic. Hence he boldly concludes, from his view of the end of man's creation, that God so disposed the creation of all men that they should all, at their creation, be made (without distinction, difference, or discrimination) partakers of his goodness and blessedness.

However, godly minds can by no means whatever be brought to reconcile God's election and reprobation of men thus. They cannot harmonize by such carnal reasoning the voluntary sin of man and the eternal purpose of God. With these human eyes they cannot see how it was that man should be placed in that condition when first created, that he himself, falling by his own will, should be the cause of his own destruction. Yet it was so ordained by the secret and eternal purpose of God that this voluntary destruction of the human race and all the posterity of Adam should be a cause for the saints' humbling themselves before God and worshiping his eternal purpose in the whole. For although it pleased God thus to ordain the whole, yet man, who had been endued with an upright nature and had been made in the image of God, did not the less willingly, on his part, hurl himself into this headlong ruin. But I would repeat my being perfectly aware how much absurdity and irreconcilable contradiction these deep things seem to carry with them, according to profane persons. Nevertheless, let one conscience suffice us in the place of a thousand such witnesses. If we duly listen to this conscience, we shall not be ashamed to confess that man perished justly, seeing that he chose to follow Satan rather than God.

The Proofs of Pighius

Let us now hear Pighius' proofs for his above views, arguments, and conclusions. In these he labors to show that salvation was ordained for all men without distinction or difference. "If it were not so," he says, "the Holy Spirit speaks falsely when he declares that God is the Father of all men" [Mal. 2:10]. The prophet is there treating of marriage, the faith of which many husbands violated at that time. Malachi is reminding such violators that God is the avenger of conjugal infidelity. Hence let our readers gather how much religion and conscience Pighius has in dealing with Holy Scripture.

Pighius then adds, "The Lord is good to all" [Ps. 145:9], from which he concludes that all were ordained unto eternal life. If this be true, the kingdom of heaven is open for dogs and asses, for the psalmist is magnifying not only the goodness of God that he shows to man, but also what he extends to all his works. Why should not Pighius thus fight for his brethren?

Then follows a third proof that, according to Paul "there is no difference between the Jew and the Gentile" [Rom. 10:12]. Now all this I receive most fully, provided there be added what the same apostle teaches: Gentiles were called to a participation of the gospel because they were ordained thereto by the eternal counsel of God [Rom. 16:26].

Pighius cites also that passage in Ecclesiasticus: "God hateth nothing that he hath made." As if we had not always maintained that God hates nothing in us that is his own, save that fallen nature only, which may be justly called a deformity of the first creation. The great question of reprobation, however, by no means turns on the hinge of whether or not God hates anything that he has made. For although long before the fall of Adam, God had, for secret reasons of his own, decreed what he would do, yet we read in Scripture that nothing was or is condemned by him but sin.

There flows from these premises, therefore, the plain and solid conclusion that God had just causes for reprobating a part of mankind—causes, however, hidden from us—but that he hates and condemns nothing in man, except that which is contrary to his justice.

The next Scripture that Pighius tacks on to his argument is that of Paul, who declares (he says) that God "included all under sin" [Gal. 3:22] "that he might have mercy upon all" [Rom. 11:32]. As if Paul were disputing about the *number* of men! Whereas Paul is abstractedly lauding the grace of God towards all of us who attain unto salvation. Most certainly nothing was less in the mind of the apostle than an extension of the mercy of God to all men. His sole object was to prostrate all glorying of the flesh so that we may clearly understand that no man will ever be saved but he whom God saves by grace alone.

Behold, then, with what glorious arguments our opponent demonstrates that none are chosen unto salvation from above in preference to others. Yet this ape of Euclid puffs himself off in the titles of all his chapters as a first-rate reasoner.

The third end of man's creation, which is so clearly and powerfully expressed by Solomon—"The Lord hath made all things for himself, even the wicked for the day of evil" [Prov. 16:4]—Pighius attacks in the following way. With reference to God's condemnation of the reprobate and his punishment of sin, Pighius argues thus:

If we say that God in his eternal decrees had any respect to what would happen to each person after his creation, we must necessarily confess that the discrimination between the elect and the reprobate was, in the divine mind, antecedent to the fall of man. Whence it will follow that the reprobate are not condemned because they were ruined in Adam, but because they were already devoted to destruction even before the fall of Adam.

To this witless argument I reply, what wonder is it that Pighius should thus (to use his own expression) *indiscriminately* confound all things in reference to the deep judgments of God when he knows not how to make the least distinction between remote and proximate causes. After men have looked this way and that way, they can never, by so doing, fix upon the cause of their destruction, nor upon the fault that produced it. And why? Because the proximate fault rests with themselves. And should they complain that the wound is inflicted on them from some other quarter, the internal sense of their mind will bind them fast to the conclusion that the evil arose from the voluntary defections and fall of the first man. I know full well that the insolence of the carnal mind cannot be prevented from immediately bawling, "If God foreknew the fall of Adam and yet was unwilling to apply a remedy, we are rather perishing in our innocence by his bare external decree than suffering the just punishment of our sin." Suppose we grant that nothing was in this way foreseen of God or thus viewed by him? The old complaint concerning original sin will still be made, and as loud as ever: "Why was not Adam left to sin for himself as a private individual so as to bear the consequences alone? Why was he made to involve us, who deserved no such calamity, in a participation of the same ruin? Indeed, under what color of justice does God visit on us the punishment of another's fault?" But after all has been said that can be said on the subject, the internal feeling in every man's heart continues to urge its conviction, nor will it suffer any child of Adam to absolve himself (even himself being his own judge) from the sin, the guilt, or the punishment consequent on the original transgression of Adam. Nor can anyone, in truth, raise a controversy on the matter. For as on account of the sin of one man, a deadly wound was inflicted on all men, all men at once acknowledge the judgment of God thereon to be righteous.

If, then, nothing can prevent a man from acknowledging that the first origin of his ruin was from Adam, and if each man finds the proximate cause of his ruin in himself, what can prevent our faith from acknowledging afar off, with all sobriety, adoring, and humility, that remote secret counsel of God by which the fall of man was thus preordained? And what should prevent the same faith from beholding, at the same time, the proximate cause within: The whole human race is individually bound by the guilt and just desert of eternal death as derived from the person of Adam, and all are in themselves, therefore, subject to death and to death eternal? Pighius, therefore, has not severed, shaken, or altered (as he thought he had done) that preeminent and most beautiful symmetry with which these proximate and remote causes divinely harmonize.

Our readers must bear in mind that both of the following propositions are equally condemned by Pighius: He denies that God from the beginning, before man had yet fallen, decreed what should take place after his fall; and he denies that God chooses out of the fallen mass those whom he willed so to choose. He laughs at Augustine and all like him; that is, at all the godly who imagine (as he terms it) that after God foreknew the universal ruin of the human race in the person of Adam, he ordained some to eternal life and others to eternal destruction. For since Pighius takes it as an acknowledged fact that the counsel of God concerning the creation of all men to salvation was *antecedent* to the fall of Adam, he maintains without a doubt that this purpose of God still remains fixed and unaltered. Otherwise, argues he, God would not be consistent with himself, and his immutable purpose would be subverted by the sin of man. He severely attacks that appearance of direct contradiction (as they term it) in our doctrine. He maintains that since God (as we teach) decreed, before Adam was created, what should happen to him and to his posterity, the destruction of the reprobate ought not to be imputed to sin committed after the fall, because it would be absurd to make the effect *antecedent* to its cause. I maintain that both these propositions that Pighius combats are true. And as to his holding before our eyes a pretended disagreement between the two sentiments, there is no such discordance at all.

We maintain that man was so created and placed in such a condition that he could have no cause whatever of complaint against his maker. God foresaw the fall of Adam, and most certainly God's suffering Adam to fall was not contrary to, but according to, his divine will. What room is there for quibbling or shuffling here? And what does such quibbling profit or effect? Yet Pighius denies the truth of this position because (he argues) the before-conceived counsel of God concerning the salvation of all men still stands unaltered. As if no solution of his pretended difficulty could be found. The truth of the matter is that salvation was not offered to all men on any other ground than on the condition of their remaining in their original innocence. For, that the decree of God concerning the salvation of all men was decisive and absolute, no one of a sound mind will hold or concede. For when man was placed in a way of salvation, his having willingly fallen from it was a sufficient ground for his just condemnation. But it could not be otherwise. Adam could not but fall, according to the foreknowledge and will of God. What then? Is Adam on that account freed from fault? Certainly not. He fell by his own full free will and by his own willing act.

If Augustine had said that it was once (or on one occasion) purposed of God to save all men, the wily argument of Pighius might have some weight in refutation of such an opinion. But when Augustine declares his mind to be that Adam was so constituted at his first creation that his proximate, or his own, rejection of life was well known to God; nay, that Adam's rejection of it was, as it were, already included in the secret counsel of God, Augustine truly and justly concludes from such grounds that the reprobate are so involved and bound up in the universal original guilt that, being left thus in death, they righteously suffer that judgment of God. The same I also hold. And I maintain that as all men are lost in Adam, those who perish, perish by the just judgment of God. Yet at the same time, I witness as my solemn confession that whatever happened to or befell Adam was so ordained of God.

The Refutation of Pighius

Now as I proceed, it will be my object not so much to consider what Pighius says, nor in what order he says it, as to take care that this worthless fellow be prostrated and buried under the ruins of his own desperate impudence. And my great concern will be to satisfy godly consciences, which we very frequently find to be disturbed by such fellows by reason of their simplicity and inexperience. To accomplish these ends, I will select out of the flowing stream of our opponent's interminable loquacity those parts that appear to be the most taking and prominent, or the most specious and plausible, so that all may witness how much such a fellow can say without saying anything.

Preaching

One reason (Pighius says) he cannot believe in particular and special election is that Christ, the redeemer of the whole world, commanded the gospel to be preached to all men, promiscuously, generally, and without distinction. But the gospel is an embassy of peace, by which the world is reconciled to God, as Paul teaches [2 Cor. 5:18, 19]. And, according to the same holy witness, it is preached so that those who hear it may be saved.

To this pretended difficulty of Pighius, I would briefly reply that Christ was so ordained the Savior of the whole world that he might save those who were given unto him by the Father out of the whole world, that he might be the eternal life of them of whom he is the head, and that he might receive into a participation of all the "blessings in him" [Eph. 1:3] all those whom God adopted to himself by his own unmerited good pleasure to be his heirs. Now which one of these solemn things can our opponent deny?

Hence the apostle Paul declares this prophecy of Isaiah to be fulfilled in Christ: "Behold, I and the children whom the Lord hath given me" [Isa. 8:18; Heb. 2:13]. Accordingly, Christ himself declares aloud: "All that the Father giveth me shall come to me, and him that cometh to me I will in no wise cast out" [John 6:37]. And again, "Those that thou gavest me I have kept, and none of them is lost, but the son of perdition" [John 17:12]. Hence we read everywhere that Christ diffuses life into none but the members of his own body. And he who will not confess that it is a special gift and a special mercy to be engrafted into the body of Christ has never read with spiritual attention Paul's Epistle to the Ephesians.

Hereupon follows a third important fact: The virtue and benefits of Christ are extended unto and belong to none but the children of God. That the universality of the grace of Christ cannot be better judged of than from the nature of the preaching of the gospel, there is no one who will not immediately grant. Yet on this hinge the whole question turns. If we see and acknowledge, therefore, the principle on which the doctrine of the gospel offers salvation to all, the whole sacred matter is settled at once. That the gospel is, in its nature, able to save all, I by no means deny. But the great question lies here: Did the Lord by his eternal counsel ordain salvation for all men? It is quite manifest that all men, without difference or distinction, are outwardly called or invited to repentance and faith. It is equally evident that the same mediator is set forth before all as he who alone can reconcile them to the Father. But it is as fully well known that none of these things can be understood or perceived but by faith, in fulfillment of the apostle Paul's declaration that "the gospel is the power of God unto salvation to every one that believeth" [Rom. 1:16]. Then what can it be to others but "the savor of death unto death?" as the same apostle elsewhere powerfully expresses himself [2 Cor. 2:16].

Further, as it is undeniably manifest, out of the multitudes

whom God calls by his outward voice in the gospel, very few believe. If I prove that the greater part of these multitudes remain unbelieving (for God deems none worthy of his illumination but
whom he will), I obtain thereby the next conclusion: The mercy of
God is offered equally to those who believe and to those who believe not, so that those who are not divinely taught within are rendered only inexcusable, not saved. Some make a distinction here,
holding that the gospel is saving to all regarding its power to save,
but not in its effect of saving. But they by no means untie the knot
by this halfway argument. We are still rolled back to the same great
question: Is the same power to believe conferred upon all men?

Paul assigns the reason that all do not obey the gospel. He refers
us to the prophet Isaiah: "Lord, who hath believed our report, and
to whom is the arm of the Lord revealed?" [Isa. 53:1; Rom. 10:16].
The prophet here, astonished at the fewness of those who believe,
seems to cry aloud that it was a thing of the highest shame and reproach that while the word of God was sounding in the ears of all
men, there were scarcely any hearts inwardly touched by it. But that
so awful a depravity in man might not terrify the contemplators of
it, the apostle Paul afterwards intimates that it is not given to all
thus to believe, but to those only to whom God manifests himself
[v. 20]. In a word, the apostle in this chapter intimates that any ef-
fort or sound of the human voice will be ineffectual unless the secret power of God works in the hearts of the hearers. Of this fact
Luke places before our eyes a memorable proof. After he had
recorded the sermon preached by Paul, Luke says, "And as many as
were ordained to eternal life believed" [Acts 13:48]. Now why was
not this same doctrine of Paul received with the same mind and
heart by all who heard it? Luke assigns the reason and defines the
number of the receivers: "As many as were ordained to eternal life
believed." The rest did not believe because they were not "ordained
to eternal life." And who is the giver of this disposition of heart but
God alone?

As to those who absurdly argue that these persons were ordained to believe by the natural impulse of their own hearts, such

silly persons are no more worthy of refutation than those would be who would affirm that the world was made by itself. The secret of the whole lies in the hidden wisdom of the gospel, which is deeper than can be penetrated by any acuteness of human intellect. "The natural man" says the apostle, "receiveth not the things of the Spirit of God" [1 Cor. 2:14]. Is it because he will not? That indeed is quite true, for all are rebellious against God who are not subdued and humbled by his Spirit. But the apostle carries the matter much deeper and higher than this, both as to man and as to God, showing that there is a "foolishness" and "ignorance" in man so that he *cannot* understand the things of the Spirit, and that the wisdom and counsel of God decreed the whole. For the apostle says, "Who hath known the mind of the Lord, and who hath been his counsellor?" [v. 16; Rom. 11:34]. No one, argues he, can know the secrets of God but by his Spirit only [1 Cor. 2:10, 11]. Whence he fully concludes that those alone are the scholars of God who are gifted, not with "the spirit of this world," but with his own heavenly Spirit, "that they may know the things that are freely given them of God" [v. 12].

What does the apostle mean by drawing this comparison between "the spirit of the world" and "the Spirit which is of God" but this: Men, while unregenerate, can only be wise in their own way and can only cleave unto the earth, but God as a heavenly Father illuminates his own children in a special manner. Yet Pighius would here thrust upon us the absurd notion that where it pleases God, each one may prepare himself by his own voluntary will and endeavor. As if Paul were not speaking to the Corinthians, whom he shortly afterwards describes as having been thieves, drunkards, slanderers, dissolute, and laden with every monstrous iniquity until they were cleansed by the sanctification of the Spirit [1 Cor. 6:9 – 11]. Now what could there be in these persons whom God had dragged out of hell itself? What could there be in these awful sinners, I say, that could help them to meet God halfway, as it were, or to deserve the illumination of his Spirit? But why should I employ a wide circle of words? The Spirit of God, who reveals to us the "mysteries of the kingdom of heaven" [Matt. 13:11], is the Spirit of adoption; and divine adoption is wholly gratuitous, the free gift of God. Therefore, the Spirit himself is freely given to whomever he is bestowed. That the Spirit is not thus freely bestowed on all men, universal experience undeniably proves. Therefore, faith is the special gift of God, and by that gift, election is manifested to and ratified in the soul who receives it.

This is what Paul means when he says that Christ, who is a "stumbling block" to the Jews and "foolishness" to the Greeks, is "to them that are called, the wisdom of God and the power of God" [1 Cor. 1:23, 24]. The next question is, where does calling come from? Whence but from God, who calls "according to his purpose" [Rom. 8:28] those whom he has chosen? From this state of things flows the conclusion (and this we hold fast) that the gospel, which is in its essential nature "a savor of life unto life" and ought to be so to all who hear it, becomes "a savor of death unto death in them that perish" [2 Cor. 2:15, 16], who thus remain in their darkness and unbelief because "the arm of the Lord" is not revealed to them [John 12:38].

If, then, amidst so universal a corruption and depravity of our nature, some few do believe the gospel, to ascribe the faith of such to their own goodness would be perfectly impious. No! Let thanks, on the contrary, be given to God continually, according to the admonition of the apostle, "because God hath from the beginning chosen such believers unto salvation, through sanctification of the Spirit and belief of the truth" [2 Thess. 2:13], in which words the apostle traces faith and sanctification to the eternal election of God as its source and cause. What shall we say then? Were these chosen because they had sanctified themselves and rendered themselves meet or worthy to be chosen? The apostle asserts most expressly that this sanctification was the work of the Spirit of God. And as the nature of faith is the same and equally the gift of God and the work of his Spirit, it incontrovertibly follows that those who are illuminated unto faith are thus illuminated and gifted with faith, in order that their election of God may be manifested and ratified by its very effects. And most certainly, when we hear that no one comes unto Christ but he that is drawn by the Father, we may safely adopt the language and argument of Augustine:

> Who can be said to be drawn who is already willing to go? And yet no one comes to Christ but he who is willing. Therefore, every comer to Christ is drawn in a wonderful way, that he may be willing, by him who knows how to work inwardly on the very hearts of men and so to work in them, not that they may believe against their wills (which would be impossible), but that they may be made willing to believe, who were before unwilling to believe.

God's Will That All Be Saved

All this Pighius loudly denies, citing the passage of the apostle Paul, "Who will have all men to be saved" [1 Tim. 2:4]. Referring also to Ezekiel 18:23, Pighius argues thus: That God wills not the death of a sinner may be taken upon his own oath, where he says by the prophet, "As I live, saith the Lord, I have no pleasure in the death of the wicked; but rather that he should return from his way and live" [Ezek. 33:11].

We reply that since the language of Ezekiel is an exhortation to repentance, it is not at all marvelous in him to declare that God wills all men to be saved, for the mutual relation between threats and promises shows that such forms of speaking are conditional. In this same manner God declared to the Ninevites, and to the kings of Gerar and Egypt, that he would do what in reality he did not intend to do, for their repentance averted the punishment that he had threatened to inflict upon them. It is evident that the punishment was announced on condition of their remaining obstinate and impenitent. Yet the announcement of the punishment was positive, as if it had been an irrevocable decree. But after God had terrified them with the apprehension of his wrath and had duly humbled them as not being utterly desperate, he encourages them with the hope of pardon, that they might feel that there was yet left open a

space for remedy. Just so it is with respect to the conditional
promises of God that invite all men to salvation. They do not positively prove what God has decreed in his secret counsel, but declare only what God is ready to do to all those who are brought to
faith and repentance.

But men untaught of God, not understanding these things, allege that we hereby attribute to God a twofold or double will,
whereas God is so far from being variable that no shadow of such
variableness appertains to him, even in the most remote degree.
Hence Pighius, ignorant of the divine nature of these deep things,
thus argues, "What else is this but making God a mocker of men if
God is represented as really not willing what he professes to will,
and as not having pleasure in what he actually has pleasure?" But if
these two parts of the sentence be read in conjunction, as they
ought to be — "I have no pleasure in the death of the wicked," and "but
that the wicked turn from his way and live" [Ezek. 33:11] — the calumny
is washed off at once. God requires of us this conversion, or turning away from our iniquity [Ezek 18:23, 30; Ezek. 33:11], and in
whomever he finds it, he does not disappoint such a one of the
promised reward of eternal life. Therefore, God is as much said to
have pleasure in and to will this eternal life as to have pleasure in
repentance; he has pleasure in repentance because he invites all men
to it by his word. All this is in perfect harmony with his secret and
eternal counsel by which he decreed to convert none except his own
elect. None but God's elect, therefore, ever do turn from their
wickedness. Yet on these accounts the adorable God is not to be
considered variable or capable of change, because as a lawgiver he
enlightens all men with the external doctrine of conditional life. In
this primary manner he calls or invites all men unto eternal life. But
he brings unto eternal life his own children, only those whom he
willed according to his eternal purpose and regenerated by his
Spirit as an eternal Father.

It is quite certain that men do not "turn from their evil ways" to
the Lord of their own accord or by any instinct of nature. Equally

certain is it that the gift of conversion is not common to all men, because this is one of the two covenants that God promises he will not make with any but his own children and his own elect people, concerning whom he has recorded his promise, "I will write my law in their hearts" [Jer. 31:33]. A man must be utterly beside himself to assert that this promise is made to all men generally and indiscriminately. God says expressly by Paul, who refers to the prophet Jeremiah, "For this is the covenant that I will make with them. Not according to the covenant that I made with their fathers; but I will put my laws into their mind, and write them in their hearts" [Heb. 8:9, 10]. To apply this promise to those who were worthy of this new covenant or to such as had prepared themselves by their own merits or endeavors to receive it, surely must be worse than the grossest ignorance and folly, and the more so as the Lord is speaking by the prophet to those who before had "stony hearts." All this is plainly stated and fully explained by the prophet Ezekiel [Ezek. 11:19; Ezek. 36:26].

That obstinacy and enmity are common to all men, I fully admit. I also maintain that the heart of no man is softened and made flexible and obedient to the will of God until God gives him the will and power to do what he commands. For why are we called "new creatures" [2 Cor. 5:17] but because "we are his workmanship, created unto good works" [Eph 2:10]. But, I ask you, what kind of a division, and how iniquitous a division of all praise and glory, would it be to make God the creator of us mortal men, and yet to make each one of us his own creator unto righteousness and eternal life? In this way God would only have for himself the praise of ineffectual and failing grace. The portion of the glory that is far more excellent would fall to our lot. But Scripture positively affirms that to circumcise the hearts of men is the work of God alone, and regeneration is not ascribed to any other than God himself. Hence it is that whatever in man is created anew, in the image of God, is called "spirit": "That which is born of the flesh *is flesh*, and that which is born of the Spirit *is spirit*" [John 3:6]. God does, indeed, frequently invite us to repentance, but he is everywhere declared to be the author of conversion; his "law" is said "to convert souls" [Ps. 19:7]. The intermediate agency of this conversion, however, is frequently transferred to the ministers of the word. But as—while they labor by praying, by sowing, by watering, it is God alone who "giveth the increase" [1 Cor. 3:6, 7]—it is not at all to be wondered at that it should be declared to be his work alone to open the heart of his own to "attend to the things spoken" by his ministers [Acts 16:14].

Hence Augustine, after having treated of the elect and having shown that their salvation is safely secured under the faithful custody of God, so that no one of them can perish, makes these solemn and blessed observations:

> All the rest of mankind, who are not of this number but are of the same fallen mass, being ordained vessels of wrath, are born for the use and service of these elect ones. For God created no one, even of them, at random, by chance, or for naught. Nor does he work ignorantly whatever good he works in or by them. For his creating in them a human nature is itself a good thing. And his adorning by them the order of this present life is a good thing. But God brings no one of these to spiritual repentance and to reconciliation with himself. Although, therefore, these are born out of the same lump of perdition as the elect of God, yet by their hardness and impenitency of heart they all, as far as in them lies, "treasure up unto themselves wrath against the day of wrath" [Rom. 2:5]. Out of this same fallen mass, God calls some to repentance by his goodness and mercy, leaving the rest, in just judgment, to their own destruction.

Thus Augustine.

That no one might imagine that there is any discrepancy, variance, or conflict between divine grace and our industry, these sentiments of the holy father everywhere meet us in his works. "Men toil" says he, "to find in our own free will what good thing there is that is our own that we have not received from God. I, for my part, know not what good things of that kind can be discovered in us at all." In another place, arguing on the same deep subject, Augustine draws this conclusion:

> Wherefore, unless we hold fast these two positions, not only that the power of will, which is free to turn this way and that and which is one of those natural good things that a bad man may badly use, is the gift of God, but also that good will, which is one of those spiritual good things of which there cannot be made a bad use, is of God. Unless, I say, we hold fast these two propositions, I know not on what grounds we are to defend the sacred position of the apostle involved in his memorable question, "What hast thou that thou didst not receive?" [1 Cor. 4:7]. But if there be in us a certain kind of free will received from God, which may yet be either good or evil, and if there be in us also a good will, rendered so by ourselves, what proceeds from ourselves is better than that which we receive from God.

Augustine arrives at this final inference from the above premises:

> Where God is pleased to give this will to obey him and to come unto Christ, it is an act of his free mercy, not according to the merits of those on whom he bestows the gift and to whom he shows the mercy. Where God is not willing to bestow the gift or to show the mercy, it is a display of his truth that declares that none can come to Christ to whom the will to come is not given. And though he has the power to draw them, he draws them not; but they are left to perish, and thus to manifest the truth of his word that "no one

can come unto Christ, except the Father draw him" [John 6:44].

The difficulty, according to Pighius, that lies in the other place of Paul, where the apostle affirms that "God will have all men to be saved and come unto the knowledge of the truth" [1 Tim. 2:4], is solved in one moment and by one question, namely, How does God wish all men to come to the knowledge of the truth? For Paul couples together this salvation and this coming to the knowledge of the truth. I would ask, Did the same will of God stand the same from the beginning of the world or not? For if God willed or wished that his truth should be known unto all men, how was it that he did not proclaim and make known his law to the Gentiles also? Why did he confine the light of life within the narrow limits of Judea? What does Moses mean when he says, "For what nation is there so great who has God so nigh unto them as the Lord our God is in all things that we call upon him for? And what nation is there so great, that has statutes and judgments so righteous, as all this law that I set before you this day" [Deut. 4:7, 8]? The divine lawgiver surely means that there was no other nation that had statutes and laws by which it was ruled like unto that nation. What does Moses extol but the peculiar privilege of the race of Abraham? To this responds the high encomium of David, pronounced on the same nation: "He hath not dealt so with any nation, and as for his judgments, they have not known them" [Ps. 147:20]. Nor must we disregard the express reason: "Because the Lord loved thy fathers, therefore he chose their seed after them" [Deut. 4:37]. And why did God thus choose them? Not because they were more excellent in themselves than others, but it pleased God to choose them "for his peculiar people" [Deut. 14:2; Deut. 26:18; 1 Pet. 2:9].

What? Are we to suppose that the apostle did not know that he was prohibited by the Holy Spirit from preaching the word in Asia, and from passing over into Bithynia [Acts 16:6, 7]? As the continuance of this argument would render us too prolix, we will be content with taking one position more. God, after having thus lighted the candle of eternal life to the Jews alone, suffered the Gentiles to wander for many ages in the darkness of ignorance, and at length this special gift and blessing were promised to the church: "But the Lord shall arise upon thee, and his glory shall be seen upon thee" [Isa. 60:2].

Now let Pighius boast, if he can, that God wills all men to be saved. The above arguments, founded on the Scriptures, prove that even the external preaching of the doctrine of salvation, which is very far inferior to the illumination of the Spirit, was not made of God common to all men. This passage of the apostle was long ago brought forward by the Pelagians and handled against us with all their might. What Augustine advanced in reply to them in many parts of his works, I think it unnecessary to bring forward on the present occasion. I will only cite one passage, which clearly and briefly proves how Augustine despised, without reservation, their objection now in question.

> When our Lord complains that though he wished to gather the children of Jerusalem as a hen gathers her chickens under her wings, but she would not [Matt. 23:37], are we to consider that the will of God was overpowered by a number of weak men, so that he who was Almighty God could not do what he wished or willed to do? If so, what is to become of that omnipotence by which he did "whatsoever pleased him in heaven and in earth" [Ps. 135:6]? Moreover, who will be found so profanely mad as to say that God cannot convert the evil wills of men which he pleases, when he pleases, and as he pleases, to good? When he does this, he does it in mercy; and when he does it not, in judgment he does it not.

The knot immediately before us, however, is not yet, I confess, untied. I have nevertheless extorted from Pighius this much: No one but a man deprived of his common sense and common judgment can believe that salvation was ordained by the secret counsel of God equally and indiscriminately for all men. The true meaning of Paul, however, in the passage now under consideration [1 Tim. 2:4], is perfectly clear and intelligible to everyone who is not determined on contention. The apostle is exhorting that all solemn "supplications, prayers, intercessions, and giving of thanks be made for all men: for kings and for all that are in authority" [v. 1]. And because there were in that age so many and such wrathful and bitter enemies of the church, Paul, to prevent despair from hindering the prayers of the faithful, hastens to meet their distresses by earnestly entreating them to be instant in prayer "for all men" and especially "for all those in authority" [vv. 1, 2]. "For" says the apostle, "God will have all men to be saved" [v. 4]. Who does not see that the apostle is here speaking of orders of men rather than of individuals? Indeed, the distinction that commentators make is not without great reason and point: *Nations* of individuals, not *individuals* of nations, are here intended by Paul. At any rate, that no other "will" of God is here to be understood than that which is revealed by the external preaching of the gospel is undeniably evident from the context. The plain meaning of the apostle, therefore, is that God "wills" the salvation of all men, considered generally, whom he therefore mercifully calls or invites unto Christ by the open preaching of the word.

Respect of Persons

Pighius renews the battle with me on the field of respect of persons. Because it is written that there is "no respect of persons with God" [Rom. 2:11], he at once concludes that all men are equally loved of God. I did, indeed, answer him, arguing that the term *persons* in Scripture signifies all those external circumstances attached to men, which external circumstances involve not the great cause of all, but which procure favor to some men and load others with hatred and contempt. Pighius, however, thunders out that this explanation of the term is absurd beyond all expression or conception. But if the matter were put to the vote, I am quite satisfied that I should have many men of the highest estimation in the church, both as companions and as leaders, in my interpretation of the term in question. Let one ground on which my explanation rests suffice for the present occasion. There is in the Hebrew language the noun *panim*, which is of the same signification as the plural Latin noun *facies*, which signifies "faces" or "appearances." The Hebrew noun *panim* is used when judges are forbidden "to accept persons in judgment." The same term is used when Moses testifies that "the Lord regardeth not persons, nor taketh reward" [Deut. 1:17; Deut. 10:17]. This same noun is also frequently used in the history of Job. Now I would ask, What else can be understood by this term than all kinds of external appearances, as we generally term them, by which we are often drawn aside from the reality with which they stand connected?

In the same manner, the apostles, when speaking of servants and masters, Jews and Gentiles, nobles and obscure, high and low, use the Greek term πρόσωπον to denote the external appearance of excellency that some have above others and that often prevents what is just and right in or towards such persons from being clearly seen. Hence it is also that Christ contrasts the judging according to ὄψιν, that is, "outward appearance," to just judgment [John 7:24], as if he had said, Wherever the favor or hatred of men rules, it cannot be but that such prejudice must pervert all equity and righteousness.

Everyone, therefore, will immediately see that Pighius, carried away by the maddened insolence of hatred against the truth, cared not what he said.

Let us listen to this admonisher's correction of our interpretation. He pronounces "respect of persons" to be a vice that has place in the administration of justice. Thus he concludes that God is no respecter of persons because he is impartial to all men, and that, as is becoming in a dispenser of the public justice and of the public good, he shows himself, as a matter of course, to be impartially liberal and beneficent. Thus prates Pighius, putting an extinguisher upon the light of Scripture and babbling what first comes into his truthless head.

The whole Scripture confirms my interpretation and view, and my opponent does not produce one passage to prove his absurd figment. And what wonder when he can bring forth his mad dreams with so much confidence and security when he has not even weighed the meaning of the very term upon which he is uttering so much vain talk. And I suppose his thus pouring out words, in contempt of all grammar and sense, is to show himself off as a great theologian. With him "person" (*persona*) signifies nothing more or less than "man." However, it is all the while more than evident that by "person" is signified an external quality, assuming which, or clothed with which, men are considered worthy of favor and respect or justly subjected to contempt. But whether God be an equal and impartial dispenser or not, the testimony of Christ, we think, is much more worthy of credit than that of Pighius. Our Lord introduces the blessed God under the person or character of the master of a household, speaking thus: "Is it not lawful for me to do what I will with mine own? Is thine eye evil, because I am good?" [Matt. 20:15]. According to which reasoning of our Lord, Paul, that he might set forth the adorable God bound and responsible to no one, nor hindered by any person or thing from dispensing his grace according to his own will, closes his argument with this interrogation: "Or, who hath first given to him, and it shall be recompensed unto him again?" [Rom. 11:35].

If there had been one grain of the fear of God in Pighius, could he ever have dared thus insolently to call God to order? For he absolutely prescribes it as a rule to the Most High that he ought to extend his bounty to all equally, as from a public treasury, thus leaving nothing to God by which to exercise his free beneficence. God judges of every individual (Pighius says) according to the dignity, merit, and works of each individual, and not according to his own good pleasure. For what merit in them, then, did God choose the family of Abraham? What dignity did he find in that race that moved him to prefer them to all the rest of the world? God himself assigns no other reason than that "he loved their fathers" [Deut.

4:37]. This he declares more expressly elsewhere: "Behold, the heaven and the heaven of heavens is the Lord's, thy God, the earth also with all that therein is. Only the Lord had a delight in thy fathers to love them, and he chose their seed after them, even you, above all people" [Deut. 10:14, 15]. In another place, God reduces all their merits to nothing by declaring Abraham and all his family to have been idolaters: "And Joshua said unto the people, Thus saith the Lord God of Israel, Your fathers dwelt on the other side of the flood in old time, even Terah, the father of Abraham and the father of Nachor, and they served other gods. And I took your father Abraham from the other side of the flood, and led him throughout all the land of Canaan, and multiplied his seed and gave him Isaac" [Josh. 24:2, 3].

From the above passages, at any rate, I obtain that which Pighius denies: The sovereign pleasure of God was clearly preached by Moses. But our opponent denies that it depends on the sovereign decree of God that one is chosen and another left, asserting that it depends on the affections of men. What, then, does this mean: "That the purpose of God according to election might stand, not of works, but of him that calleth; it was said unto her, the elder shall serve the younger" [Rom. 9:11, 12]? The blasphemy that Pighius afterwards vomits out is execrable: "God is made not only unjust, but cruel, if he be represented as ordaining any human being whatever to destruction." Pighius, however, will one day stand before the tribunal of that God, of whom Paul declares, "He will manifest his power upon the vessels of wrath fitted to destruction" [v. 22]. Our opponent even now feels, under the sense of the eternal destruction that awaits him, that God is not a being fabricated out of the opinions or thoughts of men, but that he was, is, and will be the eternal judge of the whole world. This miserable mortal (I say) is even now experiencing how true the word is: God overcomes when he is judged [Rom. 3:4].

I am willing to confess, however, that a godly and upright life is sometimes contrasted with "person" (persona), as when Peter says,

"Of a truth I perceive that God is no respecter of persons (προσω-πολήμπτης) but in every nation he that feareth him, and worketh righteousness, is accepted with him" [Acts 10:34, 35]. But the answer to those who would bring this Scripture against us is that whatever gifts God bestows on his own children, he approves and delights in, while in the whole moral nature of man he finds nothing but what deserves his righteous hatred. Therefore, in order that God may have worshipers whom he may love, he must, while they are yet devoid of all good, first bestow upon them his free love in the midst of their unworthiness of it, and thus freely give them that which he may afterwards love himself.

Says Augustine,

This first (or preventing) grace he bestows on whom he will because he is merciful, which grace, if he does not give, he is just. Where he gives it not, it is because he wills not to give it "that he might make known the riches of his glory on the vessels of mercy" [Rom. 9:23]. When Peter says that God is "no respecter of persons" [Acts 10:34], he shows at the close of the chapter what he means by it, namely, that God sometimes, passing by the children of those who do worship him, delivers from destruction the children of the reprobate.

What Augustine further says on this mighty subject is well worthy of being borne in memory:

No more glorious glass exists, in which to behold predestination, than the blessed Mediator himself, who, according to his human nature, considered as such, attained to the honor of becoming the "only begotten Son of God" by no merit of his own.

But this good pleasure of God, which God himself sets before us for our admiration in Christ, the head of the church, Pighius will not admit or suffer even in the individual members of his body. Indeed, he contends that the blessed mother of Christ was chosen on account of her own merit, as is proved, he says, from her own song: "He hath regarded the lowliness of his handmaiden" [Luke 1:48]. Such are Pighius' "proofs" that the election of God is founded on the merits of men and that it is not sovereign and free, because he chose, in the case of Mary, that which was mean and contemptible!

Election and Salvation

On this same divine principle is dissipated also another objection adduced by Pighius: "When Christ calls the blessed of his Father to inherit the kingdom, he does not state their being elected to be the cause of their right to that inheritance, but because they had done works of charity."

I would by no means hurry away men to the secret election of God that they may with open mouth expect salvation from thence, but I would exhort them to flee directly to Christ, in whom salvation is set forth before their eyes, which salvation, had it not been revealed in Christ, would have forever remained "hidden in God." For whoever walks not in the plain way of faith, to him the election of God can be nothing but a labyrinth of destruction. Therefore, if we would enjoy the certain remission of our sins, if our consciences would rest in a sure confidence of eternal life, if we would call upon God as our heavenly Father without fear, we must by no means make our beginning with the investigation of what God decreed concerning us before the world began. Our contemplation must be what God, of his Fatherly love, has revealed to us in Christ, and what Christ himself daily preaches to us through his everlasting gospel. Our deepest search and highest aim must be to become the sons of God and to know that we are such. But the mirror of free adoption, in which alone we can behold so high and unspeakable a blessing, is Christ the Son, who came down to us from the Father for the very end that by engrafting us into his body, he might make us heirs of the kingdom of heaven, of which kingdom he is himself the earnest and the pledge. Moreover, as this inheritance was once obtained for us by the blood of Christ and remains consigned to us on the sacred pages of the everlasting gospel, so the knowledge and possession of it can be attained in no other way than by faith.

In a word, I not only now freely confess, but also everywhere inculcate in all my writings, both that the salvation of men is inseparably connected with their faith and that Christ is the only door by which any man can enter the kingdom of heaven, and also that tranquil peace can be found nowhere but in the gospel. I have, moreover, ever taught that whoever shall turn aside even the shortest step from the gospel of Christ, and from faith therein, can do nothing but lose himself in doubts, ambiguities, and perplexities; that the more confidently anyone attempts to break in upon and penetrate those profound mysteries of God's secret counsel without the gospel and faith therein will ever, in so doing, get so much the farther and farther from God. Therefore, that the children of God, notwithstanding their election of God before all worlds, are to walk by faith, I deny not, but constantly affirm.

Hence on these principles another argument set against us by our opponent is done away with when he alleges: "God will crown at the last day those gifts of his Spirit that he may have bestowed on his elect in this present life." But this does not alter the truth and fact that God engrafts, by faith and by the sanctification of his Spirit, those whom he has chosen in Christ into his body. Nor does it alter the truth that he calls and justifies, in his own time, those whom he predestinated to these blessings before the foundation of the world. Therefore, Paul connects both these works of God most beautifully where he says, "We know that all things work together for good to them that love God," to which he immediately adds, "to them who are the called according to his purpose" [Rom. 8:28]. This, then, is the way in which God governs his own. This is the manner in which he completes the work of his grace in them. But why he thus takes them by the hand at all, there is another and far higher cause, namely, his eternal purpose, by which he ordained them unto eternal life. Therefore, the impudence of Pighius is the more ridiculous; for he hesitates not to grasp most insolently, for his own purpose, a testimony of Scripture that thus stands directly against him. For he would absurdly remind us that it is not said that all things "work together for good" to the *elect* or the *beloved*, but he asserts that a different cause is assigned, namely, that it was because they loved God. Whereas the apostle purposely adds the correction of all possible error upon the point by subjoining "who are the called according to his purpose," so that no one might attribute the working of all things for his good to his own merit.

In fact, the mind of the apostle in this passage is, first, to show how the faithful, for whom God causes "all things to work together for good," ought to be affected towards him. They ought to "love God." And love to God is, indeed, a peculiar firstfruit of being "called" of God. But that those who are thus "called" might not cleave to themselves and their own merits, Paul moreover teaches them that the real source of their salvation and of all things working together for their good is seated much higher than themselves—in heaven itself and in the eternal purpose of God—even because they were first chosen of God and were therefore "the called according to his purpose" [v. 28].

This knot also Pighius thinks he can loosen and settle by a single sentence, which is positively a solemn joke. He says that God "calls" all men to holiness. Whereas the apostle most plainly sets forth "calling" as being effectual only by the absolute "purpose" of God: "Who are the called" says the apostle, "according to his purpose." Over these truths, so prominently and striking plain, Pighius would spread a darkness so thick that their transparent clearness should scarcely be seen. What, for instance, can be more perspicuously clear than this passage of Scripture: "Moreover, whom he did predestinate, them he also called; and whom he called, them he also justified; and whom he justified, them he also glorified" [v. 30]?

To whatever extent our opponent may mangle and lacerate this sentence of the apostle Paul, he can never so stretch it out as to make it reach to all mankind. Hence is evident the extreme folly of the arguments of all those who labor to subvert the election of God by substituting for it faith and good works. This is making, or attempting to make, "the daughter swallow up the mother," as the old proverb has it.

The last subterfuge of Pighius in reference to the Scripture before us is this: "God predestinated none unto salvation, but they were those whom he foreknew." This way of escape I have already blocked up against these opponents, where I have shown that God could have foreseen nothing in man but what was worthy of eternal destruction until he himself should have created him anew by his Spirit. If, then, no one man has anything good that he has not received from God, what can one man bring into God's sight more than another in which he can excel his fellowman? God therefore foreknew his own, not as foreseeing their merits — for they had none — but because he cast upon them an eye of mercy and favor, thus distinguishing them from others and numbering them among his children, notwithstanding all their sin and unworthiness, according to that word of Paul: "Who maketh thee to differ?" [1 Cor. 4:7]. But Pighius' free foreknowledge, which he calls naked (that is, naked of all preference in the mind of God) is no foreknowledge at all. With what feathers of merit or acceptableness, then, will Pighius adorn his foreseen and predestined man so as to prevent him from coming before God naked and deformed in every part? For Scripture declares aloud that whatever there is in fallen and corrupt man by nature is hateful in the sight of God. And it pronounces, with a voice equally loud, that nothing is acceptable to God but his own image in those who are created anew in Christ.

Pighius next proceeds thus: "When we are anxiously inquiring the reason that the wicked are eternally condemned, Scripture does not cast in our teeth such tyrannical sentences as these in reply: 'Because they were distinguished from the elect by the eternal counsel of God,' 'because it pleased God to ordain them to eternal destruction.' We do not find in Scripture such shocking and hard answers to our inquiries as these. These are merely the reasons assigned by men in order to make such sentences as these appear to be true: 'I will it so'; 'I command it to be so'; 'My will is an all-sufficient reason.' No! The reasons we hear from the mouth of

Christ are these: 'I was an hungered, and ye gave me no meat; I was thirsty, and ye gave me no drink' [Matt. 25:42]."

Similar to this argument is what Pighius also advances in another place. Christ (says he) will not in the last day say to the wicked that they were eternally condemned because they were born of the corrupt seed of Adam, because they inherited the just desert of eternal death from his sin, and it was just and righteous that they should perish for his fault. No, says Pighius. The reasons that Christ will assign before assembled worlds in that day will be these: They did not give bread to the hungry, clothe the naked, or perform other kindred works of charity.

However, if original sin and guilt are not, in the estimation of Pighius, sufficient to condemn men eternally, and if the secret judgment of God can have no place with him, what will he make of the case of infant children who are taken out of this life before they could possibly have performed any of the works of charity above alluded to? Now there was the same natural condition of birth and of death both in those infants who died in Sodom and in those who died in Jerusalem, and their works, or rather no works, were precisely the same. How is it, then, that Christ will separate in the last day the one from the other, placing the one on his right hand and the other on his left? Who does not adore the glorious judgment of God, who ordained that the one part of these children should be born at Jerusalem, whence, through the knowledge of the truth they might afterwards be translated to a better life, while the others should be born in that wide entrance into hell, Sodom? Therefore, as I hold in truth that Christ will in the last day recompense unto the elect the reward of righteousness, so I by no means speak falsely when I assert that the reprobate will in that day pay the punishment of their unrighteousness and of all their iniquities. And though I firmly maintain that God in his eternal counsel chose those whom he pleased unto life eternal and left those whom he pleased to eternal destruction, yet there will not be found in the whole of my doctrine an assertion either that there are no punishments ordained for evil works or that there is no reward ordained for good works. No. "We must all stand before the judgment seat of Christ, that every one may receive the things done in his body, according to that he hath done, whether it be good or bad" [2 Cor. 5:10]. But the great question is, whence comes that righteousness and holiness that will then be thus crowned? Whence but from God himself, who begat these rewarded ones unto newness of life by his own Spirit? And whence is this gift of regeneration but from God's free adoption?

Pighius' argument is just like the reasoning of a man who would maintain that the day was not originally made of created light, because it is the shining of the sun that now makes the day. This comparison is not, however, I confess, strictly true in all its parts. For the light that was created "in the beginning" has properly God as its author, whereas our eternal condemnation so wholly rests in ourselves that it is not lawful for us to fetch from afar any foreign or representative colors that may tend in any way to lessen our sight of its mighty reality. My only object in adopting this comparison is to show, in a concise manner, how preposterously Pighius withdraws from our view the great remote cause by setting immediately before our eyes the proximate cause in the consideration of these momentous matters. He contends that the wicked will be eternally condemned because they have brought upon themselves the wrath of God by their own evil doings. And on this ground he concludes that their eternal condemnation does not proceed from the decree of God. Whereas I maintain that they have heaped evil deeds upon evil deeds throughout their lives because, being essentially depraved by their birth in sin, they could do nothing else but sin. Nevertheless, they sinned thus, not from any outward impulse or constraint, but knowingly and willingly from the spontaneous motion of the heart. Indeed, that the corruption and depravity of nature are the source and fountain from which all sins of every kind flow can be denied by no one who would not root out the rudiments of all godliness. But if you ask me the reason that God corrects sin in his own elect and does not deem the reprobate worthy of the same remedy, I reply, the reason lies hidden in himself.

It is in this way that the apostle Paul reasons in the ninth chapter of his Epistle to the Romans. After he had proved God to be the great disposer and ordainer of eternal life and eternal death, and had shown that those will at length be saved whom he rescues from eternal destruction; and after he had loudly declared that "it is not of him that willeth, nor of him that runneth, but of God that showeth mercy on whom he will show mercy," and that "whom he will, he hardeneth" [vv. 16, 18] — after these declarations, the apostle brings forth copious and, as it were, palpable causes of the blindness of his own nation, namely, because the greatest part of them rejected Christ, and they obstinately resisted God's "stretching out his hands unto them all the day long" [Rom. 10:21]. Therefore, these two solemn principles divinely harmonize with each other: Every man is in himself the cause of his own eternal condemnation, and nevertheless, all those who are destitute of the Spirit of God rush blindly against Christ. Agreeably to these divine principles, Paul brings in the Jews as guilty, because "going about to establish their own righteousness, they did not submit themselves to the righteousness of God" [v. 3], and they were, on this account, cast out of the church of Christ. Paul, I repeat, having thus enforced these divine principles, yet plainly teaches that it was entirely of grace that the rest stood in the truth and faith and did not thus fall, according to that remarkable declaration of God himself: "Yet have I left me seven thousand in Israel, all the knees which have not bowed unto Baal, and every mouth which hath not kissed him" [1 Kings 19:18]. For, as Augustine is careful to remark,

These seven thousand did not stand by their own strength. It was God who reserved them to himself, that they might be a remnant. But Paul still more expressly declares that the remnant gathered by the coming of Christ in his day was "a remnant saved according to the free election of grace" [Rom. 11:5]. Do you hear the term *remnant?* By this expression is signified that a small number was separated from the general mass of mankind. And the apostle affirms that these were

saved not by their own will or strength, but by the free grace
and mercy of God. He traces their salvation to God's free
election, by which he plainly means that the sole cause of
their not perishing with the rest of mankind was because
they were freely elected of God. Whence follows the plain
conclusion that if *all men* were elected, *no man* would perish.

If a mortal man should pronounce his "I will" and his "I command" and should say that his will ought to be deemed a sufficient
reason for his actions, I confess that such an "I will" would be tyrannical indeed. But to call God's "I will" and God's "I command" tyrannical is profanity, blasphemy, and madness, for no mortal dares
impute to God anything unequal or excessive to imply that there
can be in him any inordinate will, wish, or desire, as in men.

On the contrary, such honor and reverence are ever due to his
will that it is worthy of being considered as containing in itself all
the validity of a just reason, because the will of God is the source
and rule of all righteousness. As to that distinction commonly held
in the schools concerning the twofold will of God, such distinction
is by no means admitted by us. The sophists of the Sorbonne prate
about an *ordinate will* of God and an *absolute will* of God. This is a
blasphemy deservedly abhorred in its sound to all godly ears, but
plausible and pleasant to the ears of Pighius and of all his fellows.

I contend, however, that so far from there being anything inordinate in God, whatever there is of order, in heaven or in earth,
flows from him alone and from his will. Whenever, therefore, we
carry the will of God to its utmost height and show that it is higher
than all reason, far be it from us to imagine that he ever wills anything but with the highest reason. We also deeply feel that he so
possesses, as his own right, the sum of all power; so that our sacred
duty is to be content with the nod of his will alone in all things. For
if it be true what the psalmist says, "Thy judgments, O Lord, are a
great deep" [Ps. 36:6], when the mind of a man launches forth into
that height of pride that cannot rest solely in the good pleasure and
will of God, let him take solemn heed that the "great deep" swallow

him not up! Indeed, it must be so; it cannot be otherwise, and such vengeance is gloriously just.

Therefore, let that noble and solemn appeal of Augustine never fall from our memory:

> Listen to what God is and what you are. He is God. You are man. If you seem to yourself to be speaking of justice in the works and ways of God, do you think the fountain of all justice is dried up? You as a man expect an answer from me, who also am a man. Therefore, let us both hear the apostle saying, with reference to all questioning of God, "Nay, but who art thou, O man?" [Rom. 9:20]. Better is believing ignorance than daring knowledge. Search for merit, and you will find nothing but punishment. "O the depth!" [Rom. 11:33]. Peter denies; a robber believes!—"O the depth!" Do you ask the reason? I tremble before "the depth." Do you reason? I will wonder and admire. Do you dispute? I believe. I see the height, but I will not rush into the "depth." Paul quietly rests because he finds reason for wonder and admiration. He calls the judgments of God "unsearchable," and do you come on purpose "to search into them"? Paul says, "God's ways are past finding out," and do you come on purpose "to find them out"?

Akin to these holy sentiments is what Augustine says in another place:

> Will you join me in dispute? Nay, rather join with me in admiration and wonder! Rather join me in exclaiming, "O the depth!" Let us agree to tremble together so that we perish not in presumption together.

Pighius displays, in his own estimation, great acuteness when he argues thus: "There would be no deep abyss at all if the will of God were to be considered as the highest of all reason, because nothing would be easier than to say that all things were done because God so pleased, where his will ruled absolutely and alone." But by babbling thus sophistically, he ridiculously passes over the very point that forms the great question at issue. It is quite plain that all things are done because it so pleased God. But the great question is, why did it please God that one thing should be done in one way, and another thing in a way quite the contrary?

Pighius then proceeds with the same line of silly argumentation. And in order that he might show that God had a reason and a cause in all his counsels, he adduces as proof the answer Christ gave to his disciples in the case of a blind man: "He was born blind, that the works of God should be made manifest in him" [John 9:3]. Thus Pighius makes a shadow battle and then fights it out, imagining that he has gained the victory. But when and where did the monstrous idea enter my mind that any counsel of God was without God's reason for it? As I constantly make God the rule of the whole world, who by his incomprehensible and wonderful counsel governs and directs all things, will any man say that he can gather from my words that I make God to be carried this way and that way at random or make him do what he does with blindfold temerity?

It is singular that Pighius quotes some words of mine by which, if I mistake not, he is himself most evidently refuted. The words to which I allude are my assertion that God has a purpose in all his ways and works, however hidden, which purpose is that he may spread the glory of his name. But my opponent would set before the eyes of his readers a color of contradiction in my sentiments, because I hold that no reason for the goodwill of God in any of his works is to be required or investigated; and yet that I, at the same time, show what that reason is. But it is useless to waste time in exposing such cold and self-evident absurdities. The Lord has as a reason for all his works his own great glory. This is his ultimate object in them all. Hence, on the testimony of Paul, God raised up Pharaoh "so that he might show his power in him and that his name might be declared throughout all the earth" [Rom. 9:17]. Does the apostle Paul, I ask, contradict himself when he exclaims immediately afterwards that the judgments of God are "past finding out" [Rom. 11:33]? The same apostle also declares that the vessels of wrath "appointed" by the Lord "unto destruction" were "endured" by him "with much longsuffering" in order that "he might show his wrath and make his power known in them" [Rom. 9:22]. Is the wondering admiration of Paul that follows—"O the depth!" [Rom. 11:33]—contrary, I ask you, to this his sentiment? Tell me, I repeat, does the apostle here contradict himself? If he does not, neither do I contradict myself in my like solemn argument.

But Pighius goes farther into error, absurdity, and confusion in his way of arguing. He spreads a false color over the term *cause* by introducing the *final cause* in the place of the *formal cause*. Although the *end* to which God looks in his works be not obscure, namely, his great and wide glory, the *reason* it pleases him so to work by no means appears so wholly and immediately plain. The pith, however, and sum of the present point of the whole great question is this: Although God in all his works does not demonstrate to us by plain and satisfactory arguments his own righteousness, our bounden duty is to be assured that whatever he does, he does righteously. It is therefore our duty to rest in God's will alone. Thus our knowledge of his will and pleasure in whatever he does, although the cause of his doing it should surpass our comprehension, ought to suffice us more than a thousand reasons.

Hence the folly of Pighius in quarrelling with me and accusing me of inconsistency because, while I maintain that no reason for the divine will should be inquired into, I loudly affirm that God wills nothing but what he judges just and right to be done. For Pighius asserts that this latter part of my argument is really rendering a reason for the will of God as the cause of all, the rendering of which reason (he says) I elsewhere declare to be inconsistent in myself or in anyone else. But what knowledge of the cause can I be said to profess if I believe only that God does what he does with a great design and what he judges right to be done, and especially if I profess myself to be all the while unable to comprehend the certain and special reason of the divine work and counsel? Added to all this, my opponent, considering the mighty difference between the reverence of faith and the audacity of inquiry into God's will a matter of no moment at all, seizes hold of what I teach to be a matter of faith and preposterously hurls it into the circle of that common knowledge that is of human conception.

Upon this absurd principle, if anyone should affirm that God has a glorious object in his every act and should shortly after exclaim, with the apostle, that God's "judgments are unsearchable" and "his ways past finding out" [Rom. 11:33], he must, at the moment of such exclamation, be set down as a man contradicting himself. Pighius, however, is mistaken altogether. For he calls upon me to acknowledge my very own words, when the passage to which he refers is absolutely one that I had cited from Augustine. That holy man says,

> When men ask us why God did this or that, our answer is to be, "Because it was his will." If they go on to inquire, Why did he so will it? our reply should be, "Now you ask what is greater and higher than the will of God itself. You ask what none can find out." Let human rashness, then, keep itself within bounds. Let it never seek after that which is *not*, lest it should not find that which *is*.

Most truly does Augustine speak in these words, and he has my fullest assent. Nor do my sentiments above contain anything that does not perfectly harmonize with these words of the holy father. My sentiments and arguments are that the will of God is the best and most rightful adjustment of all the things that he has made and done.

The Decree of Reprobation

There is another objection of the same chaff that Pighius raises against my following published sentiments: "I deny that the reprobate are distinguished and separated from the elect by any respect of God to the merits of the elect, because the grace of God makes them worthy of his adoption of them; it does not find them worthy," as Augustine frequently remarks. In another place I express myself thus:"I deny that any injury is done to the reprobate by their reprobation, because they deserve eternal destruction."

Here Pighius spreads out his wings in tumultuous exultation, noisily exclaiming that I understand neither myself nor my own sentiments, nor do I remember at all what I have said previously. But so far am I from thinking it necessary to spend many words in my defense that I can hardly bring myself to employ even a few words. I will observe, then, that when God prefers some to others, when he chooses some and passes by others, the difference is not made on the ground of worthiness or unworthiness, either in the one or the other. Therefore, it is wrong to say that the reprobate are worthy of eternal destruction. If, therefore, in the former case there is no comparison of men with each other, nor any connection of worthiness with the reward of eternal life, in the latter case there is certainly no proof that the condition of all men is equal with reference to the election of God. Add to this that Augustine, having asserted in one part of his writings that no man ever failed of salvation who was worthy of it, qualifies this expression in his subsequent retractions, carefully excluding all idea of works and referring all acceptable worthiness to the free grace calling of God.

Pighius, however, still pushes on his violent opposition, alleging that if what I teach be true—that those who perish were ordained unto everlasting death by the eternal will of God, the reason for which is imperceptible to us—then the persons so ordained are *made worthy* of everlasting death, not *found* so.

I reply that three things are to be considered: First, the eternal predestination of God, by which he decreed before the fall of Adam what should take place in the whole human race and in every individual thereof, was unalterably fixed and determined. Second, Adam himself, on account of his departure from God, was deservedly appointed to eternal death. Third, in the person of Adam, thus fallen and lost, his whole future offspring were also eternally condemned, but so eternally condemned that God deems worthy the honor of his adoption all those whom he freely chose out of that future offspring. Of these mighty things I have neither dreamed nor fabricated any part. Nor am I called upon, in the present instance, to prove each particular, for I consider that I have most effectually done that already. All I shall do is to wash off from myself the calumny with which my opponent has soiled me when he says that these things can in no way be made to harmonize or consist with each other. Instead, what I have ever invariably taught, and still teach at this day, is that whenever election is the subject of discussion, the great point to be maintained from first to last is that all the reprobate are justly left under eternal death because they died and were eternally condemned in Adam; also, that those perish justly who are by nature the children of wrath; finally, that therefore no one can have cause to complain of the too great severity of God, seeing that all men bear in themselves and in their individual persons the guilt and just desert of death eternal.

When we come to speak of the first man in our discussion of the doctrine of predestination, my teaching is that we ought ever to consider the solemn case to be this: He, having been created perfectly righteous, fell of his own accord and willingly, and by that fall he brought eternal destruction on himself and his whole future race. And though Adam neither fell nor destroyed himself and his posterity without the knowledge or the ordaining will of God, yet that neither lessens his own fault nor implicates God in any blame whatever. For we must ever carefully bear in mind that Adam, of his own will and accord, deprived himself of that perfect righteousness which he had received from God, and of his own accord and will he gave himself up to the service of sin and Satan, and thus precipitated himself into eternal destruction. However, men will continually offer one uniform excuse for Adam: It was impossible for him to help or avoid what God himself had decreed. But to establish the guilt of Adam forever, his own voluntary transgression is enough, and more than sufficient. Nor, indeed, is the secret counsel of God the real and virtual cause of sin, but manifestly the will and inclination of man is the cause.

The folly of the complaint of Medea[16] is justly derided, even by the ancient poet, when he represents her as uttering the well-known lamentation, "O that the ship, made of planks cut down by axes from the Pelian grove, had never sailed from Egina to Colchis, my native land!" Medea had betrayed her country, carried away by the passion of a desperate love that she had conceived for a foreigner, an entire stranger. When her conscience smites her for her perfidy and barbarous cruelty, when the shame of unlawful indulgence overwhelms her, she absurdly turns her thoughts of regret to various remote circumstances as the causes of her misery. Since every human being can always find the cause of his evils in himself, of what avail is it to look about him on every side or to seek that cause in heaven? Thus Medea's fault plainly appears: She had sinned voluntarily and willingly. Why, then, does she plunge herself into a labyrinth of lost thought by rushing into the mysteries of heaven? For although mortal men may employ their thoughts in circuitous reasonings ever so long and deep, they never can delude or stupefy themselves so far as not to find and feel that they carry the originating cause of all their sins deeply seated in their own hearts. Impious reasoning, therefore, will attempt in vain to absolve from the guilt of sin that man who stands condemned by his own conscience. And as to God's having knowingly and willingly permitted man to fall, his reason for so doing may be hidden. Unjust it cannot be. Moreover, this should ever be held fast without controversy: Sin was ever hateful to God. For the praise that David loudly bestows on the Most High strictly applies to his adorable majesty in every respect: "Thou hatest all workers of iniquity" [Ps. 5:5]. Therefore, in ordaining the fall of man especially, God had a most glorious and just end, in our contemplation of which the mention or idea of sin on the part of God can never enter. The very thought of its entrance strikes us with horror.

---

16. Calvin refers to Medea, the main female character in a play with the same name, written by the Greek playwright Euripides.

Although I thus affirm that God did ordain the fall of Adam, I by no means concede that God was therein properly and really the author of Adam's fall. That I may not, however, dwell extensively on this great point now, I will only express it as my view, belief, and sentiment that what Augustine so deeply teaches on this matter was fulfilled in God's ordaining the fall of Adam:

> In a wonderful and unutterable way this was not done without the will of God, which was even done contrary to his will, because it could not have been done at all if his will had not permitted it to be done. And yet he did not permit it unwillingly, but willingly.

Therefore, the great and grand principle, on which Augustine argues, cannot be denied:

> Both man and apostate angels, as far as they were concerned, did that which God willed not, or which was contrary to his will; but as far as God's overruling omnipotence is concerned, they could not, in any manner, have done it without his will.

To these sentiments of the holy man, I subscribe with all my heart. I solemnly hold that man and apostate angels did, by their sin, what was contrary to the will of God, to the end that God, by means of their evil wills, might effect what was according to his decreeing will. If anyone should reply that this is above the capability of his mind to comprehend, I also acknowledge and confess the same. But why should we wonder that the infinite and incomprehensible majesty of God should surpass the narrow limits of our finite intellect? So far, however, am I from undertaking to explain this sublime and hidden mystery by any powers of human reason that I would ever retain in my own memory that which I declared at the commencement of this discussion: Those who seek to know more than God has revealed are madmen. Therefore, let us delight ourselves more in wise ignorance than in an immoderate and intoxicated curiosity to know more than God permits. Let all the powers of our mind restrain themselves within the bounds of the reverential assurance that God willed nothing by the sin of man except what was worthy of his infinite justice.

Pighius continues: "If the apostasy of man be the work of God, what Scripture declares is not true when it says that "all things that God doeth are very good." Now I can sacredly testify and with candor confess that this comment of my adversary never entered my mind. I have everywhere asserted that man was created in the beginning perfectly upright. I have constantly asserted this for the purpose of preventing the depravity that Adam contracted by his fall from being attributed to God. I have, with equal constancy, asserted that the eternal death to which man rendered himself subject so proceeded from his own fault that God cannot in any way be considered the author of it. If I had ever asserted that the departure of the first man from God proceeded in any way from the inspiration or motion of the Spirit of God, and if I had not uniformly contended that Adam fell by the instigation of the devil and by the impulse of his own heart, then, indeed, Pighius might justly have made his furious attack upon me. But now, removing as I do from God all the proximate cause of the act in the fall of man, I thereby remove from him also all the blame for the act, leaving man alone under the sin and the guilt. While I thus teach, why does my opponent calumniously and wickedly slander me by asserting that I make the fall of man "one of the works of God"? But how it was that God, by his foreknowledge and decree, ordained what should take place in Adam and yet so ordained it without his being in the least a participator of the fault, or being at all the author or the approver of the transgression—how this was, I repeat, is a secret manifestly far too deep to be penetrated by any stretch of human intellect. Herein, therefore, I am not ashamed to confess my utter ignorance. And far be it from anyone of the faithful to be ashamed to confess his ignorance of that which the Lord God has wholly enveloped in the blaze of his own inaccessible light!

Let my readers be assured that I offer no counsel to others that I do not follow myself with my whole heart. For the Lord is my witness, my conscience also bearing the same witness in the Holy Ghost, that daily I meditate upon these stupendous judgments of God so as not to feel the least curiosity or desire to know anything beyond what I now know and have testified. Nor does any suspicion of God's all-surpassing justice ever steal into my mind. Nor does any inclination to murmur ever entice my spirit. In a word, I fully rest, not less calmly than willingly, in the following sentiments of Augustine:

> God, who created all things very good, foreknew that evil would arise out of that good. And he also knew that his glorious and omnipotent goodness would be the more highly exalted by his producing good out of evil than by his not permitting evil at all. He ordained the life of angels and of men that he might, first of all, make it manifest by that life what free will could do, and then afterwards show what the blessing of his grace and the judgment of his justice could do.

To these divine sentiments I would merely add, repeating my heartfelt assent to them, that if the ears of any persons so continually itch that they cannot let any one of the mysteries of God remain hidden and closed, that teacher would be worse than insane who should attempt to satisfy such disciples by his instructions.

Let us rather hear and tremble at that which happened to David when he was inclined to inquire into certain unusual judgments of God that appeared in the external circumstances of persons and of this present life: "So foolish was I, and ignorant; I was as a beast before thee" [Ps. 73:22]. An exalted prophet like David could not attempt to be wise beyond what is lawful without being confounded and made to feel himself, as it were, a brute beast. Is it to be supposed, then, that we can indulge with impunity a preposterous wantonness of mind in attempting to comprehend the counsel of God, the deepest of all things in heaven or earth? After Paul had testified that God chose whom he would out of the lost mass of mankind and had reprobated whom he would, the apostle was so far from attempting to explain how or why God did so, that overwhelmed with wonder, admiration, and awe, he burst forth into the exclamation: "O the depth!" [Rom. 11:33]. Shall we, then, unawed by that depth and destitute of all reverence, dare to search into the depth of the fall and to inquire how God suffered the whole human race to fall in Adam? I have already observed that the fall of Adam is a standing lesson of humility to all his posterity, a lesson from which they may learn that they are nothing in themselves, and they can do nothing to regain eternal life. Adam was perfect and could do perfectly, yet he fell. "O the depth!" The one and only right rule of being wise is for the mind of man to restrain itself by that bridle of wonder: "O the depth!"

However, we have not, even lightly, touched upon this mighty question because an idle curiosity is not to be indulged, not because the question is abstruse and hidden in the inmost recess of the sanctuary of God. Of this curiosity, high-minded speculation is the foster mother and the nurse. And although I greatly approve all that Augustine says in his *Commentary on Genesis*, where he brings all things down to form a lesson in the fear and reverence of God, yet that other part, where he shows that God chose out of the condemned race of Adam those whom he pleased and reprobated those whom he pleased, appears to me to be far more calculated to inspire and exercise faith, and his treatment of that subject is likely to produce more abundant fruits. I, therefore, find more freedom and happiness in enforcing the doctrine that contains in its teaching the corruption, sin, and guilt of human nature. This substance of doctrine appears to me not only to be more conducive to instruction in all fundamental godliness, but also to be more theological. Let us remember, however, that in this latter substance of doctrine concerning the depravity and corruption of human nature, we must reason soberly and humbly. The greatest care must be taken that we go no farther than the Lord leads us by his word. For we know too well how captivating are the allurements of the reasonings and penetrations of human wit. Therefore, the greater caution is to be exercised in order that the simplicity of faith binds fast all our senses by her golden chain.

That God draws men unto himself by the secret inspiration and influence of his Holy Spirit, even our daily prayers bear witness. For when we pray for our persecutors, what else do we petition for them than that they may become willing to obey God who were before unwilling, that they may with us receive the truth who before resisted it, and that they may love God who before fought against him? However, it is openly manifest that it is not given indiscriminately to all men that God should suddenly deem those worthy of eternal life who had deserved eternal destruction a hundred times over.

Augustine says,

But how it is that God bestows this grace, making some, according to their just desert, vessels of wrath, and making others, according to his grace, vessels of mercy? If we ask how this is, no other reply can be given than this: "Who hath known the mind of the Lord?" [Rom. 11:34]. Though the pride and insolence of the world kick violently at such a comparison, though made by the Holy Spirit himself, it is by no means to be borne that the condition of God should be worse than that of man. For what creditor among men has not the privilege of demanding payment from one debtor and of forgiving the debts of another?

This similitude is very frequently, and most appropriately, used by Augustine.

It cannot indeed be but that the natural mind of man must immediately become ruffled when he hears that the same grace of God is denied to some who are indeed unworthy, and freely given to others who are manifestly equally unworthy. Let us, however, well consider that after all were equally under eternal condemnation, it is by no means lawful or right in us to impose on God a restraint that should prevent him from having mercy on whom he will [Rom. 9:18].

Most rightly, however, Augustine contends that the justice of God is by no means to be measured by the short rule of human justice:

After all has been said that can be said upon this stupendous subject, let the short but awe-filled exclamation of the apostle terminate all our disputations. Let us with him stand in awe of the unsearchable mind of God and breathe, "O the depth!" [Rom. 11:33]. If impudent tongues make a noise, contending or demanding more, let us never be ashamed nor grieved to utter the apostle's loud rebuke: "Nay, but who art thou, O man, that repliest against God?" [Rom. 9:20].

Election and Faith in Christ

Although I believe I have in my *Institutes* already refuted with clearness and brevity the various absurdities of opposition that my adversaries heap upon my doctrine from all quarters so that they may calumniate and defame it; although I think I have effectually met and exposed many of those figments by which ignorant persons delude and bewilder themselves; yet, as Pighius has found much delight in nibbling at my testimonies and my replies to opponents, as I proceed I will not object to wash off from myself his virulent soil.

Some of our adversaries have preposterously asked, How can men be certain of their salvation if it lies in the secret counsel of God? I have replied in these statements, which are the truth. Since the certainty of salvation is "set forth" unto us in Christ, it is useless and not without dishonor to Christ to pass over this fountain of life, which is thrown open that men may draw out of it, and to labor and toil in vain to draw the water of eternal life out of the hidden abysses of the mind and counsel of God. Paul testifies, indeed, that we were "chosen before the foundation of the world," but it was "in Christ" [Eph 1:4]. Let no one, then, seek confidence in his own election of God anywhere else than in Christ, unless he would blot out and do away with the "book of life" in which his name is written [Rev. 3:5]. God's adoption of us in Christ is for no other end than that we should be considered his children.

Scripture declares that all those who believe in the only begotten Son of God are the children and heirs of God [John 1:12; Rom. 8:16, 17; Gal. 4:7]. Christ, therefore, is the clear glass in which we are called upon to behold the eternal and hidden election of God, and of that election he is also the earnest. But the eye by which we behold the eternal life that God sets before us in this glass is faith. And the hand by which we lay hold of this earnest and pledge is faith. If any will have the matter more plainly stated, let them take it thus: Election precedes faith as to its divine order, but it is seen and understood by faith. What I just touch upon here, however, readers will find more fully explained in my *Institutes*.

Hence Christ, when dwelling on the eternal election of his own in the counsel of the Father, points out at the same time the ground on which their confidence may safely rest, where he says, "I have manifested thy name unto the men which thou gavest me out of the world: Thine they were, and thou gavest them me; and they have kept thy word" [John 17:6]. We see here that God begins with himself when he condescends to choose us and give us to Christ. But he will have us begin with Christ if we would know that we are numbered among his "peculiar people" [Deut. 14:2; Titus 2:14; 1 Pet. 2:9]. God the Father is said to have given us to his Son, to the end that each one of his chosen might enjoy the knowledge that he is an heir of God's heavenly kingdom as long as he abides in Christ, out of whom death and destruction beset us on every side. Christ is therefore said to "manifest the name" of the Father unto us [John 17:6], because by his Spirit he seals on our hearts the knowledge of our election by the Father, which is openly declared unto us by the voice of the gospel of the Son.

If we would believe what my friend Pighius says, he would make it appear that I labor and sweat, turn things upside down, confound and recast everything, so as to make it perfectly evident that I am condemned by my own conscience in all I write or say. Pighius, indeed, can pour out the flood of his characteristic loquacity with all the ease in the world, and without one drop of sweat at all. But that his tongue might have full play, he seems always to take care to wet himself well with wine so that he may be able to blow forth at random, and without any check of shame whatever, those blasts of abuse that first fill his two swollen cheeks.

Another objection of Pighius is: "If the predestination of God be the immutable and inevitable cause of salvation, all faith and confidence in us, and the need of them, are at once taken out of our hands." Without offering a word of my own argument in reply to a statement so preposterously absurd, I will merely observe that when Paul testifies that we are made partakers of divine adoption because we were chosen before the foundation of the world [Eph. 1:4], what is there, I ask, inexplicable or perplexing in this doctrine and its connection? When the apostle teaches, in the same context, that those who were thus first chosen of God and were afterwards called according to his purpose, he beautifully harmonizes, if I mistake not, the sure confidence of our faith with the immutable decree of the election of God.

Pighius further reasons thus: "If all those who are members of the body of Christ are 'written in the book of life,' then drunkards, adulterers, thieves, perjured persons, murderers, etc., will inherit the kingdom of God. All this, however, is flatly contrary to the plain testimony of the apostle Paul, for multitudes of these have been 'engrafted into Christ' by baptism and have 'put on Christ'" [Rom. 6:4; Col. 2:12; Gal. 3:27].

First, I would entreat my readers to direct their thoughts for a minute to this loose-reined profanation of Scripture in which Pighius so much delights to revel; and next, that they would mark the just judgment of God in avenging that profanation, which judgment Pighius so evidently exemplifies in himself. For with him, to trample underfoot the whole of Scripture together is nothing. Provided that he can deceive the eyes of his readers by false colors of the word of God and make himself great in the estimation of the inexperienced, he will snap his finger at uprooting the very first principles of all godliness. The Lord, however, deprives him of his common senses and exposes him to the ridicule even of children.

Now circumcision is represented by the apostle Paul as being twofold: the circumcision of "the letter" and the circumcision of "the Spirit" [Rom. 2:29]. In the same manner also, we are ever to think and speak of baptism. Many bear in their bodies only the sign, but are far from possessing the reality. Thus Peter also, after having said that we are saved by baptism, immediately declares, by way of an additional correction and caution, that the bare external washing of the flesh is not sufficient unless there be also the answer of a good conscience: "Not the putting away of the filth of the flesh, but the answer of a good conscience towards God" [1 Pet. 3:21]. Therefore, Scripture, when setting forth the sacraments, ever speaks of them in a twofold sense. When it is dealing with hypocrites, who glorying in the empty sign disregard the realty in order to prostrate the vain confidence of such, it carefully distinguishes between the reality and the sign, by which distinction the perverseness of their minds is at once exposed and defeated. In this manner Paul reminds the Corinthians that it was of no profit to the ancient people that they were all baptized in their passage through the Red Sea, "did all eat the same spiritual food, and did all drink the same spiritual drink" [1 Cor. 10:1–4]; that is, they did all partake of the same outward signs of spiritual gifts. But when the apostle is addressing believers, he speaks of the sacraments in their legitimate and efficacious use as answering the ends of their *divine* institution. When, therefore, Paul is thus speaking of the sacraments, he uses these phrases—"put on Christ," "engrafted into his body," "buried together with him," and "baptized in his name"—in their essential meanings [Rom. 13:14; Gal. 3:27; Eph. 4:24; Col. 2:12].

Pighius absurdly concludes, from Paul's use of these expressions, that all those who have been sprinkled with the visible element of water are really regenerated by the Spirit and are really incorporated into the body of Christ, so as to live unto God and in his righteousness. Pighius is not ashamed to fill page after page of his writings with such absurdities as these. Whereas when I am speaking in my writings of men generally, I call all those who have been sprinkled with the water of external baptism "members of Christ" in an external sense. Shortly afterwards, however, Pighius draws his expanded wings in a little and remarks that many fall away from Christ who had been really engrafted into his body; he makes it out that those whom Christ received from the Father as committed to his faithfulness and care are so saved by him as to have their salvation still dependent on their own free will. Pighius says, "There are many who want not the protection of the grace of Christ, but who are wanting to themselves."

Most certainly the indolence and ingratitude of those who willingly withdraw themselves from the protection of God can never be condemned with sufficient severity. It is an insult to Christ, by no means to be endured, for a man to say that the elect of God are saved by him provided they take diligent care of themselves. In this manner that protection of Christ is rendered wholly precarious and doubtful, against which, however, Christ himself declares that the devil and all the machinations of hell shall never prevail. Christ promised that he would give eternal life unto all those who were given unto him of the Father [John 17:2]. And Christ testified that he had been a safe keeper of them all up to the day on which he thus promised: "None of them is lost, but the son of perdition, that the scripture might be fulfilled" [v. 12]. In another place Christ declares that the elect of God are in his hands, and no one shall pluck them out because God is mightier than the whole world [John 8:28, 29]. If, then, eternal life is certain to all the elect, if no one can be plucked from the hand of Christ, if they can be torn away from him by no violence and no desperateness of assault, and if their salvation stands in the invincible might of God—what a brazen and audacious brow must Pighius possess to attempt to shake such a certainty and security as this?

But this is not all. He goes on to say, "Although Christ casts no one out; indeed, many of their own will depart from him. And those who were the children of God for a time do not continue such." Pighius here betrays his wickedness and perverseness as an interpreter by his refusing to acknowledge that all those whom the Father gave unto Christ are safely preserved in his hands unto the end so that they might be saved, because all those who fall away are declared by John not to have been of Christ's flock at all. "They went out from us, but they were not of us; for if they had been of us, they would no doubt have continued with us: but they went out, that they might be made manifest that they were not all of us" [1 John 2:19].

Election and Perseverance

Pighius says, "If your doctrine and argument—that all the elect are thus secure in the hand of Christ 'unto the end'—be true, the condition of salvation 'he that endureth to the end shall be saved' [Matt. 10:22], which Christ himself lays down, is proposed in vain."

Here everyone must confess that my opponent prevaricates. He had undertaken to prove that the confidence in our salvation could not consistently stand with our election of God. But now his reasoning draws us away from that point and leads us to prove that the former necessarily stands on the latter. I thus find myself so perpetually tossed to and fro by the billows of this man's violent attacks that scarcely a moment passes in which I am not in danger of being drowned. But as God ever upholds his elect to prevent them from sinking, I feel quite confident that I shall stand against all my adversary's incessant storms.

When Pighius asks me how I know that I am elected, my answer is, "Christ is to me more than a thousand witnesses." For when I find myself engrafted into his body, my salvation rests in a place so safe, secure, and tranquil that it is as if I had already realized it in heaven. If Pighius says, in reply, that the eternal election of God cannot be judged by present grace, I will not attempt to bring forward as proofs those feelings that believers experience in this matter, because it is not given unto "strangers" even to taste that bread on which the "children" of God feed [Matt. 7:6; Matt. 15:26; Mark 7:27].

But when Pighius dares to prate that it is nowhere found in Scripture that the children of God know their eternal election by their present grace, this falsehood—so bare and base—is immediately disproved by the word of God. After Paul had testified that those who were elected are called and justified and at length attain unto a blessed immortality, fortified, as it were, by a strong bulwark on every side, he thus exults and triumphs: "Who shall stand against God's elect?" [Rom. 8:31–33]. And that no one might suppose this doctrine of security to apply to all men generally, he directly afterwards applies it to the peculiar use of each believer: "For I am persuaded that neither death, nor life, nor angels, nor principalities, nor powers; nor things present, nor things to come, nor height, nor depth, nor any other creature, shall be able to separate us from the love of God, which is in Christ Jesus our Lord" [Rom. 8:38, 39]. Whereas Pighius will have it that the believer's confidence of eternal salvation may be broken short at any moment, Paul extends it into futurity and into an eternity beyond the limit of this present life and demonstrates that such a confidence proceeds from no other source than from God's election. Pighius, on the contrary, so represents the believer's confidence and his election as opposite and contradictory that he makes them destroy each other.

"What, then, does Ezekiel mean," inquires Pighius, "when he announces destruction on the righteous man if he shall turn aside from the right way" [Ezek. 18:24, 26]? We deny not that there are sometimes in the reprobate many things found also in the children of God, but however brightly the reprobate may shine with the appearance of righteousness, it is quite certain that they never proceeded from the Spirit of adoption. Such reprobate persons, thus apparently righteous, could never truly call upon God as their Father, for Paul testifies that none are ever "led" by that Spirit of adoption except the sons of God, whom he also pronounces to be "heirs" of eternal life [Rom. 8:14, 17]. Were it otherwise, that which Paul testifies in another place would not stand good, where he says, "Now we have received, not the spirit of the world, but the spirit which is of God; that we may know the things that are freely given to us of God." And again, "But we have the mind of Christ" [1 Cor. 2:12, 16]. Were it otherwise, the apostle Paul would have in vain called that Spirit by which the faithful are sealed "the earnest of their future inheritance" [Eph. 1:14]. But, so that the right knowledge of our election of God strengthens our faith in our final perseverance, that one prayer of Christ ought to furnish an abundant proof, in which he commends all the elect to his heavenly Father, separating them by name from the world and praying that when this world should be no more, they might remain saved from all its evil, being made "perfect" and "one" with himself and the Father in glory [John 17:23].

Election and Exhortations

Then follows another objection of Pighius: "It is not without purpose that Paul warns all the faithful to take heed that they 'receive not the grace of God in vain' [2 Cor. 6:1]. Nor is it without a purpose that Christ exhorts all his disciples to 'watch and pray'" [Matt. 26:41; Mark 13:33; Mark 14:38; Col. 4:2]. However, if we understand and hold fast the important difference between the unconcerned security of the flesh and the tranquil staidness of mind that faith produces, the knot of this objection is untied at once. Believers ought to rest in the certainty of their salvation. But for what end? That they might lie still in sleepy quiet? That they might throw themselves down in cowardly indolence? O no! Rather, that as they thus enjoy a quiet rest in God, they might give themselves the more unto prayer. Paul exhorts such to "work out their salvation with fear [*timore*] and trembling [*tremore*]" [Phil. 2:12].

Why is this exhortation given? Is it that they might live in fear and uncertainty as to the issue? By no means, but by nestling under the shadow of the wings of God, they might continually commit themselves to his care, depending on him alone, and so resting in his almighty power as not to doubt of their being victorious unto the end. For Paul immediately subjoins the reason the faithful should be thus anxious to shelter under the wings and omnipotent power of God: "For it is God which worketh in you, both to will and to do of his good pleasure" [v. 13]. Moreover, that the faithful might not remain in hesitation and suspense, Paul had already relieved them from all possible doubt: "Being confident of this very thing, he which hath begun a good work in you will perform it unto the day of Jesus Christ" [Phil. 1:6]. The Holy Spirit nowhere exhorts us to the care and exercise of prayer under any idea that our salvation fluctuates in a state of uncertainty or doubt, for it rests safely in the hand of God. And he nowhere imposes upon us a fear that might tend in any way to shake our confidence in the free love of God. The blessed Spirit, by such exhortations as these, designs only to quicken our natural slothfulness and unconcern.

It is to carry out and enforce this last objection of his also that Pighius calumniously twists and perverts the words of the apostle Paul:

> And if some of the branches be broken off, and thou, being a wild olive tree, wert grafted in among them, and with them partakest of the root and fatness of the olive tree; Boast not against the branches. But if thou boast, thou bearest not the root, but the root thee. Thou wilt say then, The branches were broken off, that I might be grafted in. Well; because of unbelief they were broken off, and thou standest by faith. Be not highminded, but fear: For if God spared not the natural branches, take heed lest he also spare not thee. Behold there-

fore the goodness and severity of God: on them which fell, severity; but toward thee, goodness, if thou continue in his goodness: otherwise thou also shalt be cut off" [Rom. 11: 17–22].

The real meaning of this passage is as follows: After the apostle in this chapter had spoken of the twofold election of his nation, the national and the eternal, and had shown it by the falling away of many of the Jews, it came to pass that those who before had been the legitimate and proper heirs of life, by means of the covenant that God had established with their fathers, were "broken off" and cast out, as banished from his kingdom. After speaking thus of his nation, Paul directs his word to the Gentiles, warning them neither to triumph over the Jews nor to offer them any insult, because God had taken the Gentiles into their place. We are here carefully to observe that as the universal rejection of the Jews did not at all alter or shake the fixed election of God so as to prevent him from saving some "remnant" of them, so the universal election of the Gentiles did not embrace every individual of the Gentiles so as to make them all sharers of eternal life. Paul, I repeat, is here speaking of God's twofold election of the Jewish nation. For the whole family of Abraham had been, in a certain sense, elected of God. But since many of them were not ordained unto eternal life by God's secret judgment and counsel, the greater number perished, although the election of God still rested on the "remnant." Now that the covenant of life is transferred to the Gentiles, however, the general adoption of the family of Abraham belongs to us. But this does not prevent those few of the family of Abraham who were ordained thereunto by the secret good pleasure and decree of God from still enjoying their adoption.

Paul, therefore, when thus contrasting the Gentiles with the Jews, calls the Gentiles "wild olive trees" engrafted on the original sacred root after its natural branches had been broken off. The apostle is neither speaking of individuals in a private sense, nor treating of the secret election of God abstractly. He is showing what a mighty change of things was made when the legitimate children were rejected and strangers were substituted in their place. The whole of this exhortation of Paul is not so much addressed to those believers who had truly and in heart received the grace of God, as to the whole body of the Gentiles, which was promiscuously composed of various members, believers and unbelievers. Yet there is nothing singular in God's restraining the pride and insolence of the flesh in his own Gentile children, seeing that they all labor under this corrupt infirmity. However, Pighius most ridiculously concludes from the above exhortation of the apostle that the certainty of God's election and its final accomplishment depend upon the perseverance of men. This conclusion of Pighius is, we repeat, most absurd, because in the falling away of all men generally from God, his eternal election must nevertheless stand and prevail.

The Perversity of the Reprobate

As to the profane who stigmatize the judgment of God, representing it under an utterly false color and saying, "It is in vain for the reprobate to strive after righteousness and holiness, because according to the doctrine of election, they must ultimately and inevitably perish." Such a calumny, as it is the offspring of the grossest ignorance, may be shaken off from us by a very brief reply: There can be no real desire of doing good in men that does not proceed from God's election of them. The reprobate, however, made as they are vessels unto dishonor, never cease to provoke the vengeance of God upon themselves, thereby manifestly proving, as in written characters, that they are ordained to destruction.

To Pighius, however, such a doctrine is the very climax of absurdity, so much so that he declares that there is no monstrosity equal to it to be found in all the discussions of this subject put together. But by this one declaration it is manifest that he is so carried away by a rabid lust of reviling all that is good, that abuses boil over out of his breast without any real occasion whatever.

Scripture plainly teaches that none but the elect of God are ever ruled or "led" by his Spirit [Rom. 8:14]. What rectitude or right-doing, then, can there be in man without the "leading" of the Holy Spirit? Hence it is that Paul says, "The works of the flesh are manifest, which are these: adultery, fornication, uncleanness, lasciviousness, idolatry, witchcraft, hatred, variance, emulations, wrath, strife, seditions, heresies, envyings, murders, drunkenness, revellings, and such like" [Gal. 5:19–21]. And he elsewhere declares that all the thoughts of the carnal mind are "enmity against God" [Rom. 8:7].

What inconsistency, then, is there in my affirming that all those who are not regenerated by the Spirit of God are the slaves of sin and carried headlong at the will of the flesh? Those whom God chooses, he justifies by his own righteousness. What marvel, then, if the reprobate, who are destitute of the righteousness of God, should know nothing, nor know how to do anything, but sin? But God has chosen his own for the very end that they might be "holy and without blame" [Eph. 1:4]. If, then, holiness be the fruit of free election, who can but confess that all the rest of men remain sunk in the filth and profanity of nature? Christ declares that none can hear his voice but his own sheep. And he asserts that all those who will not hear the voice of the Father sounding in his mouth are of their father, the devil [John 10:26, 27; John 8:43, 44].

When Pighius wants to show that reprobates study to do good works, he must, to be consistent, also show that their obstinacy is pleasing to God. But Pighius, in support of his doctrine that the reprobate really do devote themselves to good works, argues that Saul excelled in many virtues; indeed, even that he pleased God. That the virtues which shine in the reprobate are laudable in themselves, I by no means deny. And this is what Scripture means when it says that Saul, and others of the same character, "did what was right." As God looks at the heart, the fountain from which all works flow, a work that is in a general sense good in itself may nevertheless be "an abomination in the sight of God" [Luke 16:15]. In fact, wholly unknown to Pighius is the first principle of all godliness: "There is nothing so pure that the uncleanness of man will not defile." It is no wonder, therefore, that our opponent, looking at the works of Saul as he wore his external mask, lauds his innocence and virtues. When Pighius contends that Saul did in one instance please God, I grant it, and I make this case an exception to my general remark. God did, indeed, so honor him in his office as king that the house of Israel, as we find in Scripture, never once censured him, as Ezekiel also testifies. So Judas was chosen to the apostolic office. Will Pighius conclude that Judas was therefore numbered among the children of God? But my opponent calumniates all this, my testimony, making me to be speaking all the time of the single actions of life abstractly considered, whereas I am speaking of the continuous course and tenor of life. In a word, if we do not make all the goodness and righteousness that can be found in man to proceed from the Spirit of sanctification, the whole testimony of the Scriptures must be shaken.

Supposed Ill Effects of Predestination, Answered by Augustine

It is useless to spend more time and trouble in replying to the other cavils of our adversary. His next objection is in every enemy's mouth: "All teaching is vain, and all exhortation worthless, if strength and power to obey wholly depend on the election of God." And this additional cavil is akin to it: "Men will, as an inevitable consequence, give themselves up to indolence and unconcern when they are thus taught to rest in the eternal counsel of God."

The replies to these objections, already given by me in my answers, are so attacked by Pighius with his usual abuse that I will allow them to remain quiet and will not repeat them here to be defiled again by his hands. But if there be any ultra morose ones who are not yet satisfied, and who consider that there is more weight in the testimony of Augustine (an acknowledgment I have often and willingly made myself), I will produce Augustine's sentiments on this subject in his own words, thereby testifying my own assent to their truth. His words, as found in his book *On the Blessing of Perseverance*, are these:

Men say that the doctrine of predestination stands adverse to all preaching, rendering it altogether useless. According to this, the apostle Paul's preaching, which was full of this doctrine, was altogether useless. Did not this great teacher of the Gentiles preach the doctrine of predestination continually? But did we ever hear of his ceasing to preach the word of God because he found his preaching useless? Paul preached, "It is God which worketh in you, both to will and to do of his good pleasure" [Phil. 2:13]. But do we ever find that on that account he ceased to exhort us "to will" and to wish those things that please God and "to work" ourselves with all our power? Paul preached, "He which hath begun the good work in you will perform it unto the day of Jesus Christ" [Phil. 1:6]. But did he ever cease to persuade men to begin themselves and to persevere unto the end? No. The Lord himself called upon men to believe in him. Yet his declaration is eternally true, and his description not without its solemn purpose, when he testifies, "No man can come unto me [that is, no one can believe in me], unless it were given him of my Father" [John 6:65]. Nor is the exhortation of the Lord to believe vain because his description of those who alone do believe is true. How can it be said that the doctrine of predestination stands against preaching, exhortation, and correction, and renders them useless (which are all so frequently used in Scripture) when the same Scripture speaks so much of predestination also?

Shortly afterwards the holy father remarks,

Those hear these things and do them to whom it is given; but those to whom it is not given do them not, whether they hear them not or hear them. Neither, therefore, is the preaching of fruitful and persevering faith to be withheld because of the necessity of preaching predestination, in order that men by the preaching of fruitful and persevering faith might hear those things they ought to do, and in order that they to whom it is given might do them. "But how shall they hear," as the apostle argues, "without a preacher" [Rom. 10:14]? Nor is the preaching of predestination to be withheld because of the necessity of preaching that faith which is fruitful and perseveres unto the end, in order that he who lives in faith and obedience may not glory in his obedience as being his own, but the gift of God. As it is written, "He that glorieth, let him glory in the Lord" [2 Cor. 10:17].

Augustine continues,

As he that has received the gift so to do rightly exhorts and preaches, so he that has received the gift so to do hears and obeys. Hence the Lord so frequently says, "He that hath ears to hear, let him hear" [Matt. 11:15; Matt. 13:9, 43; et al.]. From whom those who have the gift receive it, the Lord himself shows us: "I will give them a heart to know me and ears to hear me." Ears to hear, therefore, are the gift of all obedience, with which all those who are endowed come to Christ. Therefore, we both preach and exhort. Those who have ears to hear, hear and obey; but in those who have not, that solemn Scripture is fulfilled: "That hearing they may hear and not understand" [Isa. 6:9; Mark 4:12] — hearing, indeed, with the outward ear of the body, but not with the inward ear of the heart. Why is it given to one to hear and not to another? Why is it given of the Father to some, and not to others, to come unto the Son? The reply is, "Who hath known the mind of the Lord?" [Rom. 11:34]. Are we, then, to deny what is manifest because we cannot comprehend what is hidden?

From this is plainly seen how preposterous the extreme caution of those is who, through fear of some supposed absurdity or contradiction in it, would hide or altogether suppress a doctrine most necessary to be known. But suppose that some, upon hearing the doctrine of predestination, give themselves up to indolence and unconcern and rush headlong from diligence and labor into concupiscence, following their own lusts. Is all that is said in Scripture concerning the foreknowledge of God therefore to be considered untrue? Would not those have been good if God had foreknown that they would be good, although they are now reveling in wickedness? And if God foreknew that they would be evil, evil they will be, in whatever goodness they may now appear to shine. Are, then, all those things that Scripture says in truth concerning the prescience of God to be denied or held in silence because such cases as these are found among men? And that, too, when it is certain that if these truths were not declared, men would nevertheless rush into other errors of some kind?

A reason for not declaring the truth is one thing; the necessity of declaring the truth is another. To enumerate the various reasons assigned for the propriety of not declaring the truth would exceed both our limits and our purpose. One reason assigned is this: lest those who do not understand should be made worse, while we are wishing that those who do understand may be made wiser and better. But those who are not made wiser and better by any certain doctrine of truth that we teach are assuredly not made worse. But where the reality of the case is, that when we are declaring a doctrine of truth, he who cannot understand it is rendered worse by our declaration of it, while he who can understand it is rendered worse by our keeping silence, what is to be done (it is asked) in such a case as this? Why, is it not much better that the truth should be declared in order that he who can receive it may receive it, than that it should be kept back in silence, so that neither may receive it? For by this silence both are rendered worse: he that does understand and he that does not understand. Whereas he that does understand might, by hearing the truth and receiving it, teach others also.

Hence some of us are unwilling to declare and teach that which, according to the testimony of Scripture, we ought to declare and teach. And the cause of our fear is, lest by our speaking out, he should be offended who cannot understand us. Whereas we ought also to fear, lest by our silence, he who would have understood us, had we spoken, should be left to be carried away perhaps by the false teaching of others.

This sentiment, thus briefly expressed, Augustine afterwards expands and confirms in the following manner:

Therefore, if the apostles and those teachers of the church who followed them performed the twofold service, solemnly holding forth the doctrine of God's eternal election and retaining the faithful under the discipline of a godly life, why should these men of our day think they act rightly in the matter of their teaching by keeping themselves shut up in silence within the strong tower of invincible truth, holding as they do that though what is said concerning election be eternally true, it ought not to be preached openly to the people? On the contrary, however, the doctrine of election ought to be preached constantly and thoroughly, so that he who has "ears to hear" may hear. And who has these "ears" but he who has received them from him who has promised to give them? Therefore, let him who receives not the truth reject it, but let him who hears and understands the truth receive it, drink it, and live. As therefore godliness is to be preached so that God may be rightly obeyed and worshiped, so is predestination to be preached also, so that he who has "ears to hear" the free grace of God may glory in God, and not in himself.

Hence, although there was in this holy man Augustine a singular devotedness to the edifying of the church, he so wisely tempers the system of preaching the truth that he would have offense guarded against with all prudence, where it can be done lawfully.

His admonition is that whatever truths are preached should be preached at the same time consistently:

> If anyone should address the people and say, If ye believe not, it is because ye are predestinated of God to eternal destruction, such an one would not only foster his own indolence, but would indulge malice towards his hearers. If a preacher should extend his sentiments into the future and should say that those who heard him never would believe because they were reprobates, such preaching would be imprecation, not doctrine.

Teachers of this description Augustine would have expelled from the church at once (and most deservedly) as foolish or designing prophets from whom no good can be expected. And the holy father elsewhere truly contends that a preacher then profits others when he pities them, helps them forward, and invites those whom he wishes to benefit to proceed in the right way without any appeal to them in the form of taunting rebuke. But why some profit by the preaching of the word and some profit not, far be it from us to say that this is according to the judgment or wisdom of the "clay," when it is all according to the will and wisdom of the "potter."

When men do come into the way of righteousness, or return into it by means of holy correction or rebuke, who is it that works salvation in their hearts but he who "giveth the increase," [1 Cor. 3:7], whoever sows, or whoever waters? No free will of man can resist him who wills to save. Therefore, we are to rest assured that no human wills can resist the will of God, who does all things in heaven and in earth according to his will, and who has already done by his will the things that shall be done. No wills of men, we repeat, can resist the will of God so as to prevent him from doing what he wills, seeing that he does what he wills with the wills of all mankind. And when it is God's will to bring men by any certain way that he may please, does he bind their bodies with chains? O no! He works within: He takes hold of their hearts within; he moves their hearts within; he draws them by those new wills of their own that he has himself wrought in them.

What Augustine adds in continuation must by no means be omitted.

> Since we know not who belongs to the number of the predestinated and who does not, we ought so to feel as to wish all to be saved. From this it will come to pass that whoever shall come in our way, we shall desire to make him a partaker of the peace that we ourselves enjoy. "Our peace," however, will nevertheless "rest upon the sons of peace." Therefore, as far as we are concerned, wholesome and even severe correction will ever be made use of by us as a medicine towards all men, both to save them from perishing and to prevent them from causing others to perish. But it will be of God alone to make that medicine beneficial to those whom he foreknew and predestinated.

If, then, these things be true, and if they be thus testified by a witness so eminent as the chief of the holy fathers, let them not be vomited forth from the mouths of hatred upon the head of Calvin by his ignorant and evilly disposed persecutors. I would, however, that these insipid cautious ones who so much desire to please by their teary moderation would just consider that Augustine, to whom they so willingly yield the palm of knowledge in divine things, surpasses them just as far in modesty also. This conviction would tend to prevent them from passing off their soured timidity for real modesty.

Reprobation and the Goodness of God

Now let me deal a little further with Pighius. My readers must bear in mind three special and summary particulars. First, whatever mountain of absurdities he heaps up to launch at my doctrine with a design to its suppression is hurled not so much at me as at God himself. Second, in order that he may wrest out of my hands those passages of Scripture that support my doctrine, he shows himself an ignorant trifler and manifests that he cannot support his own cause in any other way than by corrupting and subverting Scripture. Third, he rushes headlong into such an extreme of impudence and appeals without hesitation to Augustine as an authority for his absurdities. "If God," argues this worthless and daring mortal, "created any men for destruction, he is not worthy of being loved. Those poor creatures who were deprived of eternal life before they were born are more deserving of pity than of punishment." If the testimonies that this aweless being attempts to shake were mine, he would be fighting against a mortal man. But since it is God himself whom he thus insults and reproaches, I shall feel no shame in applying to him a hundred times over the solemn appeal of the apostle Paul, "Nay, but who art thou, O man, that contendest against thy maker?" [Rom. 9:20].

This miserable mortal feels now, and all his fellows will hereafter feel, the effects of the reproaches that they hurl at God from their foul and profane mouths. Such reproaches fail and fall by the weight of their own wickedness long before they reach heaven, and their only certain course is to fall back, with all their weight, upon the heads of those who utter them.

Permit me to produce just one specimen of this rebel's foul madness in adulterating Scripture: The ninth chapter of Paul's Epistle to the Romans he both confounds and dismembers in the following manner. At the commencement, to save all labor and trouble in untying the Gordian knot, Pighius cuts it right in half, as he thinks, by one word. He says that Israel was chosen of God, but not all *Israelites*, because all the descendants of Israel did not truly represent their father Israel, who received that name from "seeing." From this he concludes that God's election becomes not real and ratified in any except in those who "open their eyes." But this preeminent teacher of clear-sightedness, in interpreting the name *Israel*, is most ridiculously stone-blind himself while thus vainly attempting to make a sharp point out of a blunt log. In the meantime, this blind instructor never thinks of the fact that Israel—the "open-eyed" one, according to his lucid interpretation—was made "open-eyed" by the peculiar grace of God, for he had been chosen of God in the womb of his mother. Nor do any others ever possess "eyes" to see God or his truth except those whose minds God himself enlightens by his Spirit. And those only are deemed worthy of the light of his Spirit whom he adopted for himself even while still in their blindness and whom he makes his children.

After this, Pighius, like a wild beast escaped from his cage, rushes forth, bounding over all fences in his way, uttering such sentiments as these:

> The mercy of God is extended to everyone, for God wishes all men to be saved; for that end he stands and knocks at the door of our heart, desiring to enter. Therefore, those were elected before the foundation of the world, by whom he foreknew he should be received. But God hardens no one, excepting by his forbearance, in the same manner as too fond parents ruin their children by excessive indulgence.

Just as if anyone, by such puerile dreams as these, could escape the force of all those things that the apostle plainly declares in direct contradiction to such sentiments. And just as if it were nothing at all to his readers when Paul positively asserts that out of the twins, while they were yet in the womb of their mother, the one was chosen and the other rejected, without any respect to the works of either, present or future (the former of which there could be none), but solely by the good pleasure of God that calls. As if it were nothing when the apostle testifies, "It is not of him that willeth, nor of him that runneth, but of God that sheweth mercy," who hardens whom he will, and has mercy on whom he will [Rom. 9:16, 18]. As if it were nothing when the same apostle avers that "God sheweth forth his power in the vessels of wrath" in order that "he might make

known the riches of his grace on the vessels of mercy" [vv. 22, 23].
Paul undeniably here testifies that all those of Israel who were
saved, were saved according to God's free election, and that therefore "the election obtained it, and the rest were blinded" [Rom. 11:7].
All these solemn particulars, however, we have more fully discussed
in their order in our preceding pages.

Man's Will and God's Grace

If our opponent were a hundredfold more acute and clever than
he is, all the cavils he could muster would never prevent even the
deaf from hearing the loud thunder of the above declarations of the
apostle. And yet, after having heaped up words, mountain on
mountain, he leaves this feeble mountain of his own standing at
last: "God did not create those reprobates whom he foresaw would
be such, but he knew that some whom he would create would be
reprobates." What is all this folly, more or less, than bedaubing the
eyes of the potter, and his hands also, in order that we might not
be able to discern his real form and features or to see his work? And
it is just the same when Pighius attempts to disentangle himself
from the divine net of the apostle that lies hidden in the first chapter of his Epistle to the Ephesians. He so sports and flourishes his
bombast as if, by his loud, empty noise, he could strike even the
apostle himself dumb and force him to be silent.

This vain mortal says,

> God chose us in Christ because he foreknew that his grace,
> which otherwise was free to all, would find a place in us only,
> and that we alone should receive it. He chose us out of all
> men because he foresaw that what was set before all men for
> their reception would become peculiar to us, who alone
> would receive it. It was thus that he chose us "to the glory of
> his grace," which sanctifies us in just the same manner as the
> praise of all belongs to the preceptor, while doctrine and its
> benefit belong to the scholar.

As if that eternal purpose, which Paul elsewhere sets forth in opposition to all human works, were not the purpose of God alone. As if the glory of free grace were not, in this passage, more strikingly exhibited under the expression *the good pleasure of God* [Eph. 1:9] than by any other terms. God is said to have saved us "according to his good pleasure which he purposed in himself" [v. 9] for this very reason: Finding no cause in us, he made himself the cause of our salvation. Is it for nothing, think ye, that the apostle repeats five times over that the whole of our salvation is the effect of and dependent upon that eternal decree, purpose, and good pleasure of God? Is it with no intent whatever that the apostle declares that we were "blessed" in Christ because we were "chosen" in Christ [vv. 3, 4]? Does not the apostle refer all sanctification and every good work to the election of God, as waters are traced to their originating source? Does not Paul attribute it to the same grace that we are the "workmanship of God, created unto good works, which he hath before ordained that we should walk in them" [Eph 2:10]? Why did God choose us out and separate us from the rest but that we might know that we are what we are, and that we are blessed above all others by the free favor of God alone?

Behold then, readers, how "sweetly" God's foreknowledge of good works in us, according to the doctrine of Pighius, "harmonizes" with the apostle's context in the first chapter of his Epistle to the Ephesians. How much better would it have been, in our opponent, to have retained the character of an admirer of the apostle, which for a moment he was compelled to assume, than thus to have turned abruptly aside to haughty speculations and to have thrown off the mask of the admirer altogether to his own exposure. These great subjects, however, which I more fully digested in the former part of this work, I have now only cursorily touched with the lip.

This worthless being Pighius indeed flogs Augustine severely for being a man (as he says) who, in the discussion of this great subject, betrays more violent impetuosity than calm reason; one who dashes up against this thing and that person in his way and brings forth those things that seem to be utterly at variance with the goodness of God. Yet, this same vain mortal, devoid of every feeling of modesty, appeals to this same holy father's authority in confirmation of his own absurdities. With what impudence he does this, I will demonstrate in a few short words. He lauds the industry of the holy man for his having so carefully winnowed this important question in his book written to Simplicianus, Bishop of Mediola. But did this fellow really ever open that book? I doubt it, because he makes it to be one book instead of two. It is something rather marvelous that this very eminent interpreter should have singled out this production of Augustine from all his other works, which work the holy father acknowledges that he wrote at the commencement of his episcopate. Although he wrote that book against Pelagius, Augustine does not hesitate to confess candidly that he afterwards wrote much more fully and solidly on that subject.

His own words are these:

The predestination of the saints is, indeed, set forth by me in that book. But necessity afterwards compelled me to defend that doctrine with greater industry and labor when I was contending for the truth against the Pelagians. For I always found that each heresy, as it arose, brought its own questions into the church, against which the divine Scripture required defense with greater diligence than if no such necessity had arisen.

Let us now see what that authority is which this impudent person adduces from the works of Augustine. "My author," says Pighius, "stands in the opinion that the rejection or contempt of vocation is the cause of reprobation, and this opinion he fully affirms."

Now the fact is that the mind of Augustine is directly the contrary, for in his book *Recollections* he says, "I once labored hard for the free will of man until the grace of God at length overcame me." I will omit to notice here what Augustine further says in that book now in question and in other places before cited by me, wherein he is explaining his mind, which is of more value—to the faithful at least—than a thousand opinions of Pighius or of any others like him. How, then, does Pighius dare, with something more than impudence, to refer to Augustine as an authority for those sentiments that throughout his whole work he rejects with a determination quite as great as the candor with which he condemns them? That I may not pursue these observations too far, I only observe that those authorities which Pighius adduces are indeed extant in the work of Augustine in question, but the fact is that they are refuted on the same page on which they are found.

Augustine argues,

If Scripture says, "It is not of him that willeth, nor of him that runneth, but of God that sheweth mercy" [Rom. 9:16] because the will of man alone is not sufficient to enable him to live justly and righteously unless it be aided by the mercy of God—if this be the case, we might just as well argue, and Scripture might just as well say, "It is not of God that showeth mercy, but of man that willeth." For according to this, the mercy of God is not sufficient unless it be aided by the consent of our will. But the truth and the fact are that our willing is vain unless God has mercy. But how shall it be said (I know not) that God's having mercy is vain unless we also will? Where God has mercy, we are sure to have will, because the very nature of that mercy, when shown, is to make us willing, according to this word of the apostle: "For it is God which worketh in you both to will and to do" [Phil. 2:13]. For if it be inquired whether or not a good will is the gift of God, who will be found so daring as to deny it?

Shortly afterwards, Augustine draws this conclusion:

Therefore, the truth is that "it is not of him that willeth, nor of him that runneth, but of God that sheweth mercy" [Rom. 9:16] because although God calls many, yet he has mercy on those only whom he so calls as to make that call effectual in them that they may follow it. Hence it would be utterly false if anyone were to say, "It is not of God that showeth mercy, but of man that willeth" because God has mercy on no one ineffectually or in vain. On whomever God has mercy, him he so calls as to make the manner of his calling effectual, so that he shall not refuse him who calls.

Therefore, Pighius spoke with the greatest truth when he said, in his prefatory remarks, that this great question of predestination had been industriously winnowed by Augustine in his book addressed to Simplicianus. But Pighius most grievously transgresses in the matter, for while he is catching at the chaff blown about in the air, he disregards altogether the wheat that is evidently left upon the floor.

The Errors of Georgius

Some small space must now be found for dealing with Georgius of Sicily. All things connected with this miserable creature are so insipid, vain, and disgusting that I feel ashamed to spend any time or labor in his refutation. Nor would I condescend to enter the field with this shadow if the silly consternation of many at his pretensions did not compel me to do so. And I doubt not that there will be many who, from their considering the easy victory that I must of necessity gain over his trifling puerilities, will quite deride my needless attempt. Indeed, if he were not a mischievous person, I would consider him much more worthy of being trampled underfoot in contempt than of being refuted by the use of words. But as his books, flying throughout Italy, drive many mad on every side, I had rather, in such a kind of necessity, act a little of the madman myself with such a mad fellow than suffer by silence so much mischief to be done in the church by his madness. When of old the prophet Ezekiel saw that certain old prophetesses were blinding the eyes of the people, he felt no shame in entering into the battle with women [Ezek. 13:17]. Let us, therefore, if we would be the true servants of Christ, not feel aggrieved at being compelled to take up arms for the purpose of driving away those, whoever they may be, who are laboring with all their might to throw their chaff into the granary of the Lord.

Election Has Different Meanings

When we testify that men are predestinated either to salvation or to destruction by the eternal counsel of God, Georgius considers that we hallucinate and are deceived in that matter on three accounts in particular. The first of these, he says, is that we are ignorant that the word *election* is received in different senses in Scripture. For God, he observes, is sometimes said to elect or choose certain persons to a certain temporal office where no mention whatever is made of eternal life nor any consideration of it entertained. But by what kind of arguments will this stupid trifler attempt to persuade us that we are so inexperienced in the Scriptures as not yet to know that Saul, who was really a reprobate, was yet chosen or elected to be king? [1 Sam. 9:16, 17], and that Judas, who was one of the twelve, whom Christ declares that he himself had chosen, was called by Christ a devil [John 6:70]?

Why does not this vain fellow point out some passages of Scripture, evilly and impiously brought forward by us in support of our testimony, that will make our errors manifest? The fact is that this dreamer fabricates dreams of his own, which are the children of his own brain, and against these he wages war as if they really were our dreams. Yet it is marvelous, meanwhile, how utterly he forgets himself and his own precept concerning the different meanings of the word *election* when he attacks us and applies to us the words of the apostle: "Lest, after I have preached the gospel to others, I myself should become a reprobate [castaway]" [1 Cor. 9:27]. For Georgius concludes from this passage that Paul, according to the doctrine of election, positively uttered a falsehood when he expressed his fear

lest the immutable election of God should fail in his case, and that
he really knew not or was not certain of his own election.

This miserable being does not see that "reprobate," or "disap-
proved" in this passage is opposed to "approved." "Approved" would
signify that such an approved one had given sure evidences and
proof of his godliness. How was it that the different meanings of
the term *reprobate* did not come into the mind of our silly opponent?
For when "reprobate silver" is spoken of by the prophet Jeremiah
[Jer. 6:30], and "reprobate earth" in Paul's Epistle to the Hebrews
[Heb. 6:8], it does not mean that such "reprobate silver" or "reprobate earth" was ordained of God to eternal destruction, but that it
was silver and earth that had become alloyed, adulterated, unfruitful, and worthless. That the term *reprobate* applies to men in this
passage of the apostle, as it does also in another epistle, is at once
manifest in each place from the context.

Yet the election to any temporal office is so plainly distinct from
that eternal election by which God chooses and adopts us unto
everlasting life that Scripture sometimes joins them together in the
same person, on account of their immediate affinity. Thus, when
Paul glories that God "separated" him from his "mother's womb"
[Gal. 1:15], he is speaking of his apostolic office. But the same apostle, ascending yet higher, glories at the same time in the grace of
God also by which he had been called unto the hope of salvation.
In like manner, Christ, although he declares that one of those
whom he had chosen to the apostolic office was a devil, yet elsewhere joins the grace of adoption with the apostolic honor, saying,
"Ye have not chosen me, but I have chosen you; that ye should go
and bring forth fruit and that your fruit should remain" [John 15:16].
For he declares that his own were given to him of the Father for the
very end that he should not suffer any one of them to perish, except him who was already "the son of perdition" [John 17:12]. Although, therefore, we read everywhere in the Scriptures that God
chose these or those to this or that kind of life, or to this or that
temporal office, such facts do not at all alter the greater fact that
God chose unto salvation those whom he was pleased to save. Nor

did the one election militate against, contradict, contravene, or impede the other.

Election Is on the Basis of Faith

The second account on which Georgius declares we are in error and delusion is because we do not hold that all the believers (as he calls them) of the New Testament were chosen unto salvation, as those were of whom the apostle speaks in the first chapter of his Epistle to the Ephesians. But we have already more than fully shown that Paul in that chapter traces the faith by which the children of God enter upon the possession of their salvation unto eternal election as its true and only source; and most certainly faith is especially to be reckoned among those spiritual riches that are freely given to us in Christ. From whence does Paul testify that all and every one of our spiritual blessings flow but from that eternal and hidden fountain—the free adoption of God? Again, the apostle uses these words: "Wherein he hath abounded toward us in all wisdom and prudence" [Eph. 1:8]. How did God thus abound? And from what source did this abundance flow? The apostle tells us immediately afterwards: "According to his good pleasure, which he hath purposed in himself" [v. 9].

Therefore, if faith be the fruit of divine election, it is at once evident that all are not enlightened unto faith. Hence it is also an indubitable fact that those on whom God determined in himself to bestow faith were chosen of him from everlasting for that end. Consequently, the sentiments of Augustine are truth where he thus writes, "The elect of God are chosen by him to be his children in order that they might be made to believe, not because he foresaw that they would believe." I forbear to cite here other passages of the apostle similar to the above, because they will have to be considered very shortly in their proper place. But as there is one passage in the evangelist Matthew where the elect of God seem to be spoken of as an infinite number, where Christ says that there shall be such great signs and wonders shown by false christs and false prophets that "if it were possible, they shall deceive the very elect" [Matt. 24:24], Georgius explains "the very elect" as signifying all those who persevere in faith and righteousness. And this interpretation is perfectly right, provided that at the same time he confesses that this perseverance depends on election alone. But Georgius, to shut out all idea of special or particular election, makes each individual among men the author of his own election.

Concerning Scriptural Blindness As Punishment

The third account or cause why we are in error, according to our worthy friend Georgius, is that although Scripture does indeed make mention of men being "blinded" and "hardened," we do not bear in mind that such greater punishments are inflicted on sins of greater magnitude.

We on our part do not deny what is clearly confirmed by numberless testimonies of Scripture: God punishes with blindness, and with many other modes of judgment, contempt of his grace, pride, obstinacy, and many other kindred sins. And indeed, all those conspicuous punishments of which mention is made throughout the Scriptures ought to be referred to that general view of the righteous judgment of God in the display of which we ever see that those who have not duly feared God after knowing him, nor reverenced him as they ought, have been "given over to a reprobate mind" [Rom. 1:28] and left to wallow in every kind of uncleanness and lust. But on this deep subject we shall dwell more fully hereafter.

Although, therefore, the Lord does thus strike the wicked with vindictive madness and consternation and does thus repay them with the punishment they deserve, this does not at all change the fact that there is, in all the reprobate generally, a blindness and an obstinate hardness of heart. When Pharaoh is said to have been "hardened" of God [Ex. 7:13, 22; Ex. 8:19; et al.], he was already, in himself, worthy of being delivered over unto Satan by the Most High. Moses, however, also testifies that Pharaoh had been before blinded of God "for this very purpose" [Ex. 9:16]. Nor does Paul add

any other cause for this than that Pharaoh was one of the reprobate [Rom. 9:17]. In this same manner also does the apostle demonstrate that the Jews, when God had deprived them of the light of
understanding and had permitted them to fall into horrible darkness, suffered thereby the righteous punishments of their wicked
contempt of the grace of God. Yet the apostle plainly intimates that
this same blindness is justly inflicted of God upon all reprobates
generally, for he testifies that the "remnant" were saved "according to
the election of grace," but all "the rest were blinded" [Rom. 11:5, 7].

If, then, "the rest" in whom the election of God does not reign
are "blinded," it is doubtlessly and undeniably manifest that those
same persons, who by their rebellion and provocation of the wrath
of God procured to themselves this additional blindness, were
themselves from the beginning ordained to blindness. Hence the
words of Paul are manifestly true where he implies that "the vessels
of wrath" were "afore prepared unto destruction" [Rom. 9:22, 23],
namely, all those who being destitute of the Spirit of adoption precipitated themselves into eternal destruction by their own sin and
fault. Therefore, I hesitate not to confess that in the secret judgments of God something always precedes but is hidden. For how
God condemns the wicked and yet justifies the wicked is a mystery
that is shut up in the secret mind of God, which is inaccessible to
all human understanding. Therefore, there remains nothing better,
nothing more becoming us, than to stand in awe with the apostle
and exclaim, "How unsearchable are his judgments and his ways
past finding out!" [Rom. 11:33]. For God's judgments are a profound
abyss.

Particular Election Denied

Georgius then goes on to say,

Not one syllable can be found in the whole of Scripture from
which it can be lawfully concluded that those who were
reprobated by the eternal judgment of God were "blinded,"

and that all we testify concerning predestination rests on the mere craft of philosophic invention; for God could not be ignorant of any of those things that should come to pass, and whatever thing he did foresee could not but come to pass according to that foreknowledge.

To this lying misrepresentation of our doctrine I give no answer. My books are its standing refutation. The fact is that as the unbounded favor of the reverend abbot gave this conceited fellow the license of saying what he pleased among his silly brethren, and as he had the audacity to puff off among them all the dreams that entered his brain as the oracles of God, he really promised himself the same credit outside the monastery. But what is the benefit of my now using many words to prove what I have proved a thousand times over: We do not gather that difference between the elect and the reprobate (against which Georgius so violently but vainly wars) from the bare foreknowledge of God (according to this fellow's stupid perversion of our testimony), but we prove it to be taught in numberless, manifest, and solid passages of Holy Scripture. And yet this fellow imagines and would make it appear that we war with the prescience of God alone. Readers, however, will find above twenty plain passages already cited by me that prove the contrary to this vain imagination. He boasts that special and particular election is a fiction of our own, because God chooses no special or particular persons. Christ himself, however, declares aloud on the contrary that he knows whom he has chosen [John 13:18].

Behold then, readers, with what mighty war engines of his own fabrication Georgius labors to shake the eternal counsel of God by which some are chosen to salvation and others ordained unto destruction. Paul does indeed make the righteousness of God common to all by faith, and he does not admit any distinction whatever, testifying that "all have sinned and come short of the glory of God" [Rom. 3:23].

I also confess with my whole heart, according to Paul, that the righteousness of God is freely extended to all through faith. But whence comes faith unto men? Only from the free illumination of the Spirit. And whom does Paul consider to be those who believe in Christ? Those only whom his heavenly Father has drawn [John 6:44]. And most certainly Christ on his part reckons no one among his own but him who was given to him by his Father. Accordingly, Christ declares that those who were given to him were before his Father's [John 17:6].

Georgius, we well know, will here thrust in our faces his mad dream about natural faith, which absurdity does not belong to my present purpose to stop and refute. I shall only say that the righteousness of God is "unto all and upon all them that believe" in Christ [Rom. 3:22]. But on the testimony of the same apostle, I assert that where one believes and another does not believe, it is God alone who makes the difference; it is of God alone that some have the advantage of others in obtaining the blessing so that no one may glory. I affirm that in order that we might know the things freely given to us of God, our eternal inheritance is sealed upon our hearts by the earnest and seal of the Spirit. I also affirm that our ability to believe in Christ is given to us of God. Moreover, I maintain that "the eyes of our understanding are enlightened" by God that we might know "what is the hope of his calling" [Eph. 1:18]. And finally, I testify that faith is a fruit of the Holy Spirit.

Paul does indeed declare that "there is no difference" [Rom. 3:22–25], but his meaning is that there is no difference between the Jew and the Greek, for God invites both equally unto salvation. Now Georgius here affirms that these two races of men comprehend all mankind. Be it so, he cannot by that argument prove that righteousness is promised severally and separately to each individual of mankind. And suppose we were to grant this last point, we must come, after all, to the original proposition and fact that no one can become a partaker of the good offered him except by faith. By this argument, then, the monk must be driven to the necessity of making faith common to all men. And this, as we have before abundantly proved, is directly contrary to the mind of the apostle Paul.

Our monk will follow up his argument by saying that, according to our doctrine, the elect alone have "come short of the glory of God" [v. 23]. And how does he arrive at this conclusion? Because (says he) the grace of Christ is poured out on all who have sinned. But I so hold the grace of God to be universal as to make the great difference consist in this: All are not called "according to God's purpose" [Rom. 8:28].

Salvation for All Men

Georgius imagines himself to argue very cleverly when he says, "Christ is the propitiation for the sins of the whole world [1 John 2:2]. Therefore, those who would exclude the reprobate from a participation in the benefits of Christ must, of necessity, place them somewhere out of the world."

We will not permit the common solution of this question to avail on the present occasion, which would have it that Christ suffered sufficiently for all men, but effectually for his elect alone. This great absurdity, by which our monk has procured for himself so much applause among his own fraternity, has no weight whatever with me. John does indeed extend the benefits of the atonement of Christ, which was completed by his death, to all the elect of God throughout whatever climes of the world they may be scattered. Although the case is so, it by no means alters the fact that the reprobate are mingled with the elect in the world. It is also a fact, without controversy, that Christ came to atone for the sins "of the whole world." But the solution of all difficulty is immediately at hand in the truth and fact that it is "whosoever believeth in him" who "shall not perish, but shall have eternal life" [John 3:15, 16]. For our present question is not what the power or virtue of Christ is, nor what efficacy it has in itself, but who those are to whom he gives himself to be enjoyed. Now if the possession of Christ stands in faith, and if faith flows from the Spirit of adoption, it follows that he alone is numbered of God among his children who is designed of God to be a partaker of Christ. Indeed, the evangelist John sets forth the office of Christ to be none other than that of "gathering together all the children of God" in one by his death [John 11:52]. From all this we conclude that, although reconciliation is offered unto all men through Christ, the great benefit belongs peculiarly to the elect that they might be gathered together and be made partakers of eternal life.

Be it observed, however, that when I speak of reconciliation through Christ's being offered to all, I do not mean that that message or embassy, by which Paul says that God "reconciles the world unto himself" [2 Cor. 5:19], really comes or reaches unto all men, but that it is not sealed indiscriminately on the hearts of all those to whom it does come, so as to be effectual in them. As to our present opponent's prating about there being "no acceptance of persons with God," he must first "go and learn" what the word *person* means that agrees with our preceding explanations of it; then we shall have no more trouble with him on that score.

"But Paul teaches us," continues Georgius, "that God 'would have all men to be saved'" [1 Tim. 2:4]. It follows, therefore, according to his understanding of this passage, either that God is disappointed in his wishes or that all men without exception must be saved. If he should reply that God on his part wills all men to be saved, or as far as he is concerned, seeing that salvation is nevertheless left to the free will of each individual, I in return ask him, Why, if such be the case, God did not command the gospel to be preached to all men indiscriminately from the beginning of the world, and why he suffered so many generations of men to wander for so many ages in all the darkness of death?

It follows, in the apostle's context, that God "would have all men come to the knowledge of the truth" [v. 4]. But the sense of the whole passage is perfectly plain and contains no ambiguity to any reader of candor and of a sound judgment. We have fully explained the whole passage in former pages. The apostle had just before exhorted that solemn and general prayers should be offered up in the church "for kings and princes ..." [vv. 1, 2], that no one might have cause to deplore those kings and magistrates whom God might be pleased to set over them, because at that time rulers were the most violent enemies of the faith. Paul, therefore, makes divine provision for this state of things by the prayers of the church and by affirming that the grace of Christ could reach to this order of men also— even to kings, princes, and rulers of every description.

But it is no wonder that the more audacity this worthless fellow betrays in wresting the Scriptures, the more profuse he should be in heaping passages on passages to suit his purpose, seeing that he does not possess one particle of religion or of shame that might restrain his headlong impudence. But the more diffuse he is in his wild discussions, the briefer I shall study to be in my answers, by which I hope to curb his pretensions. He cites Isaiah 56:3: "Neither let the son of the stranger speak, saying, The Lord hath utterly separated me from his people." And he takes it for granted that this text can never be applied to the reprobate, for he judges it absurd to suppose that the elect are ever called "the sons of the stranger."

To this I reply that it is by no means unusual to find in the Scriptures those elected before the foundation of the world considered, nevertheless, "strangers" or "the sons of the stranger," until they are gathered into the family and among the children of God by faith. The words of Peter, borrowed from the prophet, are: "Which in time past were not a people; but now are the people of God" [1 Pet. 2:10, based on Hosea 2:23]. To whom is Peter here speaking? Is it not to those of whom he had testified in the beginning of the epistle that they were "elect according to the foreknowledge of God" [1 Pet. 1:2]?

Paul sets this matter forth in a still more open light in his Epistle to the Ephesians. After he had therein dwelt very largely on their eternal election by God, he subsequently reminds them, "At that time ye were aliens from the commonwealth of Israel, and strangers from the covenants of promise, having no hope and without God in the world" [Eph. 2:12]. And is it any cause of wonder if Isaiah, building thus under the inspiration of the Spirit the temple of God out of profane stones, should declare that there would be a new consecration of it? For as the calling of the Gentiles lay hidden all along in the heart of God, what else appeared in them outwardly than all damnable uncleanness? All those among them who were at length incorporated in the spiritual body of Christ by faith were, indeed, all that time really the sheep of God, as Christ himself testifies [John 10:16]. But they were sheep as yet shut out of the fold and "wandering upon the dark mountains." Although they themselves all the while knew it not, the Shepherd knew them according to the eternal predestination by which he chose his own unto himself before the foundation of the world. Augustine sets this forth very soundly and beautifully.

Georgius continues: "Now if that word of the prophet Ezekiel be true that says, 'The son shall not bear the iniquity of the father' [Ezek. 18:17, 20], no part of mankind is left in original sin."

I really will have nothing to do with this unclean beast at all. My purpose is to come to the help of the ignorant only, that they may not be taken and carried away with such worthless cavils as these. Nothing is more certain than this: All those who remain under the general destruction are not engrafted into the body of Christ. This good brother monk, prodigal of dealing with strangers, huddles all together and presses into the household even those against whom God has shut and barred the door. But that man is willfully mad, whoever he may be, who does not confess that no one of those who died naturally in Adam can be restored unto eternal life in any other way than in that ordained of God. The manifest difference between the seed of a believing and that of an unbelieving man, as determined by the apostle, is that the former is "holy," but the latter "unclean" [1 Cor. 7:14]. And on this sacred principle, before the Gentiles were engrafted into the church with the Jews by the breaking down of "the middle wall of partition between them" [Eph. 2:14], the apostle calls the branches of Abraham "holy" from their holy root [Rom. 11:16]. What need is there of a lengthened discussion of this point? Did not the same prophet Ezekiel, whose word this monk so abuses, frequently condemn the uncircumcised Gentiles to destruction as profane persons [Ezek. 28:10; Ezek. 31:18; et al.]? Nor would circumcision be the covenant of life even now on any other grounds. How, then, can it be true to assert that the son shall not bear the punishment of the sin of the father? And, I ask, How shall that man boast himself to be innocent who is born an unclean raven from an unclean egg? For original sin is so derived from Adam universally that it becomes the peculiar property of the nature of every man. No one, therefore, can justly complain under an imagination that he is bearing the guilt of another's sin and consider himself free from fault. But if it is not lawful for God to punish in their children the sins of their fathers, what is the meaning of God's "visiting the sins of the fathers upon the children unto the third and fourth generation" [Ex. 20:5; Deut. 5:9] and his "visiting the iniquity of the fathers upon the children, and upon the children's children, unto the third and to the fourth generation" [Ex. 34:7]? Moreover, the first part of this visiting vengeance is that the non-elect children of Adam, being left destitute of the Spirit of God, remain sunk in the original sin of their nature.

Georgius argues thus: "John says, 'He that sinneth, God will blot his name out of the book of life.' If you explain this as applying to the reprobate, they never were written in the book of life. If you interpret it as referring to the elect, the eternal counsel of God will be mutable and fail."

Our monk prates in this way as if God did not always address us in a manner adapted to our comprehension as men. How base a specimen of ingratitude thus to insult God for having, through the greatest indulgence towards us and our limited comprehension, expressed himself in such simple terms. If this worthless fellow goes on with his interpretation of the Scriptures at this rate, according to the letter, he will by and by fabricate for us a corporeal God, assigning as his reason that Scripture speaks of God as having ears, eyes, feet, and hands.

The meaning of the passage, however, is most simple and plain: Those are "blotted out of the book of life" who, having been considered for a time the children of God, being among them, afterwards draw back and fall away into their own place, as Peter most truly describes Judas to have done [Acts 1:16–18]. Such persons, however, as John testifies, "were never of us; for if they had been of us, they would not have gone out from us" [1 John 2:19]. That, however, which John expresses thus summarily, the prophet Ezekiel sets forth essentially and circumstantially: "They shall not be in the secret assembly of my people; neither shall they be written in the writing of the house of Israel" [Ezek. 13:9]. The same key also will unlock the difficulty that may appear in the cases where Moses and Paul express their willingness "to be blotted out of the book of life" [Ex. 32:32; Rom. 9:3]. The fact is that they were so carried out of themselves, as it were, by the excess of their grief that they uttered their readiness to perish rather than that the church of God, populous as it then was, should be extinguished. When, however, Christ bids his disciples "rejoice because your names are written in heaven" [Luke 10:20], he speaks of that as an everlasting blessing, of which they never should be deprived. In a word, Christ unites and harmonizes both meanings concerning names being written in the book of life when he says, "Every tree that my heavenly Father hath not planted shall be rooted up" [Matt. 15:13], whereby he plainly intimates that the reprobate also sometimes take root in appearance, and yet are not planted by the hand of God.

On that comparison of the apostle Paul, "As by one man sin came into the world unto condemnation; so by one man came the gift of righteousness unto life" [Rom. 5:12–19], Georgius argues thus: "If therefore, many died through one, much more must the grace of God abound, that many may reign in life by Christ."

If the apostle were proving that the grace of Christ extended unto all men, acknowledging myself vanquished, I would be silent and say no more on the subject. But as the apostle's purpose is simply to show how much more powerful the grace of Christ is in the faithful than the curse they derived from Adam, what is there in this blessed truth to shake the eternal election of those whom Christ has restored from the ruins of the fall to the possession and enjoyment of everlasting life, leaving the rest to perish in their sins?

But our monk wishes to dwell on the particular expressions of the apostle. "Paul," he says, "comprehends the whole race of mankind when he uses the words 'the sin of *one man*' and 'came upon *all men*' [v. 12]. Therefore, no one can be lawfully excluded from the participation of eternal life." But if we are allowed to reason at this rate, I would be inclined to contend that if it be so, God as a natural consequence must needs create some new worlds, so that in them things might be managed better than in this. Christ declares that the curse in Adam by no means equaled the grace in himself, because, as his apostle says, "Where sin abounded, grace did much more abound" [v. 20]. If the numbers of the sons of men — of the elect and the reprobate, of those under the curse and those under grace — be reduced into one, Christ certainly could not save more people than Adam destroyed, namely, more than these two numbers of men. Therefore, the faith of Paul must be altogether imperiled in his own election and salvation unless some new world should immediately rise out of the sea!

However, I will use in the defense of the truth no other shield than what our monk fits on my arm by another passage of Paul, which he boastingly adduces: "As in Adam all die, even so in Christ shall all be made alive" [1 Cor. 15:22]. If this worthless opponent of the truth applies the second part of this text to all the sons of Adam, Paul immediately holds up his hand to stop him. For he plainly testifies, directly afterwards, that he is therein speaking of the members of Christ only: "Christ the firstfruits; afterward they that are Christ's at his coming" [v. 23]. Paul is undeniably speaking of the resurrection, which shall be followed by a blessed immortality, which we confess in our creed when we say, "I believe in . . . the life everlasting."

Predestination Makes Preaching to All Unnecessary

That I may not, however, wear out my readers to no purpose by taking up the absurd arguments of this worthless person one after the other, my purpose now will be to lay hold of a few more out of the many that still remain unnoticed. In what sense we are to understand that God wills not the death of a sinner, but that all should turn and live [Ezek. 18:23; Ezek. 33:11], I have explained at length in former pages. For when God exhorts men to repentance and offers life to them upon their return, that exhortation and offer are common to all men. But with respect to his own children, God makes them worthy of the inestimable privilege of his taking out of them their "stony hearts" and giving them "hearts of flesh" [Ezek. 11:19; Ezek. 36:26]. Nor do I by any means concede to the monk that the Lord vainly speaks into the air all those words, by which he leaves without excuse all the wicked who are convicted of their malice against him, while he so works in his elect that the doctrine of his truth becomes effectual in their hearts by the secret power of his Spirit when the word sounds in their ears. Nor is there the least reason that common slander should distress the mind of anyone, which profanely intimates that "God merely mocks men by exhorting them to walk when he knows that they are disabled in their feet." For surely God does men no injury when he demands nothing more of them than that which they really owe him, unless the debtor who has nothing to pay may boast before his creditor that he has paid him all, and that, too, while the creditor laughs at his boasts with astonishment. But I will pursue this part of the serious battle no farther. The truth involved cannot be destroyed without the destruction of every man's conscience also.

God commands the ears of his people Israel to be stricken by and filled with the voice of his prophet. For what end? That their hearts might be touched? No, that they might be hardened. That those who hear might repent? No, that being already lost, they might doubly perish. If you, O monk, reply that the cause was mightier and so ruled over all the consequences, this confession is all I wish to be granted me in the present instance. Hence it is by no means absurd that the doctrine of the truth should, as commanded of God, be spread abroad, although he knows that in multitudes it will be without its saving effects. Nor less frivolous is the cavil when the monk declares that that word of Christ cannot be made to stand consistently with the doctrine of election where he is speaking of the "sheep" that was brought back after it had been lost [Luke 15:4–6]. I am satisfied, however, that I can, with much more propriety and effect, hurl back at the monk the javelin that he launches at me. The reason Christ represents that a sheep was thus brought back after having been lost for a time was that, being a sheep in reference to its free and eternal election of God, it was safe under the protection of the eternal Shepherd all the while it was "lost."

Of the same trash is the logical dilemma that Georgius introduces and by which he hopes to bewilder us all. He argues,

> If there were such a thing as special election, the exhortation of the prophet could not possibly be made consistent with it where he says, "Let the wicked forsake his way" [Isa. 55:7]. For if that exhortation be addressed to the elect, how can those be "wicked" in whom "all things work together for good" [Rom. 8:28]? If it be addressed to the reprobate, how can the reprobate be exhorted to repentance?

My reply is that the exhortation of the prophet is addressed both to the elect and to the reprobate—to the elect, that those among them who have for a time shaken off the yoke and have wantonly gone out of the way might, by being thus warned, return to a right mind; to the reprobate, that lying stupefied in their iniquities they might by such piercing appeals be goaded into a sense of their awful condition. For we never imagine to ourselves, nor falsely picture to others, that the elect always hold on the right course under the constant direction of the Holy Spirit. On the contrary, we ever affirm that they slip with their feet, wander out of the way, dash against various rocks of sin and of error, and frequently are quite out of the right way of salvation. But as the protection of God by which they are governed and defended is stronger than all things, it is impossible that they should fall into utter ruin.

"Men," continues the monk, "are commanded to take heed lest they perish. But it is all the while certain that the elect are placed beyond all danger. And to the reprobate, all heed or caution must be vain."

To this argument also I reply: There is nothing strange in this sacred matter at all. The elect, who are engaged in a perpetual conflict, need to be furnished with armor necessary for the battle. Moreover, the diligence of all men generally is stimulated by such exhortations, while the reprobate, by disregarding all exhortation, prove themselves at length to be incurable, for medicine is sedulously administered in diseases until despair of all cure makes its appearance without remedy.

Salvation Is Not Promised to the Elect, but to the Believing

Another objection urged by Georgius is that "Abraham is not called the father of the elect but the father of the faithful and that salvation is not promised to the elect but to the believing."

Whom, then, will he make those to be who are to be gathered together with their father Abraham into the kingdom of heaven? For Christ most certainly declares that this great blessing belongs to the elect alone. Christ also declares that a limit shall be put to the horrible coming destructions "for the elect's sake" [Matt. 24:22]. What? Shall we deny that those are the children of Abraham who, together with him, are made the members of God's household, the church? And how was it, I ask you, that so great an honor was conferred on Abraham that he was called the father of the faithful, unless it was because he was chosen of God? And how is it that those are accounted degenerate children of his who do not duly represent their believing father by their faith?

In fact, the audacity of this worthless renegade is perfectly execrable. He labors with all his might, in all his arguments, to deface, blot out, and do away with that very mark by which God—more especially than by any other—designates and distinguishes his people. I confess without any hesitation that eternal life is promised "to them that believe" [John 1:12], provided, however, that the monk

deny not that eternal life is in like manner promised to the elect;
for thus Isaiah says, "And mine elect shall possess it" [Isa. 65:9].

I shall demand also of my opponent that he confess that only
those believe whom God enlightens by his Spirit, and that he confess, moreover, that election is the mother of faith. Paul testifies that
he is ready "to endure all things for the elect's sake" [2 Tim. 2:10].
And Christ proclaims aloud that God the Father "is the avenger" of
all the elect [Luke 18:7]. Furthermore, Paul exhorts the Colossians
that they "put on, as the elect of God, and as the holy and beloved,
bowels of mercies, kindness, humbleness of mind, meekness, and
longsuffering" [Col. 3:12]. In another place the apostle declares the
elect to be free from every charge of sin or guilt: "Who shall lay any
thing to the charge of God's elect?" [Rom. 8:33]. Are, then, believers
to be robbed of all these blessings? This would be making a worse
than hostile separation of those things that God has mutually, and
indeed inseparably, joined together. "That the election of God might
stand" [Rom. 9:11], those who were once blind are "illuminated" unto
faith. By that faith they receive the righteousness of Christ, and they
are "kept" and "persevere unto the end" [1 Pet. 1:5].

Objections against Reprobation

Georgius further argues, "When Scripture denounces destruction on those who are lost, it by no means refers or attributes the
cause of that destruction to the eternal counsel of God, but declares
that it rests with the lost themselves."

However, we never so represent the reprobate to be left destitute of the Spirit of God, in his appeals to their resisting consciences, as to charge the fault of their iniquities on God. Whatever
sins men commit, let them charge all the fault on themselves alone.
And if any man should attempt to escape the fault or guilt of his
sin, I affirm that such a one would find himself bound too securely
by the chains of his own conscience ever to free himself from righteous condemnation for his transgressions. Let Adam excuse himself as long as he will by saying that he was deceived by the

enticements of the wife whom God gave him. Nevertheless, within himself will be found the deadly poison of infidelity; within himself will be found that worst of all counselors, depraved ambition; within himself will be found the flaming torch of a devilish defiance of God. Far less excusable, therefore, shall they be who attempt to force, out of the profound secrets of the eternal counsel of God, that cause of their iniquities, which is ever putting forth its awful head from the deep corruption of their own hearts. Richly do they deserve to be "given over to a reprobate mind" who have not glorified God as they ought [Rom. 1:28], even as far as he may be known by the contemplation of "his works that are seen"—the heavens and the earth [v. 20]. Those who willfully, deliberately, and maliciously reject the grace of Christ and turn their backs upon the burning and shining light of the gospel deserve still heavier punishment. Therefore, let each one acknowledge his own sins and condemn himself alone, and confessing from his heart all the fault to be his own, let him supplicate the mercy of his judge.

If any reprobate one should cavil and be inclined to make a noise, Scripture furnishes a ready and silencing reply: "O Israel, thou hast destroyed thyself" [Hos. 13:9]. For, as we have observed towards our commencement, the complaint of Medea of old in the classic poet is utterly ridiculous in lamenting that the trees were cut down from Mount Pelion to furnish wood for building the ship *Argo*, when the fact was that the flame of love, burning out of her own lustful heart, was the real cause of her destroying her father and her whole kingdom, together with herself. Much less, most certainly, are their arguments to be listened to who would fetch from afar, even from the clouds themselves, remote causes of their sin and fault when the sight of it is ever before their eyes, issuing forth continually from the deep-seated fountain of their own hearts, the evidences of which are plain and perpetual, however they may strive to hide them. Scripture therefore assigns the cause of all evils to the natural sins of men.

Indeed, the great question between me and the monk is not whether men yield necessary obedience to the secret judgment of

God, or are inevitably carried on in their sin by it without any fault of their own, which we not only declare to be a false tenet, but also a foul and detestable profanity. But the question between us is whether the wicked, who by their voluntary sins provoke the wrath of God against themselves, were afore reprobated of God (as the righteous but incomprehensible cause of all) "according to the counsel of his own will." As Paul severely condemns the sins of men, powerfully pressing them home upon their own consciences and at the same time determinately vindicating the justice of God from the profane slanders of men, so he openly declares, and dissembles not, that those who precipitate themselves into destruction by their sins are "vessels of wrath fitted to destruction" [Rom. 9:22]. Christ also charges home their guilt on the reprobate as they deserve. At the same time, he shows that the great cause of all was that they were "trees not planted by the hand of my Father" [Matt. 15:13]. In a word, we are told that the Father gave unto the Son those who were his so that he might sanctify them. In the opposite view, Paul, having shown that "the elect obtained it," namely, "the righteousness of faith" [Rom. 9:30], adds that "the rest were blinded" [Rom. 11:7]. Vain, therefore, are all the arguments of Georgius who, fixing his eyes only on the open sins of men, never thinks of the hidden source of all the wickedness of mankind: the corruption of man's nature.

The monk considers that we are implicated in a great absurdity because we make the will of man free to sin when the reprobate certainly sin of necessity. But that freedom of will in man of which we speak, and with which our monk is so familiarly acquainted, is after all quite unknown to him. Now Paul calls some "free" who are "free from righteousness" [Rom. 6:20], namely, those who, destitute of the fear of God and of all temperance, revel in iniquity. Does it follow, then, that such are not "the servants of sin"?

Our monk condemns us also for limiting and binding the power of God. "For," says he, "if God foreknows and ordains all things that shall come to pass, he has not power to change them afterwards."

A truly prodigious wonder is that God is not like a mortal man, who is ever flexible, variable, and changes his mind and purposes every hour. The very thing against which the monk so violently fights is that the adorable God is ever of one mind and consistent with himself. Hence his great hallucination is that by separating the fixed decrees of God from his power, he makes him to be divided against himself. If we were to speak as the Stoics, we should say, according to the noted sentiment of Seneca, "God is a necessity in himself." We, however, with greater reverence and sobriety, say, "God always wills the same thing, and this is the very praise of his immutability." Whatever he decrees, therefore, he effects; and this is in divine consistency with his omnipotence. The will of God, being thus inseparably united with his power, constitutes an exalted harmony of his attributes worthy of the divine providence by which all things in heaven and earth are governed.

As to this miserable being's vain display of heaping testimonies upon testimonies of Scripture that have nothing to do with each other and often have contrary meanings and applications—to all this I pay not the least regard. Although I am willing to pass by his ignorance, I am anxious to put a rein upon his impudence to prevent his causing any distress to the simpleminded. After having shown from one passage of the apostle Paul that God "sends upon those that receive not the truth, strong delusion that they should believe a lie" [2 Thess. 2:10, 11], he brings forward, on the back of this, another passage, a quite diverse reference, where the apostle says that the doctrine of the gospel is "hid in them that are lost: in whom the god of this world hath blinded the minds of them which believe not" [2 Cor. 4:3, 4]. I confess, indeed, that these blind ones are called "those that believe not." If unbelief is the sole cause of the blindness in these persons, what is the meaning of the words that immediately follow, namely, "God, who commanded the light to shine out of darkness, hath shined into our hearts" [v. 6]? We know that darkness rules everywhere, but God alone, as we here see, brings light out of darkness.

Georgius, moreover, accuses us of cruelty, averring that we block up the way of salvation against ourselves and many others also while Christ himself most kindly invites Canaanitish women, "lost sheep," and even "strange dogs." To all this we reply that we faithfully set forth before all men the doctrines of faith and repentance to the end that all men, if God will, might be profited by Christ. When our Lord himself was entreated by the wife of Zebedee that he would set one of her sons on his right hand and the other on his left, by way of restraining this foolish and untimely desire, our Lord declares that such a wish was unbecoming of her present state and calling; at the same time, he intimates by no means obscurely that there is a place decreed of his heavenly Father for everyone, which shall be revealed in its time [Matt. 20:20–23; Mark 10:35–40]. In the same manner also, the superstition of men that dwells on future events and issues, which rest with God alone, and which superstition is so plainly revealed in Scripture, ought ever to be exposed by us and not indulged by our keeping silence. For until the day of the revelation of the issues shall come, our duty is to do what God commands: to exhort all men, without exception, to repentance and faith. For the doctrine and preaching of the gospel belong to all men and are for the benefit of all men, and for those ends are they committed unto us, to be openly declared by us, even until the reprobate shall, by their deplorable obstinacy, block up our way and shut the door.

Election Is Based on Faith and Perseverance

Finding himself compelled by our testimony to admit the doctrine of predestination, confirmed as it is by the multiplied testimony of so many passages of Scripture, Georgius throws a new cavil into the field, about which nothing can be imagined more stupid or more putrid: "The believers of the New Testament are said to be 'chosen' of God, as being those to whom God made known the riches of the mystery that had been hidden from ages." To confirm this sense that he puts upon the subject by his own silly invention, Georgius collects together all those texts of Scripture that set forth the excellency of the grace revealed by Christ. And then he arrives at the conclusion that whatever is contained in the first chapter to the Ephesians has no other intent than to show that God condescended to dignify the believers of the New Testament by bestowing on them this peculiar treasure. And when pushed to state the time to which this grace refers, Georgius says that it was made common unto all men, without distinction, from the coming of Christ to the end of the world.

The words of Paul, however, show a very different boundary to this grace. The sum of Paul's testimony is that only those are illuminated unto faith who were predestinated unto eternal life "according to the eternal good pleasure of God" [Eph. 1:5]. It cannot be denied that there was, at the first preaching of the gospel, a special call of certain persons and that the gospel was published to all. And suppose it be granted that it did sound in the ears of all, as proclaimed by the external voice; yet Paul's testimony refers to a far deeper call, even to that call by which the Spirit of God penetrates into the hearts of men. When, however, we make this great distinction between the outward and the internal, effectual call, such a distinction is to Georgius all a dream. But whether the making of this difference be a trifling or a grave matter, the experience of faith furnishes a rich understanding. Moreover, the apostle does not treat of election in this chapter to the Ephesians in any other sense or with any other object than he does elsewhere, as when he gives thanks to God because he had from the beginning chosen the Thessalonians to salvation [2 Thess. 2:13]. And Paul, be it remembered, is here separating a small company of believers from the multitude of the wicked.

The monk will reply, "Lawless despisers of grace, when spoken of, are always set forth in opposition to the elect." But this is nothing whatever to the purpose, for all I am contending for in the present instance is that some are specially chosen of God in preference to others. Yet Georgius continues to prate that we are only predestinated to be born at a certain time, namely, after the coming of Christ, as he argues above. How stands the case, then, with the reprobate Judas, of whom Christ declares that he was not one of the elect but "had a devil" [John 6:70], even though Judas had heard the words of his divine master and had enjoyed his domestic fellowship? Christ immediately and distinctively adds, "I speak not of you all: I know whom I have chosen" [John 13:18]. If, however, we are to listen to this fanatical being [Georgius], the condition of Herod, who lived since Christ, was better than that of David, who was before Christ. And according to Georgius, the impious scribes and Pharisees will precede the holy prophets in the honor of election, for he will say that the latter, by reason of their age and time, were not in the number of elect believers. He everywhere clamors that the grace of election belongs generally to a certain age. In a word, he offers himself as a guarantee that the apostle Paul has nowhere spoken of predestination otherwise. What? Does the apostle include all the men of his own age when he says, "Whom God did predestinate, them he also called" [Rom. 8:30]? What? Does he not separate from the general multitude of men those of whom he speaks as being "the called according to his purpose" [v. 28]? Finally, when the apostle elsewhere says, "But God hath chosen the foolish things of the world to confound the wise" [1 Cor. 1:27], does he, when making so evident a distinction, intend his words to apply to his whole generation?

Finding himself still entangled in the net of the truth, Georgius seizes upon another way of escape: "Those are not called the elect whom God preferred above others, but those who persevere in the common election and grace." By this he means that those are at length considered of God the elect who distinguish themselves from the common multitude of men by the constancy of their faith. The passage of the apostle Paul that Georgius cites to prove his doctrine is this: "I charge thee before God and the elect angels" [1 Tim. 5:21]. What the monk requires to be granted to him from this passage is that since the elect angels did not separate themselves and fall away with the apostate angels, they procured for themselves, by such high merit, the grace of election. But suppose we would assert, on the contrary, that it was because of their being elect angels that they stood fast. How much more near the truth would be such an assertion.

When Christ predicts that the delusion of Satan shall be so great as even to "deceive the very elect, if it were possible" [Matt. 24:24], he implies the impossibility that Satan ever should carry away the elect by any violence he may adopt. By what power, then, are we to suppose that the elect will be thus secure? Georgius dreams: by their own strength. Far different, however, is the positive declaration of Christ: "No one shall pluck out of my hand those sheep which my Father hath committed to my charge. My Father, which gave them to me, is greater than all, and no one can pluck them out of my Father's hand" [John 10:27–29]. In the same manner the apostle by no means commends believers to depend upon their own faithfulness; on the contrary, he reminds them that "God is faithful, who hath called them: who also will do it" [1 Thess. 5:24].

The monk, however, makes each one the author and disposer of his own election, whereas Christ positively declares that those whom he has chosen out of the world are his own [John 15:19]. In perfect harmony with this declaration of Christ, Paul asserts aloud that "all things work together for good to them that love God, who are the called according to his purpose" [Rom. 8:28]. And he asserts the same great truth, as loudly, concerning children not yet born: "That the purpose of God might stand; not of works, but of him that calleth. As it is written, Jacob have I loved, but Esau have I hated" [Rom. 9:11, 13]. To what necessity, then, is the monk here driven? This worthless being will have to prove positively, according to his own doctrine, that Jacob, even while yet enclosed in the womb of his mother, procured for himself by his own industry the honor of his election, and that he stood in the possession of it by his own faithfulness unto the end.

Just the same amount of common reason and common sense is there in the monk's dispute: "The casting off concerning which Paul speaks does not refer to single persons, but to the whole body of the Jewish people." For his exposition of the passage is that the nation of the Jews, by rejecting Christ, deprived themselves of the inheritance of eternal life.

I am free to confess that on this one point has been founded the cause of all dispute regarding the mighty subject now in question. But no one of a sound mind will conclude or suppose that the whole great question is bounded by these narrow limits. For, first, the apostle Paul plainly teaches that the generation of Abraham consisted of both elect and reprobate individuals, promiscuously mingled together. Next, the same apostle declares, generally, that from the mixed multitude of the human race are produced by birth, as distinctive classes, the "vessels of wrath" and the "vessels of mercy," for the manifestation of the glory of God [Rom. 9:22, 23].

Paul does, indeed, make the first proximate cause of the reprobation of Israel to be their not having believed the gospel. That this cause is plainly set forth by the apostles, I by no means deny. But Paul first clearly lays down, be it remembered, the great doctrine concerning the secret judgments of God. Two things are distinctly dwelt on by the apostle. First, God was never so bound to one people as to prevent his free election from reigning in the choice or reprobation of certain individuals. Second, the Jews, by their ingratitude, shut themselves out from the family of God when they were the peculiar heirs of the covenant of eternal life. But lest the appearance of change in the purposes of God should disturb the mind of anyone, as though this later rejection of the Jews shook the secret counsel of God, Paul guards against such a consequence by the appropriate declaration: "The gifts and calling of God are without repentance" [Rom. 11:29], and therefore "the remnant according to the election of grace" should be saved [v. 5]. By these words the apostle means that the election of God, which stands in his secret counsel, remains firm and immovable.

The impudence of this worthless mortal discovers itself more basely still in his declaring that Esau was not reprobated before he sold his birthright. I willingly acknowledge the testimony of the apostle, where he says that after Esau had deprived himself of his inheritance, he was rejected [Heb. 12:17]. But are we to suppose that his rejection by his father Isaac, which he was then suffering, entirely did away with that former judgment and purpose of God that was the original cause of his reprobation? Most certainly not. No more than the faith and obedience of Jacob did away with his free and eternal adoption of God.

The observation with which I opened this discussion, I now repeat at its close: No one will ever attempt to disprove the doctrine that I have set forth herein but he who may imagine himself to be wiser than the Spirit of God. Nowadays, however, the soured opposition of men has attained to such a height that they will not willingly and quietly receive even that which is evidently taken from Scripture itself without arrogating to themselves the prerogatives of God by imposing on others the law of speech and of silence. Yet some of these insolent ones wish to conceal their real principles under the garb of modesty, professing that for themselves they would not dare to deny what had been testified by all the servants of God.

For my part, I soberly and reverently profess that I know no other law of modesty than what I have learned in the school of my heavenly master. I am, however, fully aware that all possible prudence should be adopted in tempering all things to the building up of men in the most holy faith. But as I have studied to do that throughout my ministry, and in the present treatise also, with faith and a good conscience, if the nice objections of some are not yet satisfied, I feel for myself that I have done my duty. "He that hath ears to hear, let him hear."

Introduction to God's Secret Providence

The moment I think of speaking upon the providence of God by which he governs not only the vast machinery of the whole world and each smallest part of it, but also the hearts and the actions of men, a mighty and complex subject presents itself before me. But as I have already treated of the stupendous matter in a manner calculated (I hope) to satisfy in a measure all sound minded and unprejudiced readers, I shall only touch it in a summary and passing manner upon the present occasion, adopting all possible brevity. Nor indeed can any splendor of speech or any brilliancy of thought be expected from me that shall correspond with the magnitude and excellency of the theme. I shall merely recapitulate in a few bare words those arguments that I have fully developed in my *Institutes*. But if I shall see such need, I shall interweave with these arguments some further testimonies from Holy Scripture. And I shall also, as I hope, so wash away, by a plain refutation, the designing and malignant cavils of Pighius and his fellows so that they shall not in the least degree hurt or hinder the minds of the godly.

Definition of Providence

By providence we mean not an unconcerned sitting of God in heaven, from which he merely observes the things that are done in the world, but that all-active and all-concerned ruling from his throne above by which he governs the world that he himself has made. God, then, as viewed in the glass of his providence, is not only the maker of all things in a moment, but also the perpetual ruler of all things that he has created. The providence, therefore, that we ascribe to God pertains as much to his operating hands as to his observing eyes. When, therefore, God is said to rule the world by his providence, we do not merely mean that he maintains and preserves the order of nature that he had originally purposed in himself, but also that he holds and continues a peculiar care of every single creature that he has created. True and certain is the fact that since it was the wonderful wisdom of God that originally made the world and disposed it in its present beautiful order, so unless the ever present, omnipotent power of God sustained the world thus created and disposed, it could not continue for one hour in its designed order and form.

That the sun rises upon us day by day; that in a course so rapid its rays should be tempered and its degrees adjusted; that the order of the stars, so wonderfully arranged, should never be disturbed; that the vicissitudes of the seasons should recur continuously; that the earth should open her bowels with annual regularity for the nourishment of man; that the elements and their separate particles should not cease to perform their appointed functions—in a word, that the fecundity of nature should never be worn out nor fail—all this marvelous operation, cooperation, and continuance can surely never be thought to proceed from any other cause than from the directing hand of God. What else is Psalm 104 but a long and loud praise of his universal providence? The apostle Paul lauds this same divine providence when he says, "For in him we live, and move, and have our being" [Acts 17:28]. Therefore, as the one only God has an essence peculiar to himself, the living principle of vegetation, by which all creatures subsist and without which they must soon perish, must be considered by faith as a secret infusion of God.

Particular Application of Providence to Man

The knowledge of a general and universal providence is vague and confused unless at the same time we hold the belief and contemplate that God covers under the wings of his care each one of his creatures. To teach us this glorious lesson was the object of Christ when he said that not a sparrow, which is sold for half a farthing, falls to the ground without the heavenly Father's knowledge [Matt. 10:29]. However, in considering this special providence of God, by which he secretly broods over the care of each individual creature as the work of his hands, it will be necessary that we take a sacred view of the certain degrees and distinct peculiarities that providence divinely embraces.

As man is the noblest work of God, for whose "good" all things were created which the heavens and the earth contain, Scripture sets forth the providence of God as concerned principally in the care and government of the human race. Paul, in explanation of the passage "Thou shalt not muzzle the mouth of the ox that treadeth

out the corn" [Deut. 25:4], observes, "Doth God take care of oxen?"
[1 Cor. 9:9], implying that the providential care of God does not rest
on them in particular as its peculiar sphere of action, but is more
especially employed in the care of men. In this respect, as the course
of divine providence lies in the dealings of God with men as beings
endowed with reason, its conduct assumes a surer light and a brighter
glory. For marvelous are the judgments of God: at one time, in punishing the wicked; at another, in teaching the faithful patience and
the crucifying of their flesh; at another, in purging out the wickednesses of the world; at another, in awakening the sleep and sloth of
many; at another, in breaking down the arrogance of the proud; at
another, in making the wisdom of the wise a laughingstock; at another, in destroying the machinations of the malicious. The surpassing goodness of God is brightly displayed also in succoring the
distressed, in protecting and defending the cause of the innocent,
and in coming to the assistance of those who are in despair of all
help. Psalm 107 contains a beautiful and glorious description of that
conduct of the providence of God that is manifested towards men.
In this psalm the prophet shows that those vicissitudes that men
generally consider violent floods of change are not waves of trouble
rolling over men with blind impetuosity, as it were, but bright
glasses wherein to behold the goodness, the wrath, or the justice of
God. And at the close of this blessed psalm, the penman of it draws
the concluding inference that if the godly and the "wise" would duly
"observe" these various changes in the world, they would gain understanding in the ways of God and would find abundant cause for
rejoicing [v. 43]. The psalmist also implies that the same contemplation, if exercised by the wicked, would stop their mouths by giving them an awe-striking sight of the wonderful works of God.

Four Aspects of God's Providence

Here we must take a view of other and loftier steps of the divine providence. For though God thus shows himself the Father
and the judge of the whole human race, yet as the church is his sanc-

tuary in which he resides, he there manifests his presence by clearer and brighter proofs. There he shows himself as the Father of his family and condescends to grant a nearer view of himself, if I may so speak. Scripture is filled with testimonies of this, which declare that God keeps a more special watch over the faithful. "The eyes of the Lord," says David, "are over the righteous" [Ps. 34:15]; "He preserveth the souls of his saints" [Ps. 97:10]; "He careth for you," says Peter [1 Pet. 5:7]; even "the very hairs of your head are all numbered," says the Lord himself [Matt. 10:30]. In a word, the church is the great workroom of God, wherein, in a more special manner, he displays his wonderful works, and it is the more immediate theater of his glorious providence.

For this reason God is said to have appointed angels [Ps. 104:4; Heb. 1:14], which are, as it were, his hands, to be guardians in a peculiar manner to his saints who believe in him, so that the angels also might have no separate position or office apart from the body of Christ of which they also are members. Therefore, in order that we may take a circumspective and comprehensive view of the whole divine matter, our eyes must rest, first, on the general government of the whole world by which all things are cherished and caused to vegetate, where the natural state of them all, collectively and individually, may remain and be preserved the same.

Second, our eyes must rest on the watchfulness of God in ruling and guarding the single parts and particles of all these created things, which watchfulness is such that nothing occurs unknown or unnoticed in them or concerning them.

Third, we must look at God's more special care of the human race, which is such that the life and death of men, the public destinies of kingdoms and of nations, the private cases of individuals, and whatever men usually ascribe to fortune are under his heavenly rule and disposal.

Fourth, we must contemplate that peculiar protection by which God defends his church, in which protection he more expressly manifests his presence and his power.

Reverence Required for a Discussion of Providence

The vast and multiform utility of this doctrine no words can adequately express. Nor will anyone profitably contemplate the providence of God in the government of the world as it is set before us in the Scriptures and seen by faith but he who, feeling that he has to do so with his maker and with the creator of all things, first "bows the head" with that awe, reverence, and humility that becomes one standing before such stupendous majesty. For man is ever wont to pay such honor to his fellowmen as to judge of their works with candor and modesty, especially where anything seems somewhat obscure and difficult to comprehend at the moment. Man in such cases is the more anxious and diligent in making inquiry into the truth and would rather suspend his judgment than by a hasty decision do his fellowman an injury. That being the case is it not, I ask, worse than madness and something more than ferocity to use a tenfold greater liberty with God, and to bring his stupendous works down to the scale of our puny judgment, to pronounce a precipitate opinion upon things infinitely sublime and wholly incomprehensible, to attempt to fathom God's secret counsels and, above all, to trifle with mysteries so deep and so profoundly adorable? This insolence has, indeed, stalked abroad in all ages, but it has taken greater strides and made louder boasts in the present day than in any age or time preceding. Many infidels nowadays, finding that they cannot tear God down from heaven (which, like the giants of old, they really attempt to do), strive mightily, at least, to force out of their own and all other men's consciences every particle of religion and of true worship by vomiting forth the foulest and basest blasphemies, thus betraying their profanity and their rage against God and his truth.

In the greater part of these persons, the source of all the evil is evidently this: Being persons of a light and fervid spirit, they first give indulgence to their own vain curiosity. Then, having no fixed aim or object before them, they give themselves up to utterly useless speculations. Upon the back of this comes an unbridled audacity, which instigates their tongues to speak with rashness exactly commensurate with their impudence. Others, again, are the subjects of an evil state of spirit, different indeed but just as mischievous. For bewildering themselves in absurd dreams, they drown their minds in self-will, desperation, or sloth. All these are the very wiles of the devil, and his object in adopting them is to involve the true, sound, and holy doctrine in all sorts of lying wonders of inventions, by which means he would not only rob us of all its profitableness and fruit, but would also render it contemptible, hateful, or destructive. But whatever plans the devil may adopt, be it ours ever to steer clear of the perverted caution to which some have recourse who, to meet such perils as these, find no shorter way than obscuring or corrupting what Scripture declares with all possible and naked simplicity.

A much more appropriate and effectual remedy for all these evils is to hold our minds under the constant consideration of what manner and to what end the providence of God should be contemplated. The first end is that it may keep us free from all presumptuous confidence and hold us fast in the fear of God, as well as stir us up to continual prayer. A second end is to bring us to rest upon God with still and peaceful minds and to teach us to despise, in all courage and security, the dangers that surround us on every side and the numberless deaths that constantly threaten us from every quarter. Each of these great ends I will now, with all possible brevity, endeavor to explain.

Those who imagine that there is such a thing as fortune or chance, or who expect anything from their own industry, plans, or labors, are carried hither and thither after every expedient and are driven in all directions. They turn every stone (as they say), devise every new means, and gallop about like the horse in an open field. But with all this to-do, there is no prayer, no fear of God. He, however, who knows and feels that men, their counsels, and the issues of all things are ruled and overruled by the providence of God will confess with trembling, as did the prophet Jeremiah, "I know, O Lord, that the way of man is not in himself: it is not in man that walketh to direct his steps" [Jer. 10:23]. Bearing in mind also those words of Solomon—"Man's goings are of the Lord; how can a man, then, understand his own way?" [Prov. 20:24]—he will commit himself wholly unto God and depend entirely upon him. Where there is such a state of mind, prayers will ever follow that God will begin and perfect every work that we undertake, while we thus rest on him alone in all quietness. Just in the same degree will he who dreams about the will of fortune give himself up to be driven about in fear by the devil and the wicked, as by ferocious brute animals, as if they could do anything of themselves. And thus will such a one fret and fume with perpetual anxiety, and looking at his life as hanging continually by a single thread, as it were, he will live in unending torment. He will scarcely be able to put forth one foot without despairing of his life or well-being. Whereas the faithful, having the all-ruling hand of God ever before them, will never hesitate to cast all their cares and concerns upon him. And they will all the while rest assured that the devil and all wicked men, whatever tumults they may cause, are not only held of God by their feet in chains, but also are compelled to do his pleasure, under which assurance they will pass their lives in security and peace.

The two following distinctions will also throw a divine light upon this sacred matter. The providence of God is to be viewed with reference to all time past as well as in connection with all time future. In contemplating the divine providence of all time past, all power is to be ascribed to God in all things—whether viewed with their means (*media*), without their means (*media*), or contrary to their mediums (*media*)—God ordains and appoints all things.

The consideration of the time past should be thus: If anything has taken place successfully and in fulfillment of a mortal man's wishes, let him not "sacrifice to his own drag" [Hab. 1:16], nor let him speak of his own prudence, virtue, or good fortune, nor give that praise, due to God alone, to man or any creature. But let him ever feel assured that God was the first cause and author of all his good, through whatever secondary medium it came. And in the case of all preceding adversities, let a man rest in the consolation that all took place according to the good pleasure of God, for by complaining and contending against God he shall profit himself nothing and shall bind himself in the chain of the guilt of impious obstinacy against his maker. And let a man so entertain the memory of his past life so as to acknowledge, in all the punishments he has endured, the sins he has committed that caused the punishments.

With reference to the future, the providence of God is to be contemplated by all godly minds thus: Let the minds of the godly be ever intently fixed on God's promises and threatenings, for as soon as their minds turn aside from these, they are shut up against all instruction in the fear of God, and the progress of faith ceases. But he who shall always keep his eye fixed on the omnipotence of God as seen in the glass of his word, and shall rely on his promises therein also contained, will mount on the wings of faith above all the countless perils of the world. And then, bowing before the threatenings of God also beheld in his word, he will humble himself under the sight of them as so many rods.

When I spoke of the providence of God being viewed with its mediums, my meaning was this: If anyone shall have assisted his fellowman when sunk under an extremity of distress, the deliverance rendered by the hand of man is not a human deliverance, but a divine. The sun rises day by day, but it is God who enlightens the earth by his rays. The earth brings forth her fruits, but it is God who gives bread, and it is God who gives strength by the nourishment of that bread. In a word, since all inferior and secondary causes, viewed in themselves, veil like so many curtains the glorious God from our sight (which they too frequently do), the eye of faith must be cast up far higher so that it may behold the hand of God working by all these his instruments. But in what manner the providence of God can work without any medium or instrument at all, Christ taught us by his own example when he repelled the assaulting tempter with this shield: "Man doth not live by bread only, but by every word that proceedeth out of the mouth of God doth man live" [Matt. 4:4]. For as the redeemer knew that the power of God needed no external support whatever, so he knew that he could supply that strength *without* bread, which he is nevertheless mercifully pleased to supply *by means of bread*.

O what glory is due to the providence of God, viewed contrary to all means (*media*), when I am persuaded that it is mightier than all obstacles that can oppose it! By this confidence alone, I am conqueror of every fear or apprehension. Indeed, this is the very wrestling school in which God exercises and tries our faith. When so many obstacles present themselves before us that seem likely to prevent his designs (as we view them), how many creatures appear in a threatening form, above and below, in heaven and in earth. And what, in such case, is to be done? If our faith can but mount up to the divine height of the power of God, it will combat and conquer with no great trouble all the means that stand in its way and that strive to prevent its victory. Whoever, therefore, shall restrain himself within these bounds and neither torture himself with perplexed speculations nor make an excuse for indolence because he hears that God alone does all things—such a one shall neither sink under despair nor turn aside to frivolous reasonings, which are wholly unbecoming in the presence of the majesty of God.

God's Providence Is Sovereign over All

We must now examine this sacred subject still more narrowly. Whence arise contentions about the providence of God? The divine providence itself, rightly considered and contemplated as it ought to be, genders no contention. But human reason, when considering the works of God, finding itself blind, rushes into a quarrel with its maker. But what wonder is it if those counsels of God, which the angels with uplifted eyes wonder at and adore, harmonize not with fleshly reason? However, utterly intolerable is this depravity: That we, who by nature are hardly gifted with worthiness to creep as worms on the earth, should approve of nothing but what, as if lying on the ground, we can look down upon with our natural eyes. But in order that this divine doctrine of the providence of God may become profitable, it will be, we hope, a useful labor in us thus to calm the minds of the ignorant and inexperienced and to refute the slanders of the wicked and profane.

For these ends it will be desirable to consider that the will of God is the great cause of all things that are done in the whole world, and yet that God is not the author of the evils that are done therein. I will not say, with Augustine—which, however, I readily acknowledge to have been truly said by him—"In sin or in evil, there is nothing positive," for this is an acuteness of argument that may not be satisfactory to many. I would rather assume another principle of argument and say, "Those things that are vainly or unrighteously done by man are rightly and righteously the works of God." If this should appear to some at first sight to be paradoxical or self-contradictory, let not such be so fastidious or hasty as not to inquire with me into the word of God and see how the divine matter stands as viewed in that glass.

In order that I may not defend anything with senseless pertinacity as belonging properly to God, which I have only ascribed to him myself by my own opinion, let us hear what Scripture really testifies, and let us form our definition of the works of God wholly from thence. As to all those things that God really directs by his counsel, but that as generally viewed seem to be fortuitous—concerning all such things, the clear testimony of Scripture runs thus: "The lot is cast into the lap, but the whole disposing thereof is of the Lord" [Prov. 16:33]. In like manner, if a branch falling from a tree or an axe slipping out of a man's hand unawares should fall upon the head of a passerby and kill him, Moses testifies that God, who willed that that passerby should be killed, did this according to his divine purpose [Deut. 19:5]. Other Scripture testimonies to the same purport I here advisedly leave unquoted, because my intention is only to point at them with my finger on the present occasion.

Since the Stoics found on such arguments as these their doctrine of necessity, the true doctrine of the will and purpose of God is hateful to many, even to those who dare not condemn it as false.

But this doctrine of stoical necessity is an old calumny laid upon us, under the burden of which Augustine frequently complains that he was bowed down. It ought to have ceased long ere this. But certainly for men professing any honesty, candor, or faith to lay such a reproach upon us is most unworthy of them and most disgraceful. The vain imagination of the Stoics is well known. They wove their doctrine of fate out of the Gordian's knot of complex causes in which, when they had entangled God himself, they fabricated certain golden chains (as the fables have it) to bind the very God of heaven and make him subject to inferior and secondary causes. The Stoics are imitated by the astrologers of the present day, who make their doctrine of fated necessity out of certain positions of the stars.

We leave the Stoics, then, to their doctrine of fate, while we acknowledge the will of God to be the ruling cause of all things. But to take contingency out of the world altogether would be absurd. I omit to notice here those various distinctions that are made in the schools. What I shall adduce shall be simple, in my judgment, and not strained, and that which shall be profitable for the conduct of life.

I would argue, then, in this manner: What God has decreed must necessarily come to pass, yet in such a way that what does come to pass is not in itself really and naturally a necessity. We have a familiar illustration of this in the bones of Christ our Lord. Scripture plainly testifies that Christ assumed a body in all things like unto ours. Therefore, no man in his senses will hesitate to confess that the bones of Christ's body were frangible like our own. There appears to me, however, to be another and a separate question involved in this matter: whether or not any bone of Christ's could be broken? For according to God's decree and word, it was necessary that all the parts of his body should remain whole, unbroken, and uninjured. Not that I am thus speaking and arguing because I wholly object to the received forms of expression, when men speak of necessity as being in one sense absolute, or when they speak of "the necessity of the consequent" or "the necessity of the consequence." But I speak thus, and argue thus, so that no subtlety of reasoning might prevent the simplest reader from understanding and acknowledging the truth of what I testify. If, therefore, we consider the nature of the bones in the body of Christ, they were frangible, or capable of being broken. But if we look at the decree of God, which was fulfilled in its time, the bones of Christ's body were no more subject to fracture than the angels are subject to human sorrows. In this case, therefore, when we are required to look into the law and order of nature as appointed of God, I by no means reject the contingency involved in my sense and meaning of such contingency.

God's Sovereign Use of Means

We must also carefully bear in mind the principle that I have laid down before, that when God displays his power through means (*media*) and secondary causes, that power of his is never to be separated from those means or inferior causes. It is the excess of a drunkard to say, "God has decreed all that is to come to pass and that must come to pass; therefore, to interpose any care, study, or endeavor of ours is superfluous and vain." But since God prescribes to us what we ought to do and wills that we should be the instruments of the operation of his power, let us ever deem it unlawful in us to break asunder those things that he has joined together. For instance, God "in the beginning" commanded the earth to bring forth every kind of herb and fruit without any human art or culture. But now he makes use of the hand of man as the instrument of his operation. If anyone should boastingly desire to receive bread by merely opening his indolent mouth because the blessing of God fructifies the earth, he would not only by such a boast trample underfoot the providence of God, but also would do away with it altogether, for he would separate and rend asunder those things that God has joined together by an inseparable connection.

Therefore, with reference to the time future, since the events of things are as yet hidden and unknown, everyone ought to be as intent upon the performance of his duty as if nothing whatever had been decreed concerning the issue in each particular case. Or, to speak more properly, every man ought so to hope for success in all things that he undertakes at the command of God as to be freely prepared to reconcile every contingency with the sure and certain providence of God. The Lord, moreover, promises his blessing upon the work of our hands. By this promise each godly man will acknowledge himself to be appointed of God, an instrument of his glorious providence. And such a godly one, relying on this same promise, will gird himself with alacrity to his undertaking and will be persuaded that he is not casting labor in vain into the air; but, resting on the word of God, he will believe that God, by his secret counsel, will direct all his labor to the issue that shall be best. In a word, as the providence of God, rightly considered, does not bind our hands but frees them for work, so it not only does not hinder prayer, but also strengthens and confirms its earnestness.

A like sobriety of mind ought to temper our judgments concerning the time past and in reference to things that may have already taken place. There is no exhortation more conducive to patience than our hearing that nothing happens by chance, but in fulfillment of what has been decreed by "the good pleasure" of God. Meanwhile, it by no means follows that our own indolence, rashness, thoughtlessness, or some other fault is not the immediate cause of any adversity under which we may be suffering. Although the causes of events are not always clearly seen or understood, godly minds will not, even under such ignorance, cease to render unto God the praise of his wisdom and justice in every event that transpires.

Providence Rules All the Plans and Activities of Men

Where, however, the counsels, wills, purposes, and attempts of men intervene, a greater difficulty of argument and judgment presents itself to our thoughts, especially when we desire to show how the providence of God reigns and rules in all such cases as well, not only to prevent anything from being done otherwise than according to his will, but also that men may not even agitate anything in their deliberations but what he inspires. Indeed, God gives daily and marvelous proofs of his providence where he gives full rein to the foolish counsels of men and, seeming not to notice their great preparations, frustrates by the issue all their hopes. Scripture also reveals another field wherein God manifests his dominion and the mighty working of his hand: He makes the wicked mad; he strikes them with a bewildered giddiness, deprives them of their senses, or stuns them with stupefaction; he "takes away their spirit," strips them of their courage, and so fills them with fear that they are death-struck by the fall of a leaf.

Pighius, therefore, wants common consideration when he would confine God within the narrow limits of his material creation; when he would make of God nothing more than a kind of wise manager or a skillful general who, well versed in military tactics, foresees the plans of his enemies and forms his counterplots as remedies according to circumstances. As if Scripture did not plainly represent God as he who "taketh the wise in their own craftiness, cuts off the spirit of princes, and maketh the knowledge of wise men foolishness" [Job 5:13; Ps. 76:12; Isa. 44:25]. It is therefore the grossest ignorance in Pighius when he denies that when a man is killed designedly by his fellowman, he dies by the will and decree of God. He entertains this idea, I suppose, imagining that where the will of man is engaged, the will of God is not concerned.

What is to become, then, of all those testimonies of Scripture which declare that the swords of men are wielded by the hand of God? Were the sons of Eli killed without the will of man? Yet the praise is given to God—that it was he who righteously willed that they should be slain [1 Sam. 3:11–14; 1 Sam. 4:11]. That God continually rules the hands of men, that he sometimes binds them fast and at other times turns them this way and that to execute his eternal decrees, no one will call into question who has the least acquaintance with the Scriptures. It is a fact universally admitted by common sense that whatever men undertake, the issue thereof is in the hand of God. But since even this knowledge in men is generally weak and unsettled through the dense darkness of the human mind, Scripture has erected for us a loftier place of observation, by standing on which we may look around us and behold God so ruling and overruling all the works of men as to bring them to the issue that he himself has decreed.

The sum and substance of the whole divine matter is this: Although men, like brute beasts confined by no chains, rush at random here and there, God by his secret bridle so holds and governs them so that they cannot move even one of their fingers without accomplishing the work of God much more than their own. But the faithful, who render to him their willing service as do the angels, are to be considered in a peculiar manner the hands of God. I am now, however, speaking more immediately of those men whose purposes are anything *but* a desire to do the will of God or to adopt any counsel consistent or in harmony with his counsel or in accordance with his will. The wicked do, indeed, frequently glory in themselves at any accomplishment of their wishes, but the event at length proves that they were only fulfilling all the while what had been ordained of God, and that, too, against their own will, while they knew nothing about it. Moreover, God himself very frequently makes use of the wicked to punish the sins of men, especially of his own people. And sometimes he drags the wicked by the neck, as it were, to make them the instruments of his goodness to men and saints.

To cite instances of the former marvelous dispensations of his providence would be a labor too great and too extensive for our present purpose. It would, however, perhaps be better just to touch with our finger a few examples. God, having excited the Assyrian to make war on Judah, calls him "the rod of mine anger," and declares that he was armed with "the staff of his indignation" for his weapon [Isa. 10:5]. But the same adorable God afterwards inveighs against the Assyrian's pride and rebukes him for not acknowledging himself to be "an axe" and "a saw" waged and forged by another's

(God's) hand [v. 15]. In this same manner those whom their own ambition, cruelty, or avarice urges on to violent deeds are said to be "sanctified" of God to do his work and to be his hired soldiers to accomplish his purposes. The Lord himself, moreover, testifies that he calls such together by his "hiss" and by his "trumpet" to take up arms in his cause, to perform his decrees [Isa. 5:26; Isa. 18:3]. That the way of God's goodness is prepared by the evil deeds of men, one single portion of the writings of Moses will fully demonstrate. The conspiracy of the brethren of Joseph against him was more than wicked, perfidious, and cruel when they sold him to the Midianites. But Joseph himself transfers the cause of their selling him, though with a different motive, to God himself: "Now therefore be not grieved, nor angry with yourselves, that ye sold me hither, for God did send me before you to preserve life. So now, it was not you that sent me hither, but God" [Gen. 45:5, 8]. It is evident, therefore, that though they did wickedly, God nevertheless did his work by their means so that they might find life in death. As far as their own intent was concerned, they had killed their brother, but out of their intent, life (that is, provision for their natural life and that of their whole family) shone upon them.

We may see the same working of God in Satan, the captain of all the wicked and the prince of all darkness and iniquities. God sends Satan to Ahab with his own divine command that he should be "a lying spirit in the mouth of all the king's prophets" [1 Kings 22:22]. Thus the impostor spirit becomes the minister of the wrath of God to blind the wicked who would not be obedient to his truth. The apostle Paul calls the "thorn in the flesh" that was sent upon him "the messenger of Satan to buffet me" [2 Cor. 12:7]. Here the poison of Satan is made of God an antidote to cure the apostle's pride. What kind of a physician, I ask you, is Satan in himself, who has never learned anything but to kill and to destroy? However, God, who once commanded the light to shine out of darkness, if he pleases, can marvelously bring salvation out of hell and thus turn darkness into light. But what does Satan work? In a certain sense,

the work of God! That is, God, by holding Satan fast bound in obedience to his providence, turns him whithersoever he will and thus
applies the great enemy's devices and attempts to the accomplishment of his own eternal purposes.

If Scripture did not clearly express God's secondary or instru-
mental mode of operation, this knot would not, even then, be very
difficult to untie. The other and more difficult question is whether
it is God who works in the hearts of men, directs all their counsels,
and turns their wills this way and that, and prevents them from doing anything except what he has decreed they should do. We are
not here inquiring whether or not God works all the godly and holy
affections that are found in the hearts of his people, because that is,
beyond all dispute, certain. The great question is whether he holds
also in the hand of his power all the depraved and impious affections of the wicked and turns them hither and thither so that they
might desire to do what he has decreed to accomplish by their means.

Most certainly when Solomon declares, "The heart of the king
is in the hand of God, and as the rivers of water he turneth it whithersoever he will" [Prov. 21:1], his intention is to show, generally, that
not only the wills of kings, but also all their external actions are
overruled by the will and disposal of God. Moses says that the heart
of Pharaoh was hardened by the Lord himself [Ex. 4:21; Ex. 7:3, 13].
It is vain to flee to the common refuge of God's permission, as if
God could be said to have done what he only permitted to be done.
And Moses positively affirms that the hardening of Pharaoh's heart
was the work of God. Nor, indeed, is the cruelty of the heart of
Pharaoh ascribed to the counsel of God in any other sense than
when, elsewhere, he is said to have given unto his people favor in
the eyes of the Egyptians [Ex. 3:21; Ex. 11:3; Ex. 12:36]. For who does
not see that savage and ferocious beasts were tamed and made gentle by the power of God when such men as the Egyptians were suddenly turned to clemency? From what cause and to what end, then,
can we say that Pharaoh evinced such inhuman cruelty, but because
it pleased the Lord—partly that he might thereby prove the pa-

tience of his people and partly that he might show forth his own almighty power. In this same manner God is said to have "turned the heart of their enemies to hate his people" [Josh. 11:20; Ps. 105:25]. Nor does that passage at all alter the case where it is said, "Pharaoh hardened his heart at this time also" [Ex. 8:32], because we do not make it appear that the minds of men are impelled by any outward influence to do violently, nor do we impute to God the cause of their being hardened, as if cruel and hardhearted persons do not act spontaneously from their own malice and become of themselves excited to obstinacy and presumption. What we maintain is that when men act perversely, they do so, according to the testimony of Scripture, by the ordaining purpose of God. This is also set forth in another part of Scripture where it is said that when all the people of Canaan except[17] the inhabitants of Gibeon set themselves in opposition to Israel, they did so according to the decree and purpose of God, who hardened their hearts, as it is said, "For it was of the Lord to harden their hearts, that they should come against Israel in battle, that he might destroy them utterly" [Josh. 11:20].

The very manner in which God thus works is also set forth in Scripture. For in one place it testifies that God, being angry with the people, moved the heart of David to number the people [2 Sam. 24:1]; however, in another place, it is said concerning this same act of David that the instigator of this pride in David was Satan and that he moved David to number the people [1 Chron. 21:1]. From this we see that Satan was the rod of God's wrath and that God by such means as devils and men impels the hearts of men whithersoever he will. This is still more expressly set forth in another part

---

17. The words "all the people of Canaan except" are not found in the translation of Henry Cole or of J. K. S. Reid [John Calvin, *Concerning the Eternal Predestination of God*, trans. J. K. S. Reid (London: James Clarke & Company, 1961), 175]. This phrase, however, is demanded, since Joshua 11:19 makes it plain that the inhabitants of Gibeon were not among those who opposed Israel.

of the word of God, where it is said that "an evil spirit from the Lord came upon Saul" [1 Sam. 16:14, 23]. Now Saul acted, indeed, from his own wickedness. He exercised the malice concealed within by a voluntary action. Nevertheless, it was Satan that urged him on, and not while God was a mere inactive observer, but while God willed it. Indeed, the evil spirit could not with propriety have been said to be "from the Lord" unless he had been the Lord's ordained minister to execute his vengeance and to be, as it were, his executioner. Nor is Satan the minister of God's wrath merely by his instigating men's minds to evil passions and acts, but also by effectually dragging them and leading them captive, at his will, into wicked actions.

In this same momentous sense Paul speaks when he testifies that effectual error and "strong delusions" are sent on men, "that they might believe a lie, because they would not obey the truth" [2 Thess. 2:11, 12]. Hence you see that Satan is not only "a lying spirit in the mouth of all the prophets" [1 Kings 22:22] at the express command of God, but also that his impostures so ensnare the reprobate that, being utterly deprived of their reason, they are of necessity dragged headlong into error. In this same manner also must we understand the apostle when he says that those who were ungrateful to God were "delivered over to a reprobate mind" and "given up to vile and foul affections," that they should work "that which is unseemly" and "defile their own natural bodies one among another" [Rom. 1:24–28].

Upon this Scripture Augustine remarks that these reprobate persons were not given up to the corrupt affections of their hearts by the mere permission of God as an unconcerned spectator, but by his righteous decree because they had basely profaned his glory. In what manner this was done, Scripture plainly declares: "God sent upon them strong delusion" [2 Thess. 2:11].

From this, what I have just stated is perfectly plain: The internal affections of men are no less ruled by the hand of God than their external actions are preceded by his eternal decree; moreover, God performs not by the hands of men the things he has decreed without first working in their hearts the very will that precedes the acts they are to perform.

Therefore, the sentiments of Augustine on these momentous points are to be fully received and maintained.

> When God wills that to be done which cannot be effected in the course of the things of this world without the wills of men, he at the same time inclines their hearts to will to do it, and also himself does it, not only by aiding their hearts to desire to do it, but also by decreeing it, so that they cannot but do it. Whereas these same persons had in their own minds no such purpose as "to do that which the hand and the counsel of God had afore decreed to be done" [Acts 4:28].

Augustine, moreover, most wisely proposes what ought to be considered concerning the very seeds and principles of nature—the consideration of which so many are unwilling to enter—namely, that the great diversity seen in the dispositions of men, evidently implanted in them of God, affords a manifest evidence of his secret operation by which he moves and rules the hearts of all mankind.

God's Will Is Not Merely Permission

From all that has been said, we can at once gather how vain and fluctuating is that flimsy defense of the divine justice that desires to make it appear that evil things are done not by the will of God, but by his permission only. Indeed, as far as those evil things that men perpetrate with an evil mind are in themselves evil, I willingly confess, as I will more fully explain immediately, that they by no means please God. But for men to represent God as sitting unconcerned and merely permitting those things to be done that Scripture plainly declares to be done, not only by his will but also by his authority, is a mere way of escape from the truth—utterly frivolous and vain.

Sometimes Augustine did, indeed, give way to this popular manner of speaking, but where he devotes himself more closely to the consideration of the matter and examines it more thoroughly, he by no means suffers the permission to be substituted for the act of God. I will not cite verbatim all that the holy father says on this subject in the fifth book of his discussion of it written against Julian. Let the producing of one passage suffice on this occasion:

> He who knows his own just judgments does all these things by working in a marvelous and inexpressible manner, not only in the bodies, but also in the hearts of men. He does not make wills evil, but uses the already evil wills of men as he pleases; nor can he of himself will anything that is evil.

Augustine continues:

> Just in this same manner does Scripture, if diligently considered, show that not only the good wills of men, which God himself has made good out of evil wills, but also the wills that he has made good by his grace are directed by him to good actions and to the attainment of eternal life. Moreover, those wills of men that preserve the good order of things in the world from age to age, as kings, princes, and rulers, are so under the power of God that he inclines them whithersoever he will, either to confer kindnesses on these or to inflict punishments on those, according to his will and pleasure.

The holy father then adds,

> Who does not tremble before these stupendous judgments of God by which he does whatever he will even in the hearts of men, rendering unto them all the while according to their works.

And again:

It is fully evident from the testimonies of Scripture that God works in the hearts of men to incline their wills whithersoever he pleases, whether it be to confer good according to his mercy or to inflict evil according to their just deserts, and all according to his purpose and decree, which is sometimes manifest and sometimes hidden but always just. For it ought ever to be deeply fixed in our hearts that there is no iniquity in God.

The reason that the decree of God is sometimes utterly hidden may be seen in the former part of Augustine's book where, after he had frequently testified that the sins of men are often in themselves punishments that God justly inflicts upon them on account of former sins they have committed, he at length carries up his contemplation to that higher and still more hidden secret of God, namely, that God finds just materials in all men (except those whom he has chosen by his grace) for making them the executors of his wrath. Augustine says,

As to all mortals who are not of this number of God's elect but are of the common mass of mankind (from which mass these were also chosen), they are made the "vessels of God's wrath" and are born for the use and service of God's chosen. For God does not create one of these vessels of his wrath at random or by chance. And he knows full well every particle of good that he works by their means, one part of which good is that he creates in them the excellency of human nature and adorns by their means, as kings, princes and magistrates, etc., the order of things in the world. But why God sometimes paralyzes the hearts of men with fear and dread, and sometimes inspires them with courage; why he takes away the spirit of princes and turns the counsels of the wise into foolishness; why he gifts some with the spirit of temperance and makes others drunk with the spirit of confusion

and madness—for these his marvelous judgments he sometimes manifests a plain and conspicuous reason. While it is
equally evident that his secret counsel so rules over all men
that he turns the wills of whomever he pleases wherever he
pleases...For human nature is common to all men, but not
divine grace [as the same holy father in another part of his
works also strikingly observes].

Taking, then, an honest and sober review of the whole of this
high and divine matter, the plain and indubitable conclusion will be
that the will of God is the one principal and all-high cause of all
things in heaven and earth. Our minds, therefore, ought ever to be
bridled with the knowledge of this mighty fact so that they may not
intemperately and unlawfully indulge in searching into the causes
of things. That saying of Augustine—"The will of God is the necessity of all things"—seems harsh when first heard, as does that
which he immediately adds by way of explanation: "God so ordained all secondary causes that by their means, that might be effected for the sake of which they were ordained, but not necessarily
so effected." But that "God ordained all primary and remote causes,
that by them that might of necessity be effected which he had purposed to be effected by their causation."

When the whole argument is attentively investigated, however,
its asperity soon vanishes, for what the holy father elsewhere says,
though expressed in different terms, is precisely the same in sentiment, nor does his argument contain anything that ought to offend.
Augustine says,

God retains hidden in himself the causes of some of his actions, which he has not intermingled with his created things.
These causes he brings out to their effects, not by that operation of his providence by which he has appointed certain
natures and their powers to be and to act, but by that operation by which he rules and directs as he wills the creatures
that he has made.

Herein, indeed, lies the grace by which those are saved who were lost. For what can be more true than that God, in the government of his creatures, retains hidden in himself something more than he has made visible in their nature? But of all the things that are done, *the will of God* is therefore rightly considered to be the first cause, because at his pleasure he so rules the natures of all things created by him that he directs all the counsels and actions of men to the end he had himself preordained. By this doctrine, as I have before justly observed, a rein is put upon our minds and spirits that ought to hold us within the bounds of modesty. For it is absurd in the last degree not to yield ourselves to the will of God, which is high above all other causes, unless we can see (as we think) a plain reason for our so doing.

We should ever, indeed, bear in mind what I have said before: God does nothing without the highest of reasons. But as the will of God is the surest rule of all righteousness, his will ought ever to be to us the principal reason, yea—if I may so speak—the reason of all reasons. For that humility of faith, which is the offspring of reverence for the divine justice, is by no means a stupid thing, as many imagine. For who but the man who has the persuasion deeply forced on his heart that God is just and all his works righteous will rest satisfied with God's good pleasure alone? That dogma of the Sorbonne in the promulgation of which the papal theologians so much pride themselves—"that the power of God is absolute and tyrannical"—I utterly abhor. For it would be easier to force away the light of the sun from his heat, or his heat from his fire, than to separate the power of God from his justice. Away, then, with all such monstrous speculations from godly minds that God can possibly do more or otherwise than he has done, or that he can do anything without the highest order and reason. For I do not receive that other dogma: "God, as being free from all law himself, may do anything without being subject to any blame for so doing." For whoever makes God without law, robs him of the greatest part of his glory, because he spoils God of his rectitude and justice. Not that God is subject to any law, except insofar as he is a law to himself.

But there is that inseparable connection and harmony between the power of God and his justice, so that nothing can possibly be done by him but what is moderate, legitimate, and according to the strictest rule of right. And most certainly, when the faithful speak of God as omnipotent, they acknowledge him at the same time to be the judge of the world and always hold his power to be righteously tempered with equity and justice.

God Is Not the Author of Evil

We have not yet, however, met the great objection of our adversaries: "If all things are done according to the will of God and men can do or design nothing but as he wills or ordains, God must be the author of all evils." The distinction that formerly prevailed in the schools and is now everywhere current is perfectly true provided it be rightly understood:"The evil of the punishment, but not the evil of the fault, proceeds from God." But some inexperienced ones, imagining that the matter in question can be settled in one short word, pass by in security the very point at issue: "How can God be free from blame in the very deed that he condemns in Satan and in the reprobate and that he declares men condemn in their fellowmen?" For both evils are often seen in the same work, not in different works, namely, that the praise of the punishment must, of necessity, be ascribed to God and the fault of the act to man. For instance, robbers carry off the cattle of the holy Job. The deed is cruel and disgraceful. Satan by this means drives the patriarch to desperation—a machination still more detestable. But Job declares another to be the author of it all."The Lord gave," says he,"and the Lord hath taken away" [Job 1:21]. Nor is Job wrong in attributing that to God which, in another sense, could be imputed to the robbers only. For the patriarch, as if beholding with uplifted eyes the things that are decreed on the throne of God in heaven, confesses that the Lord took away by the hands of the robbers those things that they could not have touched except by his authority and command. All this Job explains in the words that follow: "The Lord hath done whatsoever pleased him." We hear in this instance that the work of Satan was in common with that of God. We hear that nothing was done except by God's good pleasure. It may here be asked, "How shall God be exempted from that fault of which Satan and his instruments are guilty?" If a distinction be made between the works of men, derived from a consideration of their purpose and end in each particular case; if the cruelty of the man is condemned who pierces the eyes of a crow or kills a crane, while the virtue of the judge is praised who cleanses his hands by the execution of the wicked person, why shall the condition of God himself be worse than that of man? Shall not God's justice keep him separate from the wicked actions of human or satanic offenders?

Let us use an illustration somewhat more close and applicable. That prince will ever be praised among men who shall, by a just and legitimate war, repel from his dominions violence, rapine, and plunder. For this end he will hasten to arm thousands of soldiers, who will rush forward with cupidity to shed blood, to despoil the poor and helpless of their property, and to commit every act of licentiousness and violence, for which deeds of wickedness they certainly will not deserve praise. Two armies, in another part of the world, enter into a mighty battle. If you behold a prosperous issue of the skill of the general under whose conduct and command the battle is fought, you absolve him from all blame, although he is but a mortal man, while you nevertheless condemn the soldiers who lend out their hands for nefarious hire to murder their fellowmen. Will you, then, rob God of the glory of his justice because he sometimes does his works by means of Satan? Yet so it is. And as the mists that the earth exhales sometimes obscure the brightness of the sun and intercept its view from the sight of men, while the sun still really remains the same in all its brightness, so the vanity of men creates many vaporous impediments, as it were, which obstruct their sight of the equity of God, while that equity remains, nevertheless, as pure and perfect as ever. Yet these ignorant reasoners would involve God and the wicked in the same guilt where the act of God, working by the wicked, is in a sense common to him and them. But

David did not do this. When Shimei assaulted him with reproaches and stones, David did not stop at the man but looked at the command of God: "Let him curse," said David, "for God hath bidden him" [2 Sam. 16:10, 11]. And yet David does not rise up against God, but with all humility offers his back to the stripes and says, "Who shall then say, Wherefore hast thou done so?" [v. 10]. He speaks this way also in the Psalms: "I was dumb, I opened not my mouth; because thou didst it" [Ps. 39:9]. For which one of the godly will not the majesty of God immediately reduce to silence? And from which one of them will not the justice of God force the expression of praise and constrain him to break forth into that devoted exclamation of David: "So let him curse, because the Lord hath said unto him, Curse David . . . It may be that the Lord will look on mine affliction, and that the Lord will requite me good for his cursing this day" [2 Sam. 16:10, 12].

Therefore, when the wickedness of men proceeds thus from the Lord and from a just cause, but from a cause unknown to us, although the first cause of all things be his will, I most solemnly deny that he is therefore the author of sin. Nevertheless, that difference of causes on which I dwelt before is by no means to be forgotten. The one cause is proximate, another remote. The careful observance of this distinction is indispensable in order to understand clearly the wide difference and momentous distinction between the just and equal providence of God and the turbulent impetuosities of men. Our adversaries load us with illiberal and disgraceful calumny when they cast it in our teeth that we make God the author of sin by maintaining that his will is the cause of all things that are done. For when a man perpetrates anything unjustly, incited by ambition, avarice, lust, or any other depraved passion, if God by his just but secret judgment performs his works by means of such a one's hands, the mention of sin cannot be made with reference to God in those his righteous acts. It is perfidy, pride, cruelty, intemperance, envy, self-conceit, or some similar depraved desire that constitutes sin in man. But no such desire can be found in God. Shimei attacks his king with brutal insolence. The sin is at once manifest. God uses such an instrument to effect the righteous humiliation of David. Such a rod it pleases God to use. But who will dare to charge God with sin in so doing? The Arabians and the Sabeans carry off their plunder from another man's substance. The sin of robbery is evident. God exercises the patience of his servant by the violence of the plunderers. Let the heroic confession of the patriarch— "Blessed be the name of the Lord" [Job 1:21]—be heard rising from the midst of these ravages rather than the profane revilings of the wicked and the ignorant. In a word, such is God's manner of working by the sins of men that when we come to deal with him in the matter of his righteous judgments, his eternal purity immediately wipes off every spot that the wicked reasonings of men may attempt to cast upon his glorious majesty.

Here the admonition of Augustine can be listened to with profit.

> In point of oneness or agreement, there is sometimes a mighty difference between men and God in the matters of his righteous acts and judgments. As for instance, when God wills righteously what men will evilly, and when God righteously wills not what men evilly will not. In point of difference or contrariety, God and men do not ill agree, as when men will well what God righteously does not will, and when men righteously do not will what God righteously does will. For example, the son may wish for the death of his father so that he can rush upon the inheritance, while God also may will that this same father should die.

God willed that Jerusalem should be utterly destroyed, that the temple should be profaned and demolished, and that the Jews should suffer every extreme of torment. The Idumaens were all the while longing for the same. In order that the same measure might be measured to a dire and ruthless man who had spared no one,

God wills that no help whatever should be brought to him when pressed to destruction on every side by inevitable necessity. His son shall refuse him every duty of affection and have the least desire to aid him in his desperate need. God willed that the sons of Eli should not listen to the counsels of their father because he had determined to destroy them. The sons, on their part, would not hear their father. There appears here, at first sight, a certain kind of harmony and agreement, but when we consider abstractedly the evil and the good involved, there is as much disagreement and contrariety as between fire and water. A husband shall wish for a longer life of a beloved wife whom God calls out of this world. Christ shuddered at, and prayed against, the death that was a sacrifice of the sweetest odor unto God. Now the wills of each—both of the husband and of Christ—although diverse from the will of God at first appearance, were equally without blame. Therefore, far be it from any man to drag God into a participation of sin, guilt, or blame whenever any apparent similitude between the plainly depraved passions of men and his secret counsel may present itself.

Let this sentiment of Augustine be ever present to our minds:

> Therefore, by the mighty and marvelous working of God, which is so exquisitely perfect in the accomplishment of every purpose and bent of his will that in a wonderful and ineffable way, is not done without his will what is even done contrary to his will, because it could not have been done had he not permitted it to be done; and yet he did not permit it without his will, but according to his will.

God's Will Is One

Hereby is refuted either the ignorance or the wickedness of those who deny that the nature of the will of God can be one and simple if there be any other will ascribed to him than what is plainly and manifestly revealed by him in his own law. Some also ask in derision, "If there be any will of God not revealed in his law, by what name is that will called?" But those men must be deprived of their senses in whose opinion all those Scriptures signify nothing that speaks with so much wonder and admiration of the profound depth of the judgments of God. When Paul exclaims, "O the depth of the riches both of the wisdom and knowledge of God! how unsearchable are his judgments!" [Rom. 11:33], he most certainly teaches us in all plainness that the judgment of God is something more and deeper than that expressed by the simple words of Christ in the memorable ejaculation, "O Jerusalem, Jerusalem, how often would I have gathered thy children together as a hen gathereth her brood under her wings, but ye would not!" [Matt. 23:37; Luke 13:34]. And whereas God willed that the sons of Eli should not be obedient to their father, that divine will differed—in appearance—from the precept of the law, which commands children to obey their parents. In a word, wherever the apostle sets forth the wonderful judgments of God and the depth of his thoughts and ways, which are "past finding out" [Rom. 11:33], he is not speaking at all of the works of the law, which stand always plainly before our eyes. Rather, he is magnifying that inaccessible light in which is hidden God's secret counsel, which, being exalted far above the utmost stretch of the human mind, we are compelled to gaze upon with uplifted eyes and to adore.

Someone will perhaps say, "If that light is inaccessible, why do you approach it?" I do not so approach it as to wish, by an insolent curiosity, to search into those things that God wills to keep deeply hidden in himself, but that which Scripture openly declares I embrace with a sure faith and look upon with reverence. But you will say, "How can it be that God, who is ever consistent with himself and unchangeable even in the shadow of a turn, should yet will what is contrary to what he seems to be?" I reply, it is no matter of wonder that God, when speaking with men, should accommodate himself to the limits of their comprehension. Who will affirm that God ever appeared to his servants, even in visions, such as he really is? For the brightness of his glory is such that the sight of him as he is by our naked vision would immediately absorb and overwhelm all our senses. He has, therefore, ever so revealed himself as men were able to bear the revelation. But whether God talks with us in the language of a child or conceals what he knows to be beyond our comprehension — that there is anything feigned or dissembled in what he is pleased to say, I solemnly deny. Most true is that which the Psalm affirms: "Thou hatest all workers of iniquity" [Ps. 5:5]. Nor, indeed, does God there testify by the mouth of David anything else than what he exemplifies in reality every day when he punishes men for their transgressions. Nor would he punish their sins if he did not hate those sins. You here see, then, that God is an avenger, from which we are fully assured that he is not an approver. But many are deceived in these sacred matters, not rightly considering that God wills righteously those things that men do wickedly. "How will you explain this?" you may ask. I reply that God abominates all adulterous and incestuous intercourse. Absalom defiles his father's concubines in the sight of the people [2 Sam. 16:21, 22]. Was this done in every sense contrary to the will of God? No. God had predicted by his servant Nathan that Absalom should do this: "I will take thy wives before thine eyes and give them unto thy neighbour, and he shall lie with thy wives in the sight of this sun. For thou didst it secretly, but I will do this thing before all Israel and before the sun" [2 Sam. 12:11, 12].

Scripture is replete with examples of the same nature and tendency. Shall we, then, on that account either impute the cause or fault of sin to God or represent him as having a double or twofold will, and thus make him inconsistent with himself? But as I have already shown that he wills the same thing in certain cases as the wicked and profane, but in a different manner, so we must hold that he wills in the same manner with the wicked and reprobate what is in appearance different, so that in those things that are presented to our minds, the apparent diversity is tempered with the utmost oneness and harmony. Thus, inasmuch as Absalom's monstrous impiety toward his father was a perfidious violation of the law of marriage and a gross profanation of the order of nature, it is most certain that his atrocious wickedness was highly offensive to God, who can be pleased with nothing but honesty, modesty, fidelity, and chastity, and who wills that the lawful order that he has established among men should be preserved sacred and inviolate. And yet it pleased him to punish in this manner the adultery of David. And thus he wills in the same manner with men things that seem to us quite diverse. For that will of God by which he commands what shall be done, and by which he punishes all transgressions of his law, is one and simple.

We have observed before that sins are frequently punishments by which God retributively avenges men's former transgressions. In all such dispensations of his providence, there are two things that claim our deep consideration: the just judgment of God, by which he testifies that he hates the sin and thus visits with its due punishment, and the wickedness of man, which stands directly opposed to the will of God. If such infinite brightness should dazzle our mental vision, what wonder when the eyes of our body cannot endure the sight of the natural sun. For is the vision of the body stronger than that of the mind? Or is the brightness of the majesty of God less than that of the natural sun? Therefore, it behooves us not to be too acute in our penetration into the splendor of the divine majesty lest, in the meantime, we either deny that to be true which Scripture plainly teaches and confirms by experience, or lest we dare consider this or that to be, as we think, not quite consistent with the character of God.

Augustine says,

When the last day shall have come, then shall be seen in the brightest light of understanding what the godly now hold in faith until it shall be then understood by the fullest comprehension. How sure, immutable, and all-efficacious is the will of God. And how many things he can do, and yet not will. But he wills nothing that he cannot do.

Part Two

Historical Introduction to
A Brief Reply and
Reply to the Slanderous Reports

The following two works, *A Brief Reply* (1557) and *Reply to the Slanderous Reports* (1558), comprise Calvin's response from Geneva to two anonymous treatises that assailed him and the doctrine of God's sovereign counsel and providence. Calvin suspected what has since been demonstrated, namely, that both attacks were written by a former friend, Sebastian Castellio.

Castellio (1515?–1563) was a gifted Frenchman who converted to Protestantism around the year 1540. His first contact with Calvin was in Strasbourg during the three-year period of Calvin's forced separation from Geneva. Castellio, being short of funds, lodged in Calvin's home in Strasbourg for a few days in May of 1540. Shortly thereafter Castellio was appointed the rector of the school in Geneva, and he took up his work there even before Calvin returned to Geneva in 1541.

Trouble started brewing two years later when Castellio requested to be ordained a minister in Geneva. The city council agreed, provided the pastors approved of his ordination. At a colloquium with the pastors it came to light that Castellio's view of Scripture was not entirely satisfactory, for he considered the Song of Solomon to be an uninspired love poem of Solomon. Castellio also disagreed with the Genevan Catechism's interpretation of the Apostles' Creed, specifically on the meaning of Christ's descent into hell. The pastors consequently refused to admit him to the office of minister.

A few months later Castellio resigned his position at the school. He received a letter of recommendation written by Calvin so that he might seek a position in Lausanne. Calvin also wrote private letters to Viret, a pastor in Lausanne, expressing sympathy for Castellio and asking Viret to help Castellio if he could.

However, Castellio found no work in Lausanne, and he soon returned to Geneva. In May of 1544, he stood up in a public meeting in Geneva and accused the pastors of Geneva of various sins. Calvin lodged a complaint against Castellio for this, and the city council laid upon Castellio stern admonitions. Within a year, Castellio left Geneva for Basel, the city that had embraced the free-thinking Erasmus for so many years.

In Basel, Castellio labored at whatever tasks he could find to support himself and his growing family. He earned money translating, including the completion of his own translations of the Bible into Latin and later into French. In 1553, he was appointed to the position of professor of Greek at the university in Basel.

Perhaps little more would have been heard from Castellio if it were not for Michael Servetus. The same year that Castellio became professor of Greek in Basel, Geneva burned Michael Servetus at the stake for heresy and blasphemy. That ignited a war of words between Castellio and Calvin that continued to the end of Castellio's life.

The first salvo—*A History of the Death of Servetus*—came out of Basel, probably written by Castellio. Shortly thereafter Calvin published a tract defending both the doctrine of the Trinity (which Servetus had denied) and the execution of Servetus by the Genevan city council. While Calvin was writing that defense, Castellio was composing a treatise entitled *Concerning the Persecution of Heretics*,[18] which he published under the pseudonym Martinus Bellius. He criticized sharply the execution of Servetus and advocated religious liberty and tolerance. Castellio quoted numerous church fathers, as well as Luther, Zwingli, and even Calvin's earlier writings, to

---

18. This work of Castellio has been translated into English by Roland H. Bainton and published with the title *Concerning Heretics* (New York: Columbia University Press, 1935).

demonstrate that the leading lights in the church had not approved of putting heretics to death.

Theodore Beza, a close friend of Calvin, and also a fellow Genevan pastor and a teacher in the school, chose to answer Castellio's criticisms in a work entitled *Concerning the Punishment of Heretics by Civil Magistrates*. Meanwhile, Castellio wrote a reply to Calvin entitled *The Lies of Calvin* under yet another pseudonym, pressing the same theme of tolerance and setting forth proof that the Scriptures do not permit the use of the sword against heretics.

Castellio is celebrated today as an advocate for religious tolerance.[19] He insisted that salvation was not determined by what one *believed*, but how one *lived*. He had a personal stake in this venture. As time went on, it became more evident that he was opposed to the truth of the Reformation. In addition to his defense of Michael Servetus, he had a more than passing acquaintance with Faustus Sozzini, one of the founders of what would become Socinianism. Socinianism denied the Trinity and taught a universal atonement. Castellio also had a close friendship with David Joris, a radical Anabaptist living in Basel under a false identity.

Castellio's antipathy towards the truth became manifest in his attack on sovereign predestination and providence. Already in 1551 his Latin Bible translation was censored by the authorities in Basel. Castellio had added a marginal note to Romans 9, challenging Calvin's interpretation of that chapter and his teaching on predestination, and this note was removed by the Basel authorities. Later, in an anonymously published work of 1557, Castellio boldly attacked Calvin's doctrine of predestination. Calvin responded with *A Brief Reply, intended to refute the calumnies of a certain worthless person, by which he endeavored to pollute the doctrine of the eternal predestination of God*. Calvin used the term *predestination* in its broader sense, namely, that God has "predetermined" all creatures, actions, and

---

19. Roland Bainton has published much on this, including a paper, "Sebastian Castellio, Champion of Religious Liberty," in *Studies on the Reformation* (Boston: Beacon Press, 1965), 139–181.

events. Castellio charged Calvin with making God responsible for man's sin by teaching that God has sovereignly planned all things and that he executes his determinative counsel. In *A Brief Reply* Calvin repudiated the charge and at the same time maintained the absolute sovereignty of God.

Castellio was not finished attacking Calvin's doctrine. Within a year he published, again anonymously, fourteen articles that he claimed were quotations from the writings of John Calvin. All the articles had to do with fate, or predestination—*predestination* used again in the broad sense of "predetermined." In his *Reply to the Slanderous Reports* Calvin termed it God's *secret providence*, which he defined as "that free and unfettered counsel of God by which he rules all mankind, all men and things, and all parts and particles of the world by his infinite wisdom and incomprehensible justice." Calvin insisted that all fourteen articles, supposedly taken from his writings, were "partly false and partly mutilated." Calvin went on to demonstrate systematically that the articles were perversions of the biblical truth that he taught. This was the occasion for and content of his *Reply to the Slanderous Reports*. It would be Calvin's final response to Castellio.

That these replies to Castellio are two of the most acrimonious to flow from Calvin's pen is hardly surprising. The attacker had slandered Calvin, falsified his words, and published his attacks anonymously while claiming to be seeking truth. Calvin was stung, too, by the fact that he had repeatedly befriended Castellio in earlier days. Calvin alludes to this in the second of these replies when he writes,

> As far as you are concerned, poor masked monitor, I derive some consolation from the thought that you cannot be ungrateful towards the man who has treated you with much greater kindness than you deserved at his hands, without betraying at the same time your foul wickedness against God.

No doubt Castellio, among others, was on Calvin's mind when he wrote in 1557,

Because I affirm and maintain that the world is managed and
governed by the secret providence of God, a multitude of
presumptuous men rise up against me and allege that I represent God as the author of sin. This is so foolish a calumny,
that it would of itself quickly come to nothing, did it not
meet with persons who have tickled ears, and who take pleasure in feeding upon such discourse. But there are many
whose minds are so filled with envy and spleen, or ingratitude, or malignity, that there is no falsehood, however preposterous, yea, even monstrous, which they do not receive, if
it is spoken to them. Others endeavor to overthrow God's
eternal purpose of predestination, by which he distinguishes
between the reprobate and the elect; others take upon them
to defend free will; and forthwith many throw themselves
into their ranks, not so much through ignorance as by a per-
versity of zeal which I know not how to characterise. If they
were open and avowed enemies, who brought these troubles
upon me, the thing might in some way be borne. But that
those who shroud themselves under the name of brethren
…should wage such nefarious war against me, how detestable is it? In this matter I may very justly complain with
David, "Yea, mine own familiar friend, in whom I trusted,
who did eat of my bread, hath lifted up his heel against me"
(Ps. 41:9). "For it was not an enemy that reproached me; but
it was thou, a man mine equal, my guide, and mine acquaintance. We took sweet counsel together, and walked
unto the house of God in company" (Ps. 55:12, 13, 14).[20]

Calvin's concern, however, was not himself, but the truth of
God. His "only grief" was "that through [his] feeble side the solemn
and eternal truth of God is stabbed, which ought to be looked upon
with reverence and adoration by the whole world." And he added,

---

20. John Calvin, *Commentary on the Book of Psalms*, trans. James Anderson,
vol. 1 (Grand Rapids: Wm. B. Eerdmans Publishing Company, 1949), xlvi.

"But since I see that this same truth of God has ever, from the beginning, been exposed to the calumnies of the wicked, and that Christ himself by the decree of his heavenly Father must ever be a 'rock of offence' and of contradiction, I consider that the defenders of the truth must bear this offense with all patience." Consistent, therefore, with the goal of all his life, Calvin wrote these replies for the cause of God's truth and glory.

RUSSELL J. DYKSTRA
Professor of New Testament and Church History
Theological School of the Protestant Reformed Churches
Grandville, Michigan, USA

A Brief Reply

There has been cast in my way the silly script of a certain worthless mortal, who, with all his vileness, boasts of being a defender and avenger of the glory of God by waging war against the divine principle and doctrine. He says, "The world is so governed by God that nothing is done therein but by his secret counsel and decree."

Meanwhile, this miserable being sees not that when he is catching at fallacious pretenses of clearing the justice of God from imputation, he is all the while utterly subverting his power, all which is, as it were, attempting to rend in pieces God himself. But to give a color to his profanity, he prefaces his undertaking not less wickedly than maliciously with the remark: "God is not the cause of evil, nor wills sin." As if, when we claim for God the supremacy of all rule, we assert that he is the author of sin!

Now it is evident that John Calvin is attacked by this sentence.[21] But it is well known that John Calvin is too far removed from the blasphemy with which this worthless being would charge him to need any lengthened protection of himself from its malignity.

Wherever sin is the subject of discussion, John Calvin constantly declares aloud throughout his writings that the name of God is not to be mingled or mentioned with sin, because nothing is consistent with the character of God but rectitude and equity. How foul, then, is the calumny to involve a man, so long deserving well of the church of God, in the crime of making God the author of sin.

---

21. John Calvin writes this defense of himself and his teachings in the third person. At times, however, he speaks in the first person.

Calvin Falsely Charged

The object of this malicious calumny indeed affirms through-out his publications that nothing is done but by the will of God. But at the same time he asserts that those things done wickedly by men are so overruled by the secret counsel of God that his counsel has no connection whatever with the sinfulness of men.

The sum of the doctrine of the thus reviled one is that God, in wondrous ways and in ways unknown to us, directs all things to the end that he wills so that his eternal will might be the first cause of all things. But why God wills that which may seem to us inconsistent with his nature, the reviled one confesses to be incomprehensible. Therefore, he declares aloud that the *why* of God's works is not to be audaciously or curiously pried into; but that, as the counsels of God are a mighty deep and mysteries that surpass the limits of our comprehension, it becomes a man to adore them with reverence rather than to investigate them with presumption.

In the meantime, the object of all this foul calumny maintains as a sacred principle that although the reason for the counsels of God lies hidden and unknown, nevertheless the high praise of his justice is ever to be given to God because his will is, and must be, the highest rule of all equity. Therefore, let him, whoever he may be, who desires to load the man who constantly teaches these things with so atrocious a charge as making God the author of sin, first take upon himself the task of proving that when those wicked men who, by crucifying Christ, did "that which the hand of God and his counsel before determined to be done" [Acts 4:28], they made God a partaker of their wickedness and involved him in a share of their guilt. The words "that which thy hand and thy counsel before determined to be done" are not the words of Calvin (let it be remembered), but of the Holy Spirit, of Peter, and of the whole primitive church.

Let these unreasonable and extravagant men, then, cease to defile the pure and lucid doctrine of the Holy Spirit with their pollution and their filth, and thus blind the eyes of the simple so that the inexperienced who understand not the real nature of the question may not, when they hear sin mentioned, dash against the awful and abhorrent rock of making God the author of sin. After David complained that he was oppressed by the unjust violence of his enemies on every side, he failed not to add, "God has done all this" [Ps. 39:9]. When Job was despoiled of his substance by plunderers and tormented by the devil, he likewise confesses that all these evils came upon him from God [Job 1:21]. If anyone should reply that in this manner God is made the author of sin, let him wage his war with the holy prophets of God and with the Holy Spirit himself. But while the holy prophets and the witnesses of the Holy Spirit held fast the sacred distinction that though all things were thus done as ordained of God, and yet that whatever God wills or decrees is righteous and just, they, with equal plainness and firmness, set him high above all, who rules Satan himself and all the wicked with his secret and sovereign reign.

This short reply, thus far made, had John Calvin said no more, might have been sufficient to refute the iniquitous calumny of this worthless being, who so purposely and perversely corrupts and deforms his sentiments and doctrine. But that this calumniator's ends and aims may be the more completely uncovered, neither the time nor pains will be lost, perhaps, if we look into some other rising volumes of his malicious smoke. As this vain being's purpose is to deprive God of his supreme rule and government, and as with all the impudence imaginable he cuts down, at one stroke, the principle that the purpose of God is the first cause of all things, I will summarily lay hold of and examine some of the intermediate causes and reasons that he brings forward.

This abandoned mortal asserts that Plato's opinions were far above mine, because he does not suffer God to be called the author of sin, whereas this mortal knows not really what Plato either thinks or says. So abhorrent is the term *evil* to this profane scribbler that he positively denies that those numberless "evils," of which we are all the subjects, proceed from God. This is nothing more or less than despoiling God at once of his office as the judge of the world. But when Calvin, and before him Luther and Bucer, and antecedently to them, Augustine and other godly teachers, testify that the will of God is the supreme cause of all things that are in the world, it was the farthest thing from the mind of each of them and of them all to entangle God in any shadow of fault. And as to Calvin, in all his writings he repudiates with fervid zeal and pronounces to be detestable that idea of the absolute or tyrannical power of God that philosophizing theologians set afloat throughout their schools. And for this reason: that the power of God ought not and cannot be separated from his eternal wisdom. By this testimony the impudent barking of this unclean dog is at once refuted when he makes honest and faithful teachers in the church of Christ utter things that are blasphemous, abhorrent, and before unheard, and which, after all, are, with a futility equal to their malignity, brought out from the wicked workshop of his own brain.

God's Will and Evil Deeds

After vomiting forth all this foul calumny, this impure being professes to prove that God is not the cause of evils—first from the law of nature and next from the authority of the "divine" Plato, as he terms him, by whom (he says) God is called the cause of good. The solution of the whole matter is perfectly simple. The image of the rectitude that we confess to be in God is stamped upon all natural knowledge of good and evil. In proportion, therefore, as each one forms his life according to the law of nature, insofar he represents the nature of God, for righteousness is a delight to God in the same proportion as iniquity is an abomination to him. But how God rules and overrules by his secret counsel all those things that are done wickedly by man, it is not ours to define, but it is ours to be assured and to declare that in whatever God does, he never deviates from his own perfect justice.

I make the same reply to this worthless being's second argument. This noble champion for God puts forth the following question: If God is the author of sin, as he affirms that we say, why does he at all prevent sin from being committed? Why does he not throw the rein upon the necks of men altogether? What means the barking of this dog about God's being the author of sin? The fact is that this fellow fabricates monsters in his own imagination so that he might get the fame of fighting with them. What, then, if I retort, but in quite a different manner, the question that may truly be put in assertion of the omnipotence of God: If God does not will to be done the things that are done, why does he not prevent their being done? Why does he throw the rein on the necks of men to do them? But from this mode of figurative repugnance and contradiction, we may at once elicit the substance of that which Augustine testifies:

> God in a secret and marvelous way justly wills the things that men unjustly do, although according to his will, as truly expressed in his law, he hates iniquity and has pleasure only in rectitude. And from this fountain flow all the curses that are appended to the law. For if iniquities did not displease him as being utterly contrary to his nature, he would neither denounce nor exact punishments.

Therefore, all that this worthless being has heaped together to vindicate God (as he thinks) from ignominy is utterly superfluous and vain. In fact, it is himself all the while who throws upon God the idea of ignominy, while he is anxiously laboring, in a doubtful case (as he thinks), to make God appear to be good.

Having blattered forth his revilings until he was tired, our holy champion draws a little nearer, affirming that some men in these perilous times, not daring to teach openly that God is the cause of evils, intimate the same thing in varied forms of speech, asserting that Adam sinned by the will of God and that wicked men perpetrate all their wickedness not only by the permission of God, but also by his actual impulse. Upon this our noble rhetorician exclaims with great lamentation, "O miserable man! How could it have been that God willed this, who had created Adam in his own image?" As if it were mine to render an exact reason for the secret counsels of

God and to make mortals understand to a pin's point that heavenly wisdom, the height and depth of which they are commanded to look upon and adore. No! Let Moses rather break short all such foolish loquacity by that word of his: "Secret things belong unto the Lord our God, but these which I testify are revealed unto you" [Deut. 29:29]. We see how Moses, commanding the people to be content with the doctrine of the law, admonishes them to leave God's hidden counsels to him alone as mysteries to be adored, not to be inquired into.

Here, finding the point of his pen to have become somewhat bent and blunt, he sharpens it anew for a furious attack upon those who (according to his own account) assert that wickedness is perpetrated not only by the will of God, but also by his very impulse. Finding himself now entered into a boundless field, he exults and raves, leaving no kind of abuse whatever unuttered, that he might distress the minds of godly ministers, whose virtues, I would to God, he could imitate, even in a hundredth degree. He first of all classes them with the libertines, from whom, if he differed in the least degree in principle, he certainly would ruin this best of all causes by his sheer ignorance. As there exists a book of Calvin expressly written against these libertines, what kind of a face must that man possess who returns for a labor so useful and holy, so undeserved a reward? He positively contends that if God does impel men to sin, the devil himself does no more. Suppose we concede for a moment this profane comparison. What will our hero say about the servants of Christ upon whom the devil wages war ever, but God never? Let us see upon what arguments this profane being rests his profanity. "Let Satan," says he, "do what he will and tempt as he will, he cannot compel the will of man. But God, who holds the heart of man in his hand, can compel the will. If, therefore, God will force, do so he will and must, whether you will or no." Here the ignorance and its audacity are at once manifest.

All men of a sound mind are agreed that there is no sin except that which is voluntary. Therefore, you will not find one of a sound judgment who will assert that men sin against their will. But Calvin, according to the word of God, following also Augustine and other godly writers, teaches that when men sin of their own will and accord, God nevertheless gives into the hands of Satan "strong delusions" so that he may drive the reprobate hither and thither, as Paul testifies [2 Thess. 2:11]. Satan, in this manner, goes forth at the command of God to be a lying spirit in the mouth of all the prophets to deceive Ahab [1 Kings 22:21, 22].

However, it is not my purpose to accumulate testimonies from Scripture. My present object is merely to show how preposterously this barking dog howls against the innocent. "How," says he, "is a wicked man known to be such but by doing wickedly?" as if we, by attributing to the secret judgments of God all the license that he puts into the hands of Satan, thereby make the adorable God the author of sin. As if we did not, on the contrary, openly and universally testify that God is, and must be, ever utterly remote from sin because (as we show) it is in the strictest justice and righteousness that he blinds and hardens the reprobate. "But in this way," argues this hero for God, "the will of God and of the devil will be the same." Not so. There is, as I have shown before, a mighty difference, because although God and the devil will the same thing, they do so in an utterly different manner. For who will deny that Satan eagerly desires the destruction of the wicked, which destruction, nevertheless, proceeds from God? Yet the object of the righteous judge is infinitely different from that of the enemy, breathing out unmitigated cruelty. God willed that Jerusalem should be destroyed utterly; the same destruction Satan also desired.

However, I would rather untie this sacred knot by the words of Augustine than by my own. In Chapter 101 of his *Manual* addressed to Laurentius, he nobly discusses how it is that man wills with an evil will what God wills with a good will (as where a wicked son, for instance, wills the death of his father, and God wills the same death); and finally how it is that God performs what he has decreed by the wicked wills and passions of men rather than by the good wills of his own servants. I refer my readers to the exposition of the sacred matter as given by Augustine in the portion of his works to which I have alluded.

If, then, a diversity of end does not prevent the will from being the same, would it not have been according to his just desert if this champion for God had been swallowed up in the depths of hell before he had thus defiled the divine majesty and polluted it by his foul cavils? Yet he dares to charge us with denying in our hearts the justice of God that we profess with our mouths. Whereas this vile being, while he dares with unbridled insolence to assert that those against whom he wars never study uprightness of life, indulges himself in all iniquity as if there sat no judge at all upon the throne of heaven. But I would calmly ask, in which breast is it the more probable that the righteousness of God is made a laughingstock—in the breast where all desire after godliness is found, or that where the rein is given to every species of iniquity? The real fact is that there is not one thing in Calvin, and in those like him, that this goodly teacher of morality more thoroughly hates than the unswerving rigor of their moral discipline.

Insipid and unlettered as this worthless mortal is, however, he yet attempts to enlist in his base service the most scurrilous wit, demanding "whether it was God or Satan that willed the sin of Adam." Did ever godly or really serious men permit themselves to be facetious or pass jokes upon mysteries so profound—to bark at them as impudent dogs? They do indeed confess that the fall of Adam was not without the rule and overrule of the secret providence of God, but they never doubt that the end and object of his secret counsel were righteous and just. But since the reason lies hidden in the mind of God, they soberly and reverently await the revelation of it, which shall be made in the day in which we shall see that God "face to face," whom we now "behold through a glass darkly" and unintelligibly [1 Cor. 13:12]. Having thus reveled in the vilest abuse of the best and most godly of men, the next thing that this pious warrior would have done is that all their tongues should be wrenched out and thrown into the fire!

There is no slight probability, however, that the rage of this being against Calvin is all intended as a holy offering to the memory of his friend Servetus, and that lamenting the death of his kin companion and finding no other method of satisfying his revenge, he surpasses all hangmen in cruelty towards the defenders of the truth.

Twofold Will of God

Concerning the doctrine of the twofold will of God, which Calvin, following Augustine and other godly teachers, ascribes to God himself, this excellent theological judge declares that he wonders at the childish babble by which it is set forth. Everyone must surely set him down as one of the most learned of men who can talk about "the childish babble" of another. But this offensive affectation fully proves that he thus prates under a panting hunt after vainglory. He afterwards adds that this distinction, the twofold will of God, was invented by us because without it we should have laid ourselves open to the charge of blaspheming God. Whereas, by this one word of his, his own frenzied madness is expressed and exposed, for he forgets that he himself has perpetually upbraided the most innocent men with uttering open blasphemies. And was it (I ask you) any doubtful blasphemy in himself when he made God the author of sin and asserted that he not only wills sin, but also actually impels men to sin, thus representing him as renouncing his own nature and feasting upon and delighting himself in iniquities? After having impudently vomited forth these revilings, he now, forgetting himself altogether and what he has uttered, says that we cover over our blasphemies with a certain coloring that they might not be perceived.

It is worthwhile, however, to observe what arguments he cites in his attempted refutation of the twofold will of God. He accuses us of attributing, by this doctrine, unfaithfulness to God, such as making him say one thing and think another, contrary to the testimonies of Scripture wherein God says, "I am the Lord, I change not" [Mal. 3:6], and "with him is no variableness" [James 1:17]. But this silly mortal does not consider that not only Calvin and other like witnesses of the truth are attacked by this calumny, but also Moses himself, who, when declaring that the law was given unto the Jews and to their children, leaves all "secret things" with God, saying that they "belong" to him [Deut. 29:29]. Not that there is any difficulty whatever in refuting this calumny, for God, commanding that which is right, thereby testifies what truly pleases him; nor is there any other counsel concealed in his own mind by which he either loves or wills to accomplish anything whatever that he condemns in man. But he exercises his judgments in a marvelous way so that by his surpassing wisdom and equity he ordains and directs to a good end things that are in themselves evil. Nor will Calvin ever concede that God wills that which is evil—that is, insofar as it is evil—but that his secret and righteous judgments shine forth marvelously in overruling the iniquities of men. For instance, by the incestuous deeds of Absalom, God punishes the adultery of David [2 Sam. 16:21, 22]. Therefore, when God commands Adam not to taste the fruit of the tree of knowledge of good and evil [Gen. 2:17], he thereby tests his obedience. Meanwhile, he foreknew what would take place and not only foreknew it, but ordained it. If this truth be too hard and rough for the palate of our delicate theological judge, let him not blame the savor of the doctrine, but his own acerbity and disrelish. And when he attempts to thump into our hearts with all the weight of his iron mallet wielded by his ponderous words that the will of God is one only, which he reveals unto us by his prophets and by Christ, Augustine, by the force of his authority, wards off all the blows of his maul:

> These are the mighty works of the Lord, exquisitely perfect in every point of his will, and so wisely perfect that when the angelic and human natures had sinned—that is, had each done not what God had willed, but what each nature willed, though each nature did that which was contrary to the will of God in one sense—yet God, by the same will of each nature, accomplished what he willed righteously, using as the

supreme good even evil deeds to the eternal condemnation
of those whom he had justly predestinated to everlasting
punishment, and to the eternal salvation of those whom he
had predestinated unto grace. For as far as the former were
concerned, they did that which God willed not, but with reference to the omnipotence of God, which could thus bring
good out of evil, they could not by any means have willed to
do it independently of his omnipotence. For by the very fact
of their acting contrary to the will of God, the will of God
was done through them. For in this omnipotent way of
working consists the mightiness of the works of God so that
by an inexplicable manner of operation, that is not done
without the will of God what is in itself contrary to his will,
because without his will it could not have been done at all.
Yet God wills not unwillingly, but willingly. For as the God
of goodness, he would not suffer evil to be done at all unless,
as the God of omnipotence, he could out of the evil bring
good.

Therefore, let this worthless being hurl all those horrible heresies and blasphemies, which he thus directs against the most godly
ministers of our day, at the head of the eminent Augustine himself.
It is indeed perfectly true that the will of God is to be sought
nowhere but in Scripture. But while this gross hog is rooting up
everything with his snout, he does not consider that, although reverence and sobriety are ever cultivated by the faithful, yet the secret
judgments of God cannot be done away with or reduced to nothing. It is one thing to contemplate and adore that "great deep" [Ps.
36:6] with all the modesty of faith, and quite another to reject it
with contumacy because it at once engulfs all the powers of the human mind that attempt its comprehension. This vile mortal, however, in order that he might do away with all those testimonies of
Scripture, instructed by which we assert the wonderful and glorious providence of God, contents himself with broadly declaring
that all we heretics have ever abused piety, making it a mere cloak,

and have originated under the name of God every kind of evil. Why, if this round assertion is to be deemed sufficient to settle the whole matter, the same may as well be admitted as competent to disprove all heavenly doctrine and to obliterate the name of God altogether.

God's Permission or Sovereign Will?

This worthless being afterwards adds that he can answer every argument we may bring against him in two ways: by showing first that all those passages that seem to attribute the cause of evil to God do not intend his effectual will, but his permitting or his leaving a thing to be done.

Away with that calumny altogether, which is built upon the terms *good* and *evil* when used in discussing God's eternal will and decrees. For we well know that nothing is more contrary to the nature of God than sin. But men act from their own proper wickedness when they sin, so that the whole fault rests with themselves. But to turn all those passages of Scripture (wherein the affection of the mind, in the act, is distinctly described) into a mere permission on the part of God is a frivolous subterfuge and a vain attempt at escape from the mighty truth. The fathers, however, did interpret these passages by the term *permission*; for finding that the apparent asperity of the more direct terms gave offense to some at first hearing, they became anxious to mitigate them by milder expressions. However, in their too great anxiety thus to mitigate, and in their study to avoid giving any such offense, they relaxed something of that fixedness of attention that was due to the great truth itself.

But this worthless being, who professes to be so familiar with the fathers, betrays his utter ignorance of their real minds; for seizing hold of those instances of inexperience in Augustine that I have already alluded to as being found in his writings while he was as yet not deeply versed in the Scriptures, he passes over all those plain and powerful passages wherein Augustine acknowledges the secret judgments of God in their real and actual operations (if I may so express myself) of blinding and hardening the reprobate. The same ignorance and unletteredness is also manifested by this vain being when, on the authority of Hieronymus, he tells us, "When God is spoken of as doing or creating evils, the expressions are figurative." But if evils are nothing more or less than adversities (as is perfectly well known and universally acknowledged), why hunt after a figure in things that are, in themselves, perfectly manifest and plain?

Let us look into the doctrine of permission a little more closely, yet briefly. Joseph is wickedly sold by his brethren. Joseph himself declares that he was sent into Egypt by God through the means of this wickedness, not by his brethren who perpetrated it; and he declares that all this was done by the counsel of God so that the family of his father might be nourished and kept alive [Gen. 50:20]. Now is all this, I ask you, mere permission? Job also testifies that it was God who took away from him all that substance of which the robbers and plunderers had despoiled him [Job 1:21]. Does God's taking away, I ask you, declare no act on the part of God? God is said to have turned the hearts of the Gentiles to hate his people. Shall we say that this was a mere permission on the part of God? Scripture itself expresses the "turning" as a positive and open act of God. So when God is said to deliver men over "to a reprobate mind" and to give them up "to vile affections" [Rom. 1:26, 28], there cannot exist a doubt that those acts of his awful judgments are thereby declared by which he takes righteous vengeance on the reprobate. If God were merely an inactive onlooker while these mighty judgments were being effected, and merely permitted them to be executed, would he, by such mere permission of an observer, really execute the office of a judge? God calls Nebuchadnezzar the "axe in my hand" [Jer. 51:20]; he terms also the Assyrian the "staff of my indignation" [Isa. 10:5]; all wicked men he designates his "rod"; and he positively declares that by means of these he will do what he has decreed to do. What place will mere permission find here? Jeremiah, addressing the Chaldeans, exclaims, "Cursed be he that doeth the work of the Lord deceitfully, and cursed be he that keepeth back his sword from blood" [Jer. 48:10]. Behold! Whatever cruelty these bloody men commit, the prophet in another sense calls the work of God, because God by their hand executed his vengeance on the Babylonians. David in like manner testifies that whatever evil he was suffering, it was God who did it and that therefore he was "dumb" [Ps. 39:9]. By what figures or tropes, I ask you, will any man convert the words *did it* into *permitted it*, or make the doing a thing merely the permitting it to be done? Paul likewise declares that it is God who "sends upon the wicked strong delusions that they should believe a lie" [2 Thess. 2:11]. Where, therefore, the "effectual working" [Eph. 3:7] of God appears manifest, as it does here, by what alchemy or contrivance will anyone extract from such "effectual working" the divine will and purpose?

This preeminent theological teacher and judge prescribes as a canon for the interpretation of such passages as "Thou art not a God that hath pleasure in wickedness" [Ps. 5:4], that such texts are intended for all who seem to attribute evil to God. But what has this at all to do with the present question? No spot of iniquity is affixed by us on God. All we affirm is quite the reverse. All we maintain throughout our arguments is that God rules and overrules all the actions of the world with perfect and divine rectitude. If any one of us sundered the power of God from his justice, then indeed we should lay ourselves justly open to the tacit censure of those who continually and reproachfully repeat to us, "There is nothing more contrary to the power of God than tyranny." But now, while we make God "to have no pleasure in wickedness," is he, under this pretext, to be torn from his throne as the judge of the world and as having no omnipotence whereby to work good by means of evil men and their evil deeds? For the fact is that since God frequently works out his judgments by the hands of the wicked, whoever shall confine him within the bounds of permission will at once expel him from his office as judge of the world. The sons of Eli had evilly and disgracefully abused their priestly office, and they perished by the hand of the Philistines. By the canon of our great theologian, we must interpret this as meaning that all was done by the permission of God. But Scripture says that all was done because God had purposed to destroy them. Just observe to what extent of madness all madmen are driven by their madness where there is no religion, no modesty, and no shame to stop them. They rush on until they bring not only men, but God also, under subjection to their frenzied fictions.

As it would be utterly absurd to hold that anything could be done contrary to the will of God, seeing that God is at divine liberty to prevent what he does not will to be done, let us now explain in a few words how ingenious a workman this being is in getting rid of the argument that stands against him. He first of all asserts that it is ridiculous to inquire into this at all. What a pity it was that Augustine had not such a monitor by his side to save him all the holy labor he spent upon this great question, and by which labor, according to our theological hero, he made himself "perfectly ridiculous."

Whereas Augustine proves, by this very argument, that everything done on earth is effectually ruled and overruled by this secret providence of God. Nor does he hesitate to conclude that everything is done by the will of God. According to this conclusion, the psalmist testifies that God, sitting in heaven, does what he will: "But our God is in the heavens; he hath done whatsoever he hath pleased" [Ps. 115:3]. But why, I ask you, is this question a ridiculous one? Our great theological monitor replies, "Because it is not lawful to ask of God a reason for his actions." Why does not our modest monitor, then, retain this great modesty throughout his treatment of this mighty matter? Whence arise, then, this modest being's furious clamors and tumults? Whence but from the fact that the proud and ignorant reject, with hatred and disdain, the counsels of God? Certainly because their puny minds cannot grasp their profundity and immensity. Leave, then, to God the liberty to order all things according to his own will, and all strife about the matter will end at once. But it is just and right that madmen should be left thus to contend one with the other so that they may put an end to each other by a mutual destruction.

Are Many Things Done Contrary to the Will of God?

Here we are brought back to the old point of vain defense resorted to by our theological hero: "Many things are done contrary to the will of God." This we most willingly grant, provided that this contradiction to the will of God be not carried too far. God, for instance, often willed to call the Jews together, "but they would not" [Matt. 23:37; Luke 13:34], though he called them to himself by his prophets, "rising up early," as he himself forcibly expresses it [Jer. 7:13]. But as conversion is God's peculiar gift, he converts effectually those whom he wills to be converted in reality. In what sense is it that Paul says, "God will have all men to be saved" [1 Tim. 2:4]? As we have observed and explained before, let readers learn from the context. There are different degrees and kinds of salvation, as we have shown when opening this passage. But God does not deem all men (as we have before shown from the history of the world and from the few nations to whom God sent even his external word) worthy of the external word, and they are few whom he makes the partakers of his secret illumination.

Notion of Free Will

To extricate himself more easily from his perplexity, this unworthy mortal finally catches up for his defense the shield of free will. He says, "There is no wonder whatever in God's not preventing men from doing evil, who have the free will to do what they please," whereas that is the mighty wonder. And it is resolvable only by the sublime truth and its doctrine that whatever men do, they do it according to the eternal will and secret purpose of God. Why does this vain being thrust upon us a term fabricated out of nothing? What is free will when Scripture everywhere declares that man, being the captive, the servant, and the slave of the devil, is carried away into wickedness of every kind with his whole mind and inclination, being utterly incapable of understanding the things of God, much less of doing them?

In this refutation of dogfaced dishonesty, as the omnipotence of God is honestly and clearly maintained against calumnies of every kind, I feel confident that I have humbly performed a work both useful and gratifying to the church and also acceptable unto God.

Reply to the Slanderous Reports

Calumniator's Preface to Certain Articles, that is, Calumnies, Purporting to Be Extracted from the Writings of John Calvin

You are a man, John Calvin, now known throughout almost the whole world. Your doctrine has many favorers and supporters, but it has also many enemies and opponents. For myself, being one who earnestly wishes that there were but one doctrine, as there is but one truth, and who greatly desires to see all men agree, if it were possible, in that one doctrine, I have thought that you ought to be informed, in a friendly manner, of those things which are everywhere spoken against your doctrine; that if false, you might refute them and might have an opportunity of sending your refutation to me so that I might be able to make a stand against your adversaries. And I ask that you would frame your refutation of such arguments as may be plainly understood by the people.

There are indeed many who differ from you in many things. For the present, however, I will leave all other questions to other times, and I will deal with you upon that one great subject: the doctrine of fate, or predestination. For this one question is exciting vast disturbances in the church, all of which I would be glad to see quieted, and the arguments of your opponents on this mighty matter are so forcible that they cannot be refuted out of any of your books that you have hitherto published.

Certain articles connected with this vast question have been extracted from your books and spread abroad in all directions. These articles I will now place before you without any regularity of order, and to each article I will subjoin the arguments which your opponents advance against it. By this arrangement you will at once see what reply you are called upon to make.

John Calvin's Reply to the Calumniator's Preface

That there are many adversaries to my doctrine I know full well and wonder not. For it is no new thing that brawlers on every side should open their mouths against Christ, under whose banner I fight. My only grief in the sacred matter is that through my feeble side the solemn and eternal truth of God is stabbed, which ought to be looked upon with reverence and adoration by the whole world. But since I see that this same truth of God has ever, from the beginning, been exposed to the calumnies of the wicked, and that Christ himself by the decree of his heavenly Father must ever be a "rock of offence" and of contradiction [Rom. 9:33; Isa. 8:14, 15], I consider that the defenders of the truth must bear this offense with all patience. No fierce bites of the wicked, however, will at any time cause me to repent of the doctrine that I have taught, because I feel fully assured that God is its origin and author. Nor have I profited so little by those numerous conflicts in which God himself has caused me to be engaged, as now to be alarmed by your empty and futile noises.

As far as you are concerned, poor masked monitor, I derive some consolation from the thought that you cannot be ungrateful towards the man who has treated you with much greater kindness than you deserved at his hands, without betraying at the same time your foul wickedness against God. I know quite well that there is no sport more grateful to your academics than the rooting out of all faith from the hearts of the godly by casting a shade of doubt over all that they hold dear. And the sweet pleasure that you derive from all those revilings that you direct against the secret providence of God is apparent from the very point of your pen, however much you strive to hide your base gratification. But I summon you and all your fellows before that tribunal on which the judge of heaven sits, from whose mouth the blast and the bolt shall one day fall upon you all and lay you prostrate. I trust, however, that I myself, before I am done, shall make your insolent speaking against God to be as loathsome to the feelings of all good and godly men as they are inwardly gratifying to your own heart.

You demand of me a refutation of that vain scribble of yours, which you sent secretly to Paris from a town in Switzerland, in order that poison might be poured upon my name far and wide without my knowing it and without the possibility of the application of a remedy. Nevertheless, you feign the desire of learning the truth, and yet you conceal your name, for what end I know not unless it is that you well knew that I had it in my power at once to destroy any credit that men might be disposed to give either to yourself or to your fellows. In a moment I could conjecture, or rather determine, who you were from many evidences furnished by your book. But whether you wrote it with your own hand or dictated it to Scotus, the trumpeter employed by your band of madmen, that he might carry to Paris things that you dared not utter here, is a matter of utter unconcern to me. I would, indeed, that some other were the author of the book or that you yourself were another man from what you are. But that will never be until you shall have once tasted what true virtue and honesty are. For although you have ever spoken respectfully to me, yet how great your natural propensity to cavil is I have no difficulty in discovering and being fully assured. This evil inclination that you have indulged in, so many puerile and futile exhibitions of it I have endeavored to correct, but in vain, because to that natural propensity there was always appended a depraved affectation, which led you to hunt after the praise for learning and wit, even by the most frigid and more than insipid attempts at jesting on divine subjects. Nor can you by any means cover your vain attempts under the shadow of the authority of Socrates, who (you say) was accustomed to attack with sharp sarcasm many things that were said against his doctrines. That excellent man was endowed with many eminent virtues, all of which, however, he marred the brightness of by this one frailty and defect, which you thus, with as much failure as anxiety, attempt to imitate.

Moreover, you ask me to send you a refutation of your vain script as shall be understood by the people. I have never done otherwise than study to accommodate myself to the capacity of the most humble and unlettered reader by adopting the purest and simplest language of instruction. But if you will acknowledge no other mode of reasoning than that which the natural mind of an earthly mortal can receive, you at once shut up against yourself, by pride and disdain, the only way of approach to the comprehension of that doctrine, to the knowledge of which the first step is reverence. I am by no means ignorant of the sarcastic sneers of yourself and of all like you who treat the deep mysteries of God with a contempt that indicates, in your estimation, that everything loses its grace and authority that does not at once meet your opinion and approbation. For what is the meaning of all this: The moment anyone chooses to open his mouth against me, I must be called upon to furnish a refutation of his slanders? Socrates, whose name you thus brandish before you, would not have suffered himself to be put in such a position. He would not have yielded to anyone dictating such a law to him. Not that I would follow any man in everything. But if anyone, not only in this but also in any other age, was ever permitted constantly to set himself with indignation against the wicked and to refute their calumnies against him as Socrates did, surely even the most malevolent and iniquitous will grant me also a fair opportunity of exercising the same kind of diligence in my defense. Your barking, therefore, is the more intolerable, for you trample with blind ignorance on my numerous books of self-defense and of reply to my adversaries, and you call upon me to do the same work of refutation twice or thrice over.

However, you affirm that there is one question in particular on which the arguments of my enemies are too powerful to be refuted by the contents of any of my books that I have written on the subject. That question, you say, is the great subject of predestination or fate. I wish that you could resolve either to inquire into that subject modestly or to argue upon it honestly rather than to cast off all shame and to confound, in one, things that are the most diverse from each other in order to prevent all true light from falling upon them. *Fate* is a term given by the Stoics to their doctrine of necessity, which they had formed out of a multiplex labyrinth of contradictory reasonings—a doctrine calculated to call God himself to order and to set him laws whereby to work. *Predestination* I define, according to the Holy Scriptures, as that free and unfettered counsel of God by which he rules all mankind, all men and things, and all parts and particles of the world by his infinite wisdom and incomprehensible justice. If the depravity of mind and the lust of cavils and diabolical pride have so blinded you that you can see nothing in the midday light, to readers who really have eyes that can see, the distinction I have laid down immediately shows the great injustice and inequity of your quarrelling with God in the profound matter of his secret providence.

Added to this, had you but been willing to look into my books, you would have been convinced at once how offensive to me is the profane term *fate;* indeed, you would have learned in reading my writings that this same abhorrent term was cast in the teeth of Augustine by the malignity and hatred of the wicked and the worthless of his day. You would also have discovered in my testimony that these objections were replied to by that holy father and godly teacher in a manner that would fully answer every purpose of my own cause and defense upon the present occasion.

In your articles also (purporting to be extracts from my books), which you say you will give the public in your proposed order, you will find that my manner and substance of argument are precisely the same as those of that holy father of happy memory. Malevolent ones, however, knowing that this doctrine was not well known nor generally received, have boastingly published abroad these articles, which are partly false and partly mutilated, so that the ignorant and inexperienced might be fired with hatred of their contents and might not be able to form any but the most unfavorable judgment concerning them. And though many persons thought, at the first sight of them, that the articles put forth in Augustine's day were really extracts from his writings, yet the holy father bitterly complains that they were imputed to him falsely. For the compilers of them had either put together short portions of sentences with evil industry or had with wicked art corrupted sentences that were whole, true, and godly by the crafty introduction of a few words, thus wholly altering the original in order to create offense in the minds of the simple. All honest and sincere readers (many of whom will gladly take the pains to compare my doctrine with your base calumnies) will discover that the articles that you now boast you will put forth as extracted from my writings are of precisely the same description as those published abroad in Augustine's day, purporting to be true extracts from his books.

First of all, I take this stand against you: You act neither kindly nor honestly in not affixing any marks of designation or reference to the passages purporting to be extracts from my books so that readers might refer to the originals and assure themselves that I really had written as the extracts represent. And what can be more iniquitous than to state confusingly that in the course of fifty or more volumes written by me, some fourteen articles were found of such and such a description? Now had you possessed one drop of common honesty, you would have cited, as a matter of course, my sentences verbatim; or if you had met with any doubt or danger in so doing, from want of the realities and originals, you would have warned your readers against the doubtfulness of the text in such cases, whereas now you cast a shade of doubt over all my writings together, hoping thereby to destroy all good memory of them from the earth. And thus, so that my books, which might have been read

without any offense at all, you have for your own convenience malignantly corrupted and exposed to hatred and contempt. Although
I do not altogether condemn Augustine for his prudence, where
wishing to meet the craft and iniquity of his enemies he tempers
his modes of reply to them in order to escape odium, according to
my views, my reply to you will be more generally useful in this great
cause if I refute your revilings freely, openly, and unreservedly than
if I write so as to convey the least idea of retreat or desertion.

Articles [Purported to be] Extracted from the Latin and French Books of John Calvin on Predestination

ARTICLE I
God of his pure and mere will created the greatest part of the
world to perdition.

Statements and Observations of the Calumniator

This is the first article I shall produce. Now hear what arguments are brought by your adversaries against it.

Your opponents maintain that this article is contrary to nature
and to Scripture. With respect to nature, they affirm that every animal loves its own offspring. Now this nature is given of God,
whence it follows that God also loves his own offspring; for God
would not cause all animals to love their own offspring unless he
himself loved his own offspring. And this position they prove in the
following manner from Isaiah 66:9: "Shall I bring to the birth, and
not cause to bring forth?" As if he had said, "That which I cause
others to do, I also do myself. Now I cause others to bring forth;
therefore, I also bring forth."

By a parity of reasoning, therefore, they derive this argument
and its conclusion: God causes all animals to love their own off-

spring. Therefore, he himself also loves his own offspring. Now all men are the offspring of God, for God is the Father of Adam, from whom all men sprung. However, to create men to perdition is not an act of love, but of hatred. Therefore, God did not create anyone to perdition.

Again, they argue: "Creation is a work of love, not of hatred. Therefore, God created all men in love, not in hatred."

And again, "No beast is so cruel (to say nothing of man) that it would desire to create its young to misery. How much less, then, shall such a desire be found in God? Would not God in such a case of creation be less kind and merciful than the wolf that he has created?"

Christ argues in this way: "If ye then, being evil, know how to give good gifts unto your children, how much more shall God?" [Matt. 7:11]. It is thus just that your adversaries argue. They say, "If Calvin, though an evil man, would not wish to beget a child unto misery, how much less shall God desire to do so?" These and like arguments your opponents bring forward with respect to nature.

But with reference to Scripture, they reason thus: God saw that "all things" which he had made were "very good" [Gen. 1:31]. Such, therefore, was man, whom also he had made "very good." But what if God created him to destruction? If such be the case, God created that which "was very good" to destruction and perdition, and therefore he must love to destroy. But that is a thing impious, even in thought.

Again, they argue: God created one man and placed him in paradise, which is a life of happiness. Therefore, God created all men for a happy life, for all men were created in the one man. And if all men fell in Adam, it follows that all men stood in Adam and in the very condition in which Adam stood. Further, God says, "I would not the death of a sinner"; and it is written, "God willeth not that any should perish, but that all men should come to the knowledge of the truth."[22] Further, if God created the greatest part of the

---

22. The first part of this "quotation" is from 2 Peter 3:9; the last part is a paraphrase of 1 Tim. 2:4.

world to perdition, it follows that his anger is greater than his mercy, and it consequently follows also that his anger is shown "unto the third and fourth generation" [Ex. 20:5; Num. 14:18]. Whereas, on the contrary, "it is evident" that his mercy extends "even unto the thousandth generation."

Reply of John Calvin

That on which you seize as your first article is that God, *of his pure and mere will, created the greatest part of the world to perdition*. All this — *the greatest part of the world unto perdition* and *of his own pure and mere will* — is a perfect fiction and a production from the workshop of your own brain. For although God did certainly decree from the beginning everything that should befall the race of man, yet such a manner of speech as the saying that the end or object of God's work of creation was destruction or perdition is nowhere to be found in my writings. Just like an unclean hog, therefore, you root up with your foul snout all doctrine that is of sweet odor, hoping to find in it something filthy and offensive.

Next, although my doctrine is that the will of God is the first and supreme cause of all things, I everywhere teach that wherever in his counsels and works the cause does not plainly appear, yet that there is a cause which lies hidden in God, and that according to it he has decreed nothing except what is wise, holy, and just. Therefore, with reference to the sentiments of the schoolmen concerning the absolute, or tyrannical, will of God, I not only repudiate but also abhor them all, because they separate the justice of God from his ruling power. See, then, you unclean dog, how much you have gained and how far you have advanced your cause by your impudent barking. For myself, while I subject the whole human race to the will of God, at the same time I ever affirm that God never decrees anything but with the most righteous reason, which (though it may at the present time be unknown to us) will assuredly be revealed to us at the last day in all its infinite righteousness and divine perfection.

You thrust in my face and impudently upbraid me with the *pure and mere will* of God, an idea that I in a hundred or more passages of my books utterly repudiate. Meanwhile, I freely acknowledge my doctrine to be this: Adam fell not only by the permission of God, but also by his secret counsel and decree; and by his fall Adam drew all his posterity with himself into eternal destruction. Both of these positions, it seems, give you great offense as being, according to your account, "contrary to nature and to Scripture." You attempt to prove it to be contrary to nature because every animal naturally loves its own offspring; therefore, you argue that God, who gave such a natural affection to brute beasts, certainly ought not to love all men less because they are his offspring. Your argument and thought are infinitely too coarse and low, and infinitely beneath the mightiness of the matter when you demand of God, the eternal author of nature, just what he rightfully demands of the ox and the ass that he has created. As if God himself ought to be bound by the same laws as those he has appointed for the creatures that he has made! In order that every animal might propagate its own kind, he has implanted in each animal the desire of that propagation. Go, then, and expostulate with God and ask him how it is that from all eternity he has remained content with himself and has retained his own native excellency and glory, barren, as it were, and unpropagated. God ought certainly ever to be consistent with himself. Therefore, if you are to be our judge in this mighty and stupendous matter, God has violated the order by choosing to be without all offspring rather than to exercise his fruitfulness.

Moreover, as all brute beasts fight for their offspring, even unto death, how is it (according to your doctrine) that God permits his helpless offspring to be torn in pieces and devoured by tigers and bears and lions and wolves? Is it because his hand is too short, so that he cannot stretch it down out of heaven for their defense? Do you not see how wide a field lies open to me if I were inclined to expose and condemn all your idle and absurd reasonings? But I will content myself with dwelling on one point only, and let that suffice. Proofs of the love of God toward the whole human race exist innumerable, all of which demonstrate the ingratitude of those who perish or come "to perdition." This fact, however, forms no reason whatever that God should not confine his special or peculiar love to a few whom he has in infinite condescension been pleased to choose out of the rest.

When God was pleased to adopt unto himself the family of Abraham, he thereby most plainly testified that he did not embrace the whole of mankind with an equal love. When, again, God rejected Esau, the elder, and chose Jacob, the younger brother, he gave a manifest and signal proof of his free love, of that love with which he loves none others than those whom he will. Moses declares aloud that one certain nation was beloved of God, while all other nations were passed by and disregarded as to any peculiar love of God for them. The prophets everywhere testify that the Jews exceeded and surpassed all other nations in excellency and importance for no other reason than God freely loved them.

Again, Christ is not addressing the whole human race, nor indeed the whole Jewish nation, but God's little chosen flock alone when he says, and not in vain, "Fear not, little flock; for it is your Father's good pleasure to give you the kingdom" [Luke 12:32]. By this Christ intimates that none experience the favor of God unto the hope of eternal life but those whom he has rendered acceptable and well-pleasing unto himself by his only begotten Son. But if you are determined to make God subject to the laws of nature, you must necessarily accuse and condemn him of injustice because, on account of the fault of one man, we are all involved in the guilt and just desert of eternal death. One man sinned, and we are all dragged to punishment. And not only that, but by the pollution of one we are all drawn into the contagion and are born corrupt and infected with a deadly disease. What have you to say to this noble teacher and judge? Will you accuse the blessed God of cruelty because he has thus precipitated all his offspring into ruin by the fall of one man? For although Adam destroyed both himself and all his offspring, the corruption and guilt of the fall of one man must necessarily be ascribed to the secret counsel and decree of God. For the fault of one man could have had nothing to do with us had not our heavenly judge been pleased to consign us to eternal destruction on that account.

Only reflect for a moment how craftily you apply those passages of the prophet Isaiah as a covering for your error [Isa. 49:19–21; Isa. 54:1, et al.]. As it seemed beyond all belief that the church of God in her Babylonian captivity, being not only bereft of her children but also barren in her power to produce more, should, by the recovery of her strength, become even more fruitful than she was before, God in these passages speaks, as it were, thus to her: "Am not I, by whose power women conceive and bring forth, able to raise up an offspring to thee also?" Because God speaks thus to his church, you, under this pretext, would force him to assume the affections of any kind of animal. And you daringly reason that because God causes all animals to love their own offspring, he also loves all his own offspring, namely, the whole race of mankind. And suppose for a moment that I grant you this; it will not, therefore, at once follow that God loves his own in the same manner as beasts love their own. And if God does love his own, it does not the less follow that he has a right to reject, as a just judge, those to whom he had in vain shown his love and indulgence throughout their whole lives as the kindest Father.

But you are ready to reply, "To create is a work of love, not of hatred, and God therefore, created in love, not in hatred." However, you perceive not that although all men are hateful to God in fallen Adam, in their original creation the love of God shines in all its brightness. That argument, therefore, which you think is so plausible, any other person endowed with the most moderate judgment and common equity immediately acknowledges to be frivolous and vain.

That which you add next, I do not consider it my duty to refute as to cut down at once with the stroke of the sword. It is indeed evident that men are born to misery, but is the cause of this to be imputed to my writings? Whence arises this miserable condition of us all, that we are subject not only to temporal evils, but also to eternal death? Does it not arise from the solemn fact that by the fall and fault of one man, God was pleased to cast us all under the common guilt? In this miserable ruin of the whole human race, therefore, it is not my opinion only that is plainly seen, but also it is the work of God himself that is so openly and undeniably manifest.

Meanwhile, you hesitate not to vomit forth your profane and abhorrent opinion that God, who thus wills to create men to misery, is worse than any wolf. Some men, be it remembered, are born blind, some deaf, some dumb, and some of monstrous deformity. If we are to go by your opinion as the judge in these sacred and deep matters, God is also cruel because he afflicts his offspring with such evils as these, and that before they have seen the light. But be assured, the day will come when you will heartily wish that you had been blind rather than being so wonderfully sharp-sighted in thus penetrating into these secrets of the eternal God.

You accuse God of injustice; indeed, you declare him to be nothing above a monster if he dares to decree anything concerning men otherwise than we ourselves should determine concerning our own children. If so, how shall we account for God's creating some dull of comprehension, others of greater incapacity, and others quite idiots? Do you really think that the work of God's creation, with reference to such imperfect mortals, was really according to the fables of some Jews about the fauns and satyrs? For they say that God was prevented from completing the form of these latter monsters by the intervention of the Sabbath, and therefore that they fell half-made from his hands. No. It rather becomes us to receive a deep and humbling lesson from such sad spectacles as these defective human beings and not to commence a quarrel with the maker of heaven and earth from the conceptions of our own brain concerning his works, or what in our opinion they ought to have been. When any idiot happens to meet me, I am admonished to reflect upon what God might have made me, had he been so pleased. As many dull of comprehension and idiots as there are in the world, so many spectacles does God set before me in which to behold his power, which is not less a subject of awe than a subject of wonder.

But as for you, you brawl against God with all impiety and profanity as being less merciful than a wolf because, in your opinion, he has so little considered the good and happiness of his offspring. Before the saying of Christ—"God, because he is good, acts more kindly towards his children than men do, who are evil" [Matt. 7:11]—can be called in to favor your opinions and arguments, you must prove that all men are equally the children of God. But it is evident that all men lost eternal life in Adam, and that therefore the adoption of God is an act of special grace. From this it will follow that all those are hated of God who are thus estranged and alienated from him. All the testimonies of Scripture that you cite are mere javelins hurled at random by the hand of a madman, as where you quote: "And God saw every thing that he had made, and behold it was very good" [Gen. 1:31]. For from this text you conclude that man was also "very good." And from this you next infer that God was unjust in creating for perdition that which was "good."

In what sense, however, man was created upright by nature I have explained in many parts of my writings. Man certainly was not better than the devil was before the devil lost his angelic uprightness. Now, suppose I were to cede to you for a moment that both men and apostate angels were created unto salvation, and yet that God, having respect to their future fall, condemned both to eternal destruction. What would you gain from this concession to help you in supporting your arguments? God most certainly knew what would take place, both in men and in apostate angels, and he decreed at the same time what he would do.

With reference to the doctrine of permission, we will speak of that hereafter in its place. But for the present, if you should be disposed to reply that the foreknowledge of God is not the cause of evils, I would ask you only this one question: If God foresaw the destruction both of man and of the devil before he created them, and did not at the same time decree their destruction, why did he not apply, betimes, an adequate remedy that should prevent their fall and their liability thereto? The devil, from the very beginning of the world, alienated himself from the hope of salvation. And man, as soon as he was created, destroyed both himself and his posterity with a deadly destruction. If, therefore, the preservation of both was in the hand of God, how was it that (if he had not decreed their destruction) he permitted their ruin? Moreover, why did he not furnish each with at least some small degree of ability to stand? To whatever circuitous reasonings you have recourse, therefore, I shall be able to hold you fast to this principle: Although man was created weak and liable to fall, this weakness contained in it a great blessing, because man's fall immediately afterwards taught him that nothing outside of God is either safe, secure, or enduring. Hence it is made evident that all you prate about men having been created unto salvation is an argument mutilated and halt and laid down without adequate consideration. For the truth is that when I am confessing that there was nothing in man, when created, contrary to salvation, I am thereby and therein proving that salvation was predestinated for all men.

Let me repeat this same argument very briefly in other words. What I mean is that if we argue on that perfection of nature with which Adam was gifted at his first creation, we may say that he was created unto salvation, because in that perfection of his first created state, there was found no cause of death. But if we carry the question up to God's secret predestination, we are met by that deep abyss that ought at once to transport us into wonder and admiration. The fact is that had you but been gifted with the least feeling of godly reverence, you would immediately acknowledge that this is not a question concerning the completeness of man's original perfection, but concerning the will and decree of God. The state of the sacred case is as if the Holy Spirit had said to you, "Nothing of excellency was wanting in any of the creatures at their creation, but all occasion was taken away from you, and from all like you, of contending against God." For however loudly you and yours may deny that there was any "good" in man's being so created and conditioned that he should by his immediate fall destroy himself and the whole world, yet God himself declares that such a condition of things pleased him. Therefore, it was most just and righteous.

And that you may the more correctly understand Moses, he

does not (remember!) declare how upright and perfect man was, but in order to stop the barkings of all dogs like yourself, he teaches that the whole order of the creation was so tempered of God that nothing more just or perfect can be imagined. Therefore, when Moses comes to speak of all the several works of God collectively, he says, "God saw everything that he had made, and behold it was very good" [Gen. 1:31]. But Moses affirms no such thing concerning man, individually, specially, and absolutely, in every sense. Having narrated man's creation, the sacred historian concludes by saying, in words applying generally to the whole creation, that all the things God had made were "very good." In these words are doubtlessly to be comprehended, as in harmony with them, the words of Solomon, where he affirms that the wicked were created for the day of evil: "The Lord hath made all things for himself; yea, even the wicked for the day of evil" [Prov. 16:4].

Take, then, the sum of the whole matter to be this: Although man at his first creation was in his newly created nature "good," this rectitude, which was weak, frail, and liable to fall, militates not against, nor stands contrary to, the predestination of God, by which predestination man perished by his own sin and fault, although his nature was pure by creation. Looking at and arguing from his primitive natural excellency, man was created in this view and sense to salvation. Yet from this line of argument, you vainly, absurdly, and preposterously infer that man was created "good" so that he might perish though "good," or as a good man. Whereas, it is openly and undeniably manifest that he perished by his infirmity and sin, and therefore that he perished as one liable to righteous condemnation and destruction. How these two propositions and positions agree and harmonize with each other we will show hereafter, as we have indeed shown again and again before.

Here you throw in the common objection: "God has no pleasure in the death of a sinner," as declared by the prophet Ezekiel [18:23, 32; 33:11]. But listen, I ask you, to what in the prophet immediately follows: "Because God inviteth all men to repentance" [Ezek. 18:30–32]. To all such, therefore, as return into the way of life, pardon is freely offered. The next and principal thing to be considered is whether the conversion or "returning" that God requires [v. 30] is in the power of man's free will or is a peculiar and sovereign gift of God. Inasmuch, therefore, as all men are invited and exhorted by God to repentance, the prophet, on that ground, justly declares that God "hath no pleasure in the death of a sinner."

Why it is that God does not turn or convert all men to himself, equally and alike, is a question the reply to which lies hidden in himself. And as to your usual way of citing the passage of the apostle Paul — "God would have all men to be saved and to come to the knowledge of the truth" [1 Tim. 2:4], how vain a prop to put under your error to support it. I think I have already shown this with sufficient plainness and that repeatedly. For it is, so to speak, more certain than certainty itself that the apostle is not in that passage speaking of individuals, but of orders of men in their various civil and national vocations. He had just before commanded that the public prayers of the church should be offered up for kings, others in authority, and for all who held magisterial offices, of what kind and degree they may be. But as nearly all those who were then armed with the sword of public justice were open and professed enemies of the church, and as it might therefore seem to the church singular or absurd that public prayers should be offered for them, the apostle meets all objections, so very natural, by admonishing the church to pray even for them and to supplicate God to extend his grace and favor even to them for the church's quiet, peace, and safety.

There is, perhaps, a stronger color in some of the words of Peter, which might have better suited your purposes, where he says that God is "not willing that any should perish, but that all should come to repentance" [2 Pet. 3:9]. And if there be anything in the first part of the passage that seems difficult of comprehension at first sight, it is made perfectly plain by the explanation that follows. For insofar as God "willeth that all should come to repentance," insofar does he will that no one should perish. In order that they may thus be received of God, they must "come" [John 6:37, 44]. Scripture everywhere affirms, however, that in order to come, they must be prevented of God; that is, God must come first to draw them, for until they are drawn of God, they will remain where they are, given up to the obstinacy of the flesh.

If there were one single particle of right judgment in you, you would immediately acknowledge that there is a wide and wonderful difference between these two things: The hearts of men are made by God "fleshly" out of "stony" hearts [Ezek. 11:19], and thus they are made to be displeased and dissatisfied with themselves and are brought as suppliants to beg of God mercy and pardon; after they are thus changed, they are received into all grace. God declares that both these things are of his pure goodness and mercy. He gives us hearts that we may repent and then pardons us graciously upon our repentance and supplication. For if God were not ready to receive us when we do truly implore his mercy, he would not say, "Turn ye unto me, and I will turn unto you" [Zech. 1:3]. If repentance were in the power of the free will of man, Paul would not say, "If peradventure God will give them repentance to the acknowledging of the truth" [2 Tim. 2:25]. In truth, if God himself, who exhorts all men to repentance by his voice—if God himself, I repeat, who thus exhorts, did not draw his elect by the secret operation of his Spirit, Jeremiah would not thus describe those who do return: "Turn thou me, and I shall be turned; for thou art the Lord my God. Surely after that I was turned, I repented" [Jer. 31:18, 19]. I repeat that the solution of the matter—if there were any shame or modesty in so impudent a dog as yourself—ought to have been known to you as existing in my writings in a hundred different places. Although you may take it upon yourself to reject such a solution, it nevertheless stands supported and confirmed both by the apostle Paul and by the prophet Ezekiel.

How and in what sense God wills all men to be saved is a matter not here to be inquisitively discussed. One thing is certain: These two things—salvation and the knowledge of the truth—are always inseparably joined together. Now, then, answer me: If God had willed that his truth should be known unto all men, how is it that from the first preaching of the gospel until now, so many nations exist unto whom his pure truth has never been sent by him and unto whom, therefore, it has never come? Again, if such had been the will of God concerning all men, how is it that he never opened the eyes of all? For the internal illumination of the Spirit, with which God has condescended to bless so few, is indispensably necessary unto faith. There is also another knot for you to untie: Since no one but he who is drawn by the secret influence of the Spirit can approach unto God, how is it that God does not draw all men indiscriminately to himself if he really "wills all men to be saved," in the common meaning of the expression? [1 Tim. 2:4].

It is, therefore, an evident conclusion, flowing from this discrimination that God makes: There is with him a secret reason that he shut so many out from salvation. How it is, then, that the mercy of God is shown unto the thousandth generation, you will never acknowledge as long as the pride by which you are inflated blinds and blunts your faculties. For no such mercy is promised as that which shall utterly abolish the curse under which the whole race of Adam lies; yet such a mercy is promised as shall, where all naturally existing obstacles are removed, break forth and endure forever upon the most unworthy.

In this manner God passed by many of the children of Abraham when he chose one of them: Isaac. So also, when the twin sons of Isaac were born, the same God willed that his mercy should rest on one of them only: Jacob. Again, although God shows forth proofs of his wrath in many, it nevertheless remains eternally true that he is "abundant in goodness" and "slow to anger" [Ex. 34:6; Ps. 103:8; Rom. 2:4]. Therefore, in that very longsuffering with which God endures the reprobate, there shines forth no dim refulgence of his great goodness. Observe, then, in what an effectual manner your frivolous and captious objections, from which I can disengage myself in a moment, do entangle, ensnare, and imprison you.

In order to make the mercy of God greater than his anger, you desire to have more chosen to salvation than to destruction. Suppose I should for a moment cede this to you. What greater glory will thereby be secured to God? None whatever. God will nevertheless be as unjust as ever to those few who are lost (if your calumnies are to be received and believed). Unless God loves all his created offspring alike, you will still profanely and awfully pronounce him to be less kind and merciful than a wolf. If there be but one person only against whom God shall righteously exercise his wrath, how shall God escape or avoid the accusation of cruelty in your blind and unholy judgment? Further still, you will not even allow as exceptions from the impious and profane charges of cruelty in God that there are gross provocations of his divine wrath in the men themselves. But comparing alone wrath with mercy, you merely contend for the magnitude of the one or the other, just as if God, by choosing more to salvation than to destruction, would thereby alone prove himself to be a merciful God. However, God commends the greatness of his grace to us in a manner far different from this. He not only pardons so many and such various sins in his elect, but even contends with and bears with the obstinate malice of the reprobate until it has filled up the measure of its iniquity [Matt. 23:32].

ARTICLE 2

God not only predestinated even Adam to damnation, but to the causes of that damnation also, whose fall he not only foresaw, but he also willed by his secret and eternal decree and ordained that he should fall, which fall, that it might in its time take place, God placed before him the apple that should cause that fall.

Statements and Observations of the Calumniator

Your opponents say that this second article is the doctrine of the devil, and they demand Calvin to tell them where in the divine Scriptures the substance contained in this article is written.

Reply of John Calvin

Under this second article you appear again exactly the same man as before. Now just produce the passage from my writings where I teach that the apple was placed by God before Adam, that it might be the cause of his fall. This, in fact, is the very source of all your popularity—the drawing of a cloud of obscurity across the minds of the inexperienced to prevent them from rising to the height of the truth that is removed out of the reach of the common understanding of the flesh and of the carnal mind.

But not to wrangle about words, I willingly and immediately confess that what I have written is this: "The fall of Adam was not by accident, nor by chance, but was ordained by the secret counsel of God." And this is the doctrine that you positively pronounce to be "the doctrine of the devil." You are in your own eyes, I know, a judge of the highest authority, and therefore it is in your self-conceit that you imagine you can, by five words of the foulest abuse, knock down that firm fabric of truth that I have erected and supported by the most impregnable arguments. You call upon me to produce a testimony from Scripture where it is manifest that Adam did not fall except by the secret decree of God. Had you read even a few pages of my writings with any attention, that sentiment of mine could not have escaped you which everywhere occurs in my books—that God governs all things by his secret counsel and decree. You ascribe a prescience to God after your own fashion, representing him as sitting in heaven as an idle, inactive, unconcerned spectator of all things in the life of men.

Contrary to this, God himself, ever vindicating to himself the right and the act of holding the helm of all things that are done in the whole world, never permits a separation of his prescience from his power. This manner of reasoning is not mine only, but most certainly is Augustine's also. That holy father says,

If God foresaw what he did not will to be done, he holds not the supreme rule over all things. God, therefore, ordained that which should come to pass, because nothing could have been done had he not willed it to be done.

If you judge this to be absurd, you will be just as far off as before and will fall back into the same confusion into which you fell by making my doctrine to be "the doctrine of the devil," for you ought to have applied that remedy for your evil case that might have been ready at your hand. But that you did not this, nor could do it, is perfectly plain. You might have thought thus: "God foresaw the fall of Adam, and it was in God's power to have prevented it if he would, but he did not will to do so. Why did he not will to do so? No other reason can be assigned for his unwillingness than that his will had quite another bent or inclination." But, if you will permit yourself to enter into a contention with God, you had better profanely accuse him at once and condemn him for having so made man of constitutional frailty as to leave him liable to fall into eternal ruin on that account. But you will reply that Adam fell by his own free will. My reply to you, in return, is that Adam had need of being gifted with that fortitude and constancy with which the elect of God are gifted whom God wills to "keep" safe and sound "from falling" [Jude 24].

Most certain it is that if fresh strength were not supplied to us from heaven every moment, such is our liability to fall that we should perish a thousand times over. But God supplies all those whom he has chosen with an invincible fortitude, by which they are so holden up as to persevere unto the end. How was it, then, I again ask, that God did not bestow this same fortitude and perseverance on Adam if he had willed that he should stand fast and in safety? Here, most assuredly, every mouth must be silent and dumb, or all must confess with Solomon that "God hath made all things for himself; yea, even the wicked for the day of evil" [Prov. 16:4]. If this offend you as being an absurdity, think within yourself whether the Scriptures in vain declare so often that the judgments of God are a great deep. If it were possible for us to measure the incomprehensible counsel of God by the standard of our own human capacity,

Moses would have said in vain: "Secret things belong unto the Lord our God, but those things which are revealed belong unto us and to our children for ever" [Deut. 29:29].

You demand of me to cite the place in the Holy Scriptures by which I prove that God did not prevent the fall of Adam because his will was not to prevent it. Just as if that memorable reply of God to all such inquiries and inquirers did not contain in itself an all-sufficient proof: "I will have mercy on whom I will have mercy" [Rom. 9:15, from Ex. 3:19]. From this the apostle Paul at once concludes, and justly so, that God does not have mercy upon all, because he wills not to have mercy upon all [Rom. 9:16]. And most certainly these words, without the aid of any interpreter, plainly and loudly declare that God is not bound by any law that should compel him to show mercy unto all men indiscriminately and alike, but that he is the Lord of his own will, to impart pardon to whom he will and to pass by others as he will. It is, moreover, certain that God was the same then as now, when the prophet said of him, "He doeth according to his will" [Dan. 4:35].

If, therefore, God permitted the fall of Adam against his will, as you would have it, you will say next that he was overcome by Satan in the conflict. Thus you will make, like the Manicheans, two ruling principles. But Paul, pleading also this great cause of God, soberly and solemnly compares him to a potter, who of his own will could form different kinds of vessels from the same mass as he pleased [Rom. 9:21].

Had the apostle been so led, he might have begun his argument from sin. But he does not. He commences the mighty subject by defending the free right of God from the beginning of his glorious workmanship, even from his secret, eternal, and sovereign will. And where he afterwards adds "All were concluded under unbelief" [Rom. 11:32], does he teach that this took place contrary to or without the will of God? Does he not, on the contrary, teach that God was the author of that state of unbelief? If you reply that all were condemned to unbelief as they deserved, the context will not admit even that interpretation, because Paul is there speaking of the se-

cret judgments of God. And that solemn exclamation "O the depth
…!" [v. 33] directly militates against such an interpretation. Therefore, as God from the beginning predestinated Christ to succor
those who were lost, so by his inconceivable and inestimable counsel, he decreed a way by which he might manifest his glory by the
fall of Adam.

I willingly confess that where God is vindicating the free course
of his mercy, he speaks of the whole human race generally, which
had already perished in Adam, but this same view and consideration held good before Adam fell, so that God's will was then all-sufficient to show mercy when and as he pleased. Moreover, although
his eternal will depends on none and on nothing but himself and
has no prior cause to influence it, nevertheless it is founded in the
highest reason and in the highest equity. For though in the case of
men they require a law to rein and restrain their intemperateness,
it is far otherwise with God. He is his own law—a law unto himself. And his will is the highest rule of the highest equity.

ARTICLE 3

Sins are committed not only by the permission, but even by the
will of God. For it is frivolous to make any difference between the
permission of God and the will of God as far as sin is concerned.
They who attempt to make this difference merely attempt to gain
God over by flattery.

Statements and Observations of the Calumniator

Concerning the difference between the will and the permission
of God, the arguments of your opponents are these: Calvin professes to be a prophet of God, but we say that Calvin is a prophet
of the devil. One of these assertions must be false; both parties cannot speak the truth. If Calvin is a prophet of God, we lie; if Calvin
is a prophet of the devil, he lies, for he asserts that he is a prophet

of God. But suppose (by the will of God) that both positions are true: If God wills that Calvin should say that he is a prophet of God while we say that Calvin is a prophet of the devil, it follows that contradiction is a will, which is impossible. For if God wills that which is false, he does not will that which is true. Again, if God wills that which is true, he does not will that which is false. From this it will follow that if God wills that the one party should speak the truth, it must be contrary to his will that the other party should lie. But the one party certainly does lie. Therefore, the one party lies by the permission, but not by the will, of God. The next consequence is that there is a difference even in God himself, for there is a discrepancy between his permission and his will.

Moreover, your adversaries cite many conspicuous examples of this discrepancy between the will of God and his permission, especially from Ezekiel 20, where God, after he had reproved his people very fully and severely for not obeying his commandments, at last concludes with these words: "Go ye; serve ye every one his idols, and hereafter also, if ye will not hearken unto me" [v. 39]. As if God had said, "I permit you to serve your own lusts, since ye will not obey my precepts." And this indeed seems to be exactly the same as what he had said in the former part of the same chapter: "Because they despise my statutes, therefore I gave them also statutes that were not good" [vv. 24, 25]. Now God did not in reality, we are assured, give to the Israelites statutes that were not in themselves good, for all the statutes of God are good. But because they despised the good precepts of God, he forsook them; and they, being thus forsaken of God, fell away into evil statutes, just as that prodigal son, being forsaken by his father, or rather having forsaken his father, fell into luxury and every evil. Thus also Paul teaches that because men did not love the truth, God sent them strong delusions, that they might believe a lie.

Of the same description also seems to be that passage of Amos 4: "Go ye to Bethel, and transgress, for this liketh you" [vv. 4, 5]. So it is also in the present day, as in the case of yourself and your disciples. As men would not obey God, who says that he hates sin, therefore God has permitted spirits of delusion such as yours to exist, who teach that God wills sin so that they who would not obey the truth might be left to obey a lie.

Your opponents cite that passage from Zechariah, where God says he is angry with the nations that are at ease because, when he was lightly angry with the Israelites, they helped forward the calamity; that is, they afflicted the Israelites more grievously than the anger of the Lord against them required or could endure [Zech. 1:15]. This was, therefore, done by the permission, not by the will, of God.

They produce also a similar example from the prophet Oded, who reproves the people of Israel because they oppressed the people of Judah more heavily than the anger of the Lord required [2 Chron. 28:9ff.].

They bring forward also the example of the prodigal son, concerning whom, if you say that he ran into riotous living by the will of his father [Luke 15:13], it will be the greatest possible absurdity. The son, therefore, thus acted by the permission of the father. In the same way also your opponents affirm that the wicked are prodigal sons of God, and that they sin not by the will but by the permission of God.

They refer, moreover, to that saying of Christ, "And ye, will ye also go away?" [John 6:67]. Christ most certainly did not will that they should go away, but he permitted them to do so.

They argue, finally, from the nature of common sense, which dictates that there must be a difference between willing and permitting. They affirm that it was according to common sense that Christ taught divine things, and that if you take away common sense from his teaching, all his parables must fall at once, for it is by common sense that those parables are to be judged and understood.

Reply of John Calvin

This third article shows, equally with the preceding, how greedily and to what extent you feed on calumnies. If you did wish thus fiercely to gnaw at my doctrine, why did you not at least cite my words honestly? In the vast cause now before us, I affirm that to make a difference between the permission and the will of God is indeed "frivolous." But you interpose a witty and clever argument, as you imagine, although it is an empty sophism. If all things are done by the will of God, you assert that God wills things that are contrary in nature and in principle, which is proved, you maintain, by saying that I really am a prophet of the devil, while I affirm that I am a true servant of God. This appearance of contradiction is that which dazzles and blinds your eyes. But God, who well knows in himself how he wills the same thing in one sense that is contrary to his will in another sense, pays no regard to your dullness of understanding and stupidity. As often as God called forth the true prophets, he most certainly willed that they should contend zealously and earnestly in declaring the doctrine of the law. Upon this there secretly rose up false prophets, who strove to overthrow that doctrine. That there should be a conflict, therefore, between the true and false prophets was inevitable. But God did not therefore contend with or contradict himself, although he willed that both these true and false prophets should come forth. You thrust upon me the longsuffering of God, but God declares that no false prophets arise except those whom he ordains to be such, either to prove the faith of his own people or to blind the unbelieving. "If there arise among you a false prophet," says Moses, "your God proveth you by that prophet" [Deut. 13:1, 3].

Now you, by a most perverse and preposterous comment, transfer to some other that which Moses ascribes expressly to God. Therefore, either deny at once that God searches the hearts of his people or admit that which is the evident and indubitable truth: False prophets are instruments of God by which he proves, as by a touchstone, that of which he will have himself acknowledged to be the author. Ezekiel sets this forth still more clearly and remarkably: "And if the prophet be deceived when he hath spoken a thing, I the Lord have deceived that prophet, and I will stretch out my hand

upon him, and will destroy him from the midst of my people Israel" [Ezek. 14:9].

You would have us rest content with the permission of God
only. But God by his prophet asserts that his will and his hand are
in the whole matter as the moving cause. Just consider, then, which
of the two is the more worthy to be believed: God, who by his
Spirit, the only fountain of truth, thus speaks concerning himself,
or you, prating about his hidden and unsearchable mysteries out of
the worthless knowledge of your own carnal brain? What? When
God calls in Satan for his purposes, as the instrument of his
vengeance, and openly gives him commandment to go and deceive
the prophets of Ahab, does this positive command differ nothing
from a mere permission? The voice of God contains in it no ambiguity whatever: "Who," says God, "will go and deceive Ahab for me?"
[1 Kings 22:20]. Nor does God command Satan in any obscure
manner: "Go thou and be a lying spirit in the mouths of all his
prophets" [v. 22].

I wish to know from you whether doing a thing is the same as
permitting it to be done. When David had secretly abused the wife
of another man, God declares that he will cause all of David's wives
to be dragged forth, to make an example of the same disgraceful sin
openly in the sight of the sun [2 Sam. 12:11, 12]. God does not say,
"I will permit it to be done," but "I will do it." But you, in your wondrous defense of God (as you think), would aid him by your fallacious help in thrusting forward your imaginary permission. How
very differently does David think and act. While revolving in his
mind the fearful judgment of God, he exclaims, "I was dumb... because *thou* didst it" [Ps. 39:9].

In like manner Job blesses God and confesses that he was plundered by the robbers, not only through the permission but also by
the will and act of God; for he plainly affirms that it was the Lord
who gave and the Lord who took away what he had himself given
[Job 1:21]. If, upon your authority, giving and receiving are to be understood in the same way as willing and permitting, riches are not

blessings actually bestowed of God, but they fall into our hands at random by the permission of God. But if you and your foul band should continue thus to cry out against God until doomsday, he will nevertheless, in due time, fully justify and vindicate himself. But as for us, we will adore with all reverence those mysteries that so far surpass our comprehension, until the brightness of their full knowledge shall shine forth upon us in that day when he, who is now seen "through a glass darkly," shall be seen by us "face to face" [1 Cor. 13:12]. "Then," says Augustine, "shall he be seen in the brightest light of understanding what the godly now hold fast in faith. How sure, certain, immutable, and all efficacious is the will of God! How many things can he do that he yet wills not to be done? But he wills nothing that he cannot do!"

With reference, however, to the present article, I will answer you from the mouth of the same godly writer.

> These are the mighty works of the Lord, exquisitely perfect according to every bent of his will. And so perfect in exquisite wisdom that when both the angelic and human natures had sinned—that is, had done not what God willed but what each nature willed, even by a like will in each creature—it came to pass that what God as the creator willed not, he himself accomplished according as he had willed, thus blessedly using, as the God of perfect goodness, even evils to the damnation of those whom he had righteously predestinated unto punishment and to the salvation of those whom he had mercifully predestinated unto grace. For as far as these transgressing natures were concerned, they did that which God willed not; but with respect to the omnipotence of God, they could by no means have done what they did without it or its involvement. For by the very act of their doing what was contrary to the will of God, they were thereby fulfilling the will of God. Therefore, these mighty works of God, exquisitely perfect according to every bent of his will, are such that in a wonderful and ineffable way that is not

done without the will of God which is even done contrary
to his will, because it could not be done at all unless he permitted it to be done; yet he does not permit unwillingly, but
willingly. Nor, as the God of goodness, would he permit a
thing to be done in an evil way unless, as the God of omnipotence, he could work good even out of the evil done.

As to the testimonies of Scripture that you cite, they have no
more to do with the present mighty question and cause than oil has
to do with wine to make a mixture or to dilute the one with the
other. Speaking to the Jews by the prophet Ezekiel and addressing
them as disobedient, God says, "Go ye, worship every man his own
idols" [Ezek. 20:39]. This I openly profess is not the voice of God
commanding or exhorting, but of God rejecting an impious mixture
of worship by which the Jews had profaned his sanctuary. Now what
else can you conclude from this passage but that God sometimes
permits to exist that of which he disapproves and condemns? As if
it were not evident to all that God sometimes commands and permits by using the same forms of expression. God says in the law, "Six
days shalt thou labor" [Ex. 20:9]. Here is a permission. For sanctify-
ing every seventh day to himself, he leaves the other six free to men.
In a manner somewhat different, he permitted of old divorce to the
Jews, which he nevertheless by no means approved. In the present
case, recorded by the prophet Ezekiel, he gives up the double-
minded and the perfidious to idols because he will not suffer his
name to be polluted. But how is it that you have forgotten here that
all this is wrought by the secret providence of God, by which he ordains and turns to the accomplishment of his own purposes all the
movements and tumults of the world, according to his own will?
Moreover, corrupting vainly and ignorantly as you do that other
passage [Ezek. 20:24, 25], you demonstrate how everything sacred
is disregarded by an impure and profane person like yourself. The
words of God are, "Because they despised my statutes, I gave them
precepts that were not good." Here you trifle by observing that
when they were forsaken of God, they fell into idolatry. But God

undoubtedly means that the Jews were given over to the Chaldeans into slavery, and that the Chaldeans, who were idolaters, were oppressing them by their tyrannical laws.

Our question now is, did God merely permit the Jews to be dragged into exile by the Chaldeans or did he use the Chaldeans as rods, chosen by himself, to scourge the Jews for their sins? If you will still make the doctrine of mere permission a pretext, you might as well commit all the prophets to the flames at once, for at one time they declare that Satan was sent by God to deceive, at another that the Chaldeans or Assyrians were sent by God to destroy, and at the same time assert that God "hissed for" the Egyptians so that he might use their might in punishing his people; at another time they declare that the Assyrians were his hired soldiers, and Nebuchadnezzar was his servant in plundering Egypt, and the Assyrians were the axe in his hand and the rod of his anger in utterly devastating Judea. I do not multiply, as I might do, kindred examples lest I should exceed all moderate bounds of proof.

Nor is your inebriated audacity the less manifest where you would vainly make it appear that God's sending "strong delusion" on the unbelieving, that they might believe a lie, means that he permits false teachers to exist; and that, as he permitted the prodigal son to fall into riotous living when he had deserted his father, so he permits his prodigals to fall into error and delusion when they forsake him. And when you spout forth all this folly, you imagine that your readers are so blind that they do not see things to be quite otherwise in the words of Paul, where he says, "God shall send upon them strong delusions, that they might believe a lie" [2 Thess. 2:11]. But it is no marvel that he should prate thus, at will and at random, who imagines that there are no judgments of God at all, who does not know what the judgment means, or who holds it in perfect contempt if he does. For no man who is not insane would say that a judge had no hand in the judgment of the wicked or that he would sit down in unconcern and leave others to perform the duty that belonged properly to him alone.

You attempt, however, by your barking, either to frighten me or

to provoke me, when you say that by the permission of God, spirits of error and delusion exist who teach that God wills sin. But as
this same reproach was cast in the teeth of the apostle Paul himself, why should I grieve or complain at being a partaker of the same
reproach with him? You cite a passage from the prophet Zechariah,
where the nations are described as punishing God's people beyond
the extent that God's wrath required. Are you, then, really such a
simpleton as not to believe that there was protection enough in God
to prevent this excess of his people's affliction by their enemies, and
to have made their punishment less had he been pleased or had he
willed to do so? You reply that the words of the prophet intimate
this excess of punishment. But you must be twice or thrice dipped
in stupidity if you do not perceive that God tries the patience of his
people in a marvelous manner by the severest proofs, sometimes in
one way and sometimes in another, and that he is often at the same
time offended by the insolence of their enemies, when he sees them
become too much elated with their victories and when they insult
and cruelly use the conquered. Your foolish comments and reasonings fall to the ground of their own accord, directly militating
against and mutually destroying each other. For the truth and fact
must be either that God positively commanded those profane nations or he merely permitted them to gently chastise his people. If
you reply that he commanded them to do so, I then obtain the conclusion that though these neighboring enemies were, without cause,
afflictive to the miserable exiles who dwelt with them, yet they
would have been without blame if they had not exceeded due
bounds in their cruel treatment of them as the conquered and as
captives. For who would attribute that to them as iniquity which
they had done at God's command?

   You are laboring all the time to establish a difference between
the permission of God and his command, thus making it appear
that though God commanded their enemies to inflict punishment
on his people, yet it was by his permission only that they exceeded
all due bounds in the punishment they inflicted. In this same way
of reasoning, the Israelites also were deserving of censure, for they

also afflicted their brethren of Judah more severely than the wrath of God against them required (according to your reasoning). But your insanity blinds you so far as to cause you to assert that they would have been free from all guilt and blame if they had been moderate in their vexation of their brethren. I have to bring you back again and again to this point: The Israelites sinned not only because (by the permission of God, as you imagine) they exercised too great severity towards their brethren, but also because they took up arms against them at all. You, however, hesitate not to declare that there was no sin in their commencing war against their brethren, because God was angry with the people of Judah, and he himself armed the Israelites so that they might execute his vengeance upon them at his own command. I maintain that the Israelites sinned in a twofold sense: first, because they had themselves no intent or desire to do the will of God, although they were really the instruments of his vengeance; second, because their atrocity proves that they were destitute of all sense of equity. Indeed, at the outset you betray your shameless ignorance in your pretending that men, as far as they are themselves concerned, err and fall by the permission of God, whereas such a representation of the sacred matter is impious and profane. It is making God to give permission to men to do evil in reference to their own actions, as considered in themselves, while the reality and truth are that God severely prohibits and solemnly forbids the doing of anything that is contrary to his commands. Why God of his will permits men to do wrong and by his secret decree gives men over to evil whom he nevertheless commands to continue in the right way, it becomes our sobriety and modesty of mind to remain willingly ignorant. To search into this profound secret insolently, as you do, is rashness, audacity, and madness.

How cleverly and appropriately you interpret that passage where Christ (as you make it appear) permits his disciples to go away [John 6:67], learn from the following reality of the case. When Christ, referring to those who had gone away, turns to his disciples and says to them, "Will ye also go away?" he is positively exhorting them to persevere and continue with him. Asking them in grief whether they also would go away, he puts, as it were, a gentle rein upon them to prevent them from falling away with apostates. And is this, I ask you, the manner in which you convert all such forms of speech as these into permissions? Common sense does, at first sight, I acknowledge, take *to command* to be one thing and *to permit* to be another. But the fact is that this difference, or this sameness, is not the real question at issue. The question between us is whether God, in unconcern and inactivity, merely observes as an uninterested, unconcerned, and idle spectator all the things that are done upon earth, or whether from his all-high throne he rules, overrules, and governs by his divine command every single action of the sons of men. Or if the term *permission* gives you so much satisfaction and pleasure, answer me this question: Does God permit things to be done willingly or unwillingly? That God permits unwillingly is positively denied by Psalm 115:3: "The Lord hath done whatsoever he has willed," or "whatsoever he hath pleased." If, therefore, God permits willingly, then to represent him as sitting on his throne as a mere unconcerned and unengaged spectator is utterly profane. Therefore, it follows that God determines and rules by his counsel whatever he wills to be done. But you are for bringing, with child's talk, this sublime mystery of God down to the rule and measure of common sense!

As to your objecting and arguing that Christ taught all the divine lessons of his teaching so as to accommodate himself to the capacity of people of common sense, Christ himself flatly denies this and convicts you at once both of lying and of impudence in the matter. Hear you not Christ himself declaring that he spoke in "parables" so that the common people, or people in general, "might hear, and yet not understand" [Matt. 13:13]? It is, indeed, true that the Holy Spirit does, for our sakes, everywhere speak as a nurse would speak to children, but this is a widely different matter from representing, as you do, that common sense is a capable and competent judge of those profound doctrines that exceed in their incomprehensibility the capacity of angels. Paul proclaims aloud, "The natural man receiveth not the things of the Spirit of God, neither can he know them" [1 Cor. 2:14]. He therefore admonishes all those to become fools, and to resign all their own wisdom, who would profit in the heavenly school. In a word, God everywhere vindicates to himself as his own all true light of understanding. Indeed, both days and volumes would fail me if I were to attempt the accumulation of those testimonies of Scripture that condemn common sense as perfect darkness, for they are numberless, and they all declare that light can be obtained from heaven alone and that whoever would be wise in the things of God and of his own salvation must renounce all his own wisdom, however much human light it may contain. I will content myself, therefore, with one example only. God willed not that the doctrine of the gospel should be preached unto the Gentiles, and he withheld it from them even until the coming of Christ. That is why the apostle calls the gospel "the mystery that was hidden from ages." Indeed, it was unknown to the angels in heaven [Col. 1:26; 1 Pet. 1:12].

Notwithstanding such testimonies as these, however, you will persist in thrusting upon us the sufficiency of common sense, which by its own natural will and judgment subverts this very doctrine of the apostle altogether. For you will grant nothing to be even probable but that of which common sense may be the estimator, arbiter, and judge. Yet the prophet, when speaking of the secret providence of God, exclaims, "O Lord, how great are thy works! and thy thoughts are very deep" [Ps. 92:5].

You, on the contrary, deny that anything is divine but that which you can measure by the rule of your own reason. What becomes, then, of the remonstrance of the apostle when he is discussing the mighty question now before us? Why does he make the appeal, "Nay, but who art thou, O man" [Rom. 9:20]? What does his wonder and admiration mean when he says, "O the depth!... How unsearchable..." [Rom. 11:33]? The apostle commands us to wonder and be astonished, because whenever we come to the incomprehensible counsel of God, all mortal senses and powers fail before it, while you, all the time, will admit nothing that you cannot see with your own natural eyes.

ARTICLE 4
All the crimes committed by any man are by the operation
of God good and just.

Statements and Observations of the Calumniator

Against this fourth article all your opponents utter aloud that passage of Isaiah 5:20: "Woe unto them that call evil good, and good evil." Now if sin is a good and righteous work of God, it follows that righteousness is an evil and unrighteous work of God, for righteousness is altogether contrary to sin. Again, if sin is righteous, it follows that unrighteousness is righteous, for sin is unrighteousness. Further, if sin is a work of God, it must follow (your opponents argue) that God does what is sinful.

Reply of John Calvin

In this fourth article also you go on grossly lying as before. Of this fact I would, at the outset, cautiously warn my readers, and for the reason that they can form their judgments from the reality of the case rather than from your foul calumnies. Nor do I so much condemn your objections in themselves as I indignantly complain that by altering and perverting my words, you malignantly wrest what I did say for the purpose of fanning the flame of hatred against my doctrine, which doctrine is far different from your false representations of it. You enter into a quarrel with me as if I had said that sin was a just or righteous work of God. Yet such a doctrine and the idea of it I hold in the utmost detestation throughout my writings. Therefore, the more clever the argument you imagine yourself to possess, the greater is your real puerility. In your argument on this mendaciously stated fourth article, you arrive at the conclusion that righteousness is evil and that unrighteousness is good. You also conclude that God as the author and (as you awfully state) the doer of sin is unjust in punishing what is his own work. Yet all these monstrous profanities are the fabrications of your own brain. All such enormities of profaneness I have ever most carefully, and with abhorrence, condemned and refuted in all my writings.

You yourself, however, will one day find to your sorrow how abhorrent a crime it is to trifle and lie in this manner concerning the secret mysteries of God. That you may clearly understand that you are not dealing with me in this, your war against the truth, but with the supreme judge of heaven, whose tribunal, you may be assured, you can never escape, listen to what Job testifies, under no other influence certainly than the inspiration of the Holy Spirit: The doings of Satan and of the robbers who plundered him were the works of God himself [Job 1:21]. Yet Job never, in the extremest idea, charges God with sin; not even the most distant intimation of this is found in the patriarch. On the contrary, Job blesses God's holy name for what he had done by Satan and these robbers [v. 21]. So also when the brethren of the innocent Joseph sold him to the Ishmaelites, the deed evidently was a most wicked one. But when Joseph ascribes this to God as his work, so far is he from imputing sin to God that he considers and lauds his infinite goodness, because by this very means God had given nourishment to his father's whole family [Gen. 45:5]. Again, when Isaiah declares that the Assyrian is the "staff of God's wrath" in his righteous hand, with which he was about to work that terrible slaughter by means of the same Assyrian, the prophet thereby makes God the author of that awful destruction, but without the least imputation of sin to God nor the most distant idea of it [Isa. 10:5, 15]. In like manner, when Jeremiah curses those who do the work of God negligently, the prophet by his phrase "the work of the Lord" [Jer. 48:10] means all the cruel destruction that the enemies of the Jews wrought upon them. Go, therefore, and expostulate with the prophet, and declare to him that he has made God to commit sin. In a word, all who are in the least acquainted with Scripture know full well that a whole volume might be made of like passages of the Holy Scriptures where God is made the author, as commander, of the evil and cruel deeds done by men and nations. But it is utterly vain to spend more words upon a subject so well known and self-evident.

Was it not a signal manifestation of the grace of God when he spared not his own Son? Was it not an equally marvelous exhibition of grace in Christ when he delivered up himself? Now will you really affirm, with your foul and profane mouth, that God sinned in thus ordaining the deed of the crucifixion of his Son and in ordaining the men also who should do the deed [Acts 4:28]? Was God's work of the offering up of his only begotten Son a sin in him? O no! All godly persons very easily untie this knot, as Augustine does in the following clear and striking manner:

> When the Father gave up the Son, when the Lord gave up his own body, when Judas delivered up the Lord—how was it in this same "delivering up" that God was righteous and man guilty? The reason was that in this same thing that both God and man did, the motive was not the same from which God and man acted. Hence it is that Peter, without hesitation, declares that Pontius Pilate and Judas and the other wicked people of the Jews had done "what God's hand and his counsel had afore determined to be done" [Acts 4:28], as Peter had just before that said of Jesus, "Him being delivered by the determinate counsel and foreknowledge of God" [Acts 2:23].

If you turn your back on the term *foreknowledge*, the definitiveness of the term *determinate counsel* will floor you at once. Nor does the former passage leave the least degree of ambiguity behind it, namely, that Pontius Pilate, Judas, and the wicked people of the Jews did "whatsoever God's hand and his counsel had before determined to be done." Now if your understanding cannot hold a mystery and a secret as deep as these, why do you not wonder and exclaim with the apostle Paul, "O the depth!"? Why do you daringly trample upon them as an infuriated madman? Had you been of a teachable mind, you would have found in my writings explications of this deep matter far more copious that I can repeat here. My present object is only to blunt the edge of your impudence so that it may not disturb the minds of the weak.

ARTICLE 5
No adultery, theft, or murder is committed without the intervention of the will of God (*Institutes* 14.44).

ARTICLE 6
Scripture openly testifies that evil doings are designed not only by the will, but also by the authority, of God.

Statements and Observations of the Calumniator

Against these fifth and sixth articles your opponents bring these and many other arguments. If (they say) God wills sin, God is the author of sin. And again, if God wills sin (they argue), it is not the devil that wills sin, for the devil is the mere servant of God. And they affirm that if God wills sin, he must be inferior to many men, for many men are unwilling to sin. Indeed, the nearer any man approaches to the very law of nature, the less he will sin; otherwise, how is it that Paul says, "The good that I would, I do not; but the evil that I would not, that I do" [Rom. 7:19]? If Paul wills sin by nature (as Calvin says), how is it that Paul does not will what God wills? And how is it that Paul wills that good which God (according to Calvin) does not will? Finally, your opponents ask of you, what Scripture testifies that evil doings are designed of God, not only by his will, but also by his authority?

Reply of John Calvin

In the case of this fifth article, it is not without the peculiar intervention of the providence of God that you have pretended to give the reference to the passage in my *Institutes* (14.44) from which you falsely assert it is extracted. In this instance readers will see that I state the things in these articles—that is, calumnies—that my adversaries bring against my doctrines just as faithfully as if they themselves had stated them.

Seizing, as you do, upon this mutilated passage, do you not deserve that everyone who passes you should spit in your face? Although you do not attempt to offer any reference in the case of the sixth article, your real audacity takes a wider leap still. Tell me, did I, who in all my writings so reverently and solemnly declare that whenever and wherever sin is mentioned, the name of God should be kept in all solemnity wide out of the way—did I ever or anywhere assert that evil doings are perpetrated not only by the design but also by the authority of God? Most certainly nothing can be uttered too powerfully or too severely in condemnation of such monstrous blasphemy. I am willing to hear all that you or any men can say in its abhorrence. Let not my name, therefore, ever be associated with its horrible profanity.

How successful you are in deceiving fools I know not, but of one thing I am certain: If anyone will just take the pains to compare your foul inventions with my genuine writings, your dishonesty and wickedness will leave you painted in your true and execrable colors. You profanely contend that if God loves sin, he must hate righteousness; and you utter many things in the same line of profanity. And why do you utter them but that you might be forced at last to subscribe under your own convictions to my written doctrines? For not yesterday only, nor the day before yesterday, but for these many years past I have written and spoken concerning Job thus: If in the spoliation of that patriarch by robbers, the work of God, Satan, and the plunderers were one and the same in the act, abstractedly considered, how is it that God is clear of all the fault, as he sacredly is, of which Satan and the robbers are guilty? The reason is that in the actions of men, an entire difference exists when the motives and ends of those actions are duly considered, so that the cruelty of a man is condemned who barbarously pierces the eyes of a crow, or the sacrilege of him who kills a crane (a bird held in so much religious veneration among the ancients), while the sentence of the judge, who sanctifies his hands by putting to death a murderer, is lauded? Why should the position of God be held inferior to that of man? Why should not his infinite righteousness vindicate him and hold him separate from a participation in the guilt of evil-doing men? Only let readers cursorily observe what I am now about to add. Let them carefully read the whole of that part of my *Institutes* where I discourse on the providence of God, and they will immediately see all your cloudy-minded objections discussed, exposed, answered, and refuted.

Let readers consider also, if they please, what I have written in my commentary on the second chapter of the Acts of the Apostles. Men, I have there shown, when they commit theft or murder, sin against God because they are thieves and murderers, and because in their theft and in their murder there is wicked design. But God, who makes sovereign use of their wickedness, stands in an infinitely different and in an all-high position above all men, acts, and things. And the objects and ends of God are infinitely different from and higher than those of men. God's purpose is, by the wicked acts of men, to chastise some and to exercise the patience of others. Hence, in all of his uses of the evil doings of men, God never deviates in the remotest degree from his own nature, that is, from his own infinitely perfect rectitude. If, then, an evil deed is thus to be estimated according to its end and object, it is fully manifest that God is not, nor can be, the author of sin.

The sum of the whole great matter is this: Since an evil will in men is the cause of all and every sin, God, in performing his righteous counsels by the hands of men, is so far from being involved in the same sin and fault with men that in a marvelous manner he causes, by their means, the light of his glory to shine forth out of darkness. Indeed, in that book of mine, *On the Providence of God*, which lighted all these very flames of the deepest pits of hell against me, there will be found continually occurring the distinctive declaration that nothing is more impious or more preposterous than to drag God into a participation of sin or guilt with man while he is performing his secret judgments by means of the hands of men and of the devil, because there is no affinity whatever between the motives and ends of God and those of men and devils.

There was published by me more than twelve years ago a book that clearly vindicates both me and my doctrine from all these foul calumnies, and that ought to preserve me free from all this present trouble also, if there were but one spark of honesty or humanity in either yourself or your fellows. But with reference to that mad and impious dream of the libertines concerning God's being the author of sin, which fascinated so many, how fully I have refuted that horrible idea I will not now boast.[23] Most certainly I purposefully undertook to defend the cause of God therein, and I proved with all possible clarity that God was not, in any sense, degree, or manner whatever, the author of sin.

ARTICLE 7
Whatsoever men do when and while they sin, they do according to the will of God, seeing that the will of God often conflicts with his precept.

Statements and Observations of the Calumniator

On this seventh article your opponents ask you this question: If the will of God is often at variance with his precept, in what way can it be known when God wills and when he does not will what he commands? For, say they, if Calvin asserts that what God commands ought always to be done whether God wills it or does not will it, it will follow that God wills in order that his will might sometimes be resisted. For if God commands me not to commit

---

23. John Calvin, *Treatises against the Anabaptists and against the Libertines: Translation, Introduction, and Notes*, trans. and ed. Benjamin Wirt Farley (Grand Rapids: Baker Book House, 1982).

adultery, and yet wills that I should commit adultery even though I ought not to commit adultery, it follows that I ought to do that which is contrary to his will. For when God commands the people of Israel generally, "Thou shalt not commit adultery" [Ex. 20:14; Deut. 5:18], does he mean that none of them should commit adultery, or that some should commit adultery but others should not?

On this point, Calvin, your adversaries ask of you for a direct answer. If you reply that God wills that some should commit adultery, but that he at the same time wills that others should not, you will make God inconsistent with himself in the one and the same precept. If you reply to these arguments of your adversaries by asserting that God has a twofold will—the one open and manifest, the other secret—they next inquire: Who was it, then, that made this secret will known to Calvin? For if Calvin and his followers know this secret will, it cannot be secret; and if they know it not, how dare they affirm that which they know not?

Your opponents again inquire whether God commands according to his will when he enjoins his people to pray, "Thy will be done" [Matt. 6:10], and where Christ also says, "He that doeth the will of my Father which is in heaven, the same is my brother and sister and mother" [Mark 3:35]? There is also this passage of Paul: "Behold, thou art called a Jew, and restest in the law, and makest thy boast of God, and knowest his will, and approvest that which is excellent, and art a teacher of the law" [Rom. 2:17, 18]. Surely we have here the will of God and that which is commanded in the law, which will, if it be good, which it certainly is, it must necessarily follow that what is contrary thereto is evil, for whatever is contrary to good must be evil. There is, moreover, that memorable ejaculation of Christ: "How often would I have gathered thy children together... but thou wouldest not" [Matt. 23:37; Luke 13:34]. Christ most certainly speaks here of the open or manifest will of God, namely, the will that Christ himself had explained in so many ways. Now if Christ had in his mind another will of God contrary to this will, his whole life must have been a contradiction.

Reply of John Calvin

I am utterly unconcerned to make any reply at all to this seventh article. Produce me the place in my writings where I have asserted that "the will of God is frequently at variance with, or conflicts with, his precept." Such an idea never entered my mind—no, not even as a dream. On the entire contrary, among many other kindred explanations, I have faithfully expounded and set forth how simple and uniform and one the will of God is, although between the secret counsel of God and his general doctrine there is to ignorant and inexperienced persons, at first sight, a certain appearance of difference. But whoever modestly, soberly, and reverently submits and commits himself to God and his teaching will immediately see and acknowledge, as far as the human mind's capacity can see and acknowledge it, how God, who forbids adultery and fornication, punishes David's sin of adultery with the wife of Uriah by the incestuous intercourse of Absalom with the wives of David. God ever wills one and the same thing, but frequently in different forms. Therefore, in order that the foulness of your lies may not cast any filth on me or my doctrine, let my readers receive in one word this solemn declaration: That which you cast in my teeth as promulgated by me concerning the two wills of God is an entire fiction of your own. For as to myself, I have ever proclaimed that there is between the secret or hidden counsel of God and the openly revealed voice of his doctrine the most perfect, divine, and consummate harmony.

Augustine did, indeed, by way of concession and explanation to his adversaries, make mention of a twofold will, or of different wills of God—a secret will and an open or revealed will—but he so represented that twofold will as to show that they are in such consummate harmony with each other that the last day will make it most gloriously manifest that there never was nor is the least variance, conflict, or contradiction in this multiform way of God's workings and doings, but instead, the most divine and infinite harmony and oneness.

Having laid down this solemn principle and taken this immovable stand, I will now, if you will have it so, draw swords with you
in battle for the truth. You argue thus: If God forbids a man to do
what he really wills him to do all the time, or if God commands
men to do what he really wills not, he must command for the very
purpose that his will may be resisted.

In none of all this filth of argumentation are either myself or my
doctrines the least concerned. I acknowledge nothing whatever of
the profane sentiments which it refers to be mine. On the contrary,
the sum of my doctrine is this: The will of God set forth in his law
clearly demonstrates that righteousness is his delight and iniquity
is his hatred, and it is most certain that God would not pronounce
punishment against evil doers if their evil doings pleased him. This,
however, by no means prevents God from willing, by his secret and
inexplicable counsel, that those things should be done in a certain
sense and manner that he yet wills not to be done and that he forbids to be done.

If you will here raise the objection that I make God inconsistent with himself, in return I would ask you whether it belongs to
you to prescribe a law or a bound for God, forbidding him to do
anything that surpasses your judgment and comprehension. Moses
declares aloud, "The secret things of God belong unto himself
alone; but that whatever things are useful for man to know are revealed in the law" [Deut. 29:29]. Will you, therefore, deny God the
right of doing anything except the reason of which you can fully
comprehend and explain? After the depth of the counsel of God,
which engulfs all human capacities of comprehension, has been
fully declared in the Book of Job, the sublime description closes
with this significant intimation: "Lo, these are parts of his ways; but
how little is heard of him?" [Job 26:14]. As for you, you will not permit God to have any counsel to himself, except what you can plainly
see as something that you behold with your natural eyes. You are
more than blind, however, if you cannot see that when God, by his
voice, forbids you to commit adultery, his will is that you should not
be an adulterer. Yet he, the same great God, regarding those same

adulteries that he condemns, most certainly exercises his righteous judgments, but not without his full knowledge and will.

To state this matter more briefly and succinctly, God wills that adultery should not be committed, inasmuch as it is a pollution and violation of the holy bond of matrimony and a great transgression of his righteous law. But insofar as God uses adulteries, as well as other wicked doings of men, to execute his own acts of vengeance on the sins of men, he certainly executes the office and performs the sacred duty of a judge, not unwillingly but willingly. Therefore, in whatever instances either the Chaldeans or Assyrians acted cruelly in their terrible victories and horrible slaughters, we by no means praise them for such awful barbarities. Further, God himself declares that he will be the avenger of the afflicted and inhumanly treated [Rom. 12:19; 1 Thess. 4:6]. Yet the same righteous God elsewhere declares that these slaughters are sacrifices that he has in this way prepared for himself [Isa. 29; Isa. 34:6; Jer. 46:10; Ezek. 39]. Will you deny that God wills what he thus dignifies with the honored designation of a "sacrifice"? Awake, then, from your slumber, open your eyes from your blindness, and at length acknowledge that God, by secret and inexplicable ways, rules and overrules his righteous judgments.

You, however, by a subtlety of argument that you deem marvelously wise, inquire whether God, from the time that he first forbade men to commit adultery, willed that all should be adulterers or only a part of them. Take this as a sure and certain reply: God demands of all men chastity, because God loves chastity in all men. Experience itself, however, manifests (without our entering into any proof or mention of the important facts themselves) that there are in God different reasons, motives, and manners of his willing. For if he equally and effectually willed that all men should be chaste, he would, without all doubt, make and render all men chaste. Therefore, since chastity is a singular gift of God, the prompt and evident conclusion is that he wills what he commands in his word differently from what he effectually works and fulfills by his regenerating Spirit. Hence your impure and profane tongue has no ground whatever for charging God with inconsistency. God is neither dubious nor ambiguous in anything that he commands or forbids, but he plainly discovers his pure and holy nature in both. Neither will you find anything contrary to his purity, holiness, and righteousness in that secret and hidden will of his by which he rules and overrules all the actions of the sons of men.

Whoredom is highly displeasing to God as the author of all chastity. Yet the same holy God's will was to punish the adultery of David by the incestuous lust of Absalom. God forbids man's blood to be shed, for as he greatly loves his own image, so he defends it by his own protection. Yet he raised up out of the wicked nations slaughterers of the sons of Eli because it was his will that they should be killed; so the sacred history plainly and literally teaches us [1 Sam. 3:10–12; 1 Sam. 4:10, 11]. If your blindness is as a stone wall in your way, all who really have eyes see a perfectly holy and harmonious consistency in God when he—the same divine being who hates whoredom and slaughter insofar as they are sins, or (which is the same thing) who hates the sins of whoredom and murder because they are transgressions of his righteous law—exercises his secret and righteous judgments in justly punishing the wickednesses of nations and men by means of the cruelties and sins of other nations and men.

As to your own conceit about your acute wisdom when you ask the question, "If there be any secret will of God, when and how shall that will be revealed to me?" the answer to your impious question will contain no difficulty when you have granted to me the acknowledgment that we are to follow the Holy Spirit alone as our teacher. For if God, according to the testimony of Paul, "dwelleth in the light that no man can approach unto" [1 Tim. 6:16], and if the same apostle reverentially declares, "God's ways are past finding out" [Rom. 11:33], why am I not freely permitted to wonder at and adore the secret will of his that is hidden from my comprehension? The wisdom of God is exalted in the Book of Job with the highest praises, so that mortals may know and confess that it cannot be spanned by any human intellect. Are you, then, purposed to laugh at everything that is said concerning a matter so sublimely secret? Will you upbraid David with folly for solemnly proclaiming and adoring those judgments of God that he confessed to be a "great deep" [Ps. 36:6]? I hear from all the prophets and apostles that the counsels of God are incomprehensible. What they all declare I embrace with a firm and unhesitating faith, and what I believe I freely and undoubtingly profess and teach. Why, then, is this my reverence for God's secret will charged upon me as a fault and a crime?

And that you may not turn around upon me and say that I adduce from the Scriptures examples and proofs wholly irrelevant, Paul's case and mine are surely one and the same. Paul, when speaking of the secret election or reprobation of God and adoring the riches and profundity of his wisdom, the incomprehensibility of his judgments, and the unsearchableness of his ways, still ceases not to affirm openly that God has mercy on whom he will and consigns whom he will to eternal destruction [Rom. 9:18]. In a word, I ask you not to exult anymore in the irreconcilable inconsistency that you imagine you have discovered in my doctrines, for the Scriptures furnish an abundance of testimonies concerning the secret and hidden will of God. What I have from them learned, I fearlessly assert and speak of as a thing sure and certain. But as my human intellect cannot soar to a height so stupendous, I adore with reverence, fear, and trembling, the mystery that is too high and too deep for the angels to penetrate. And this is my reason for offering so frequently in my writings the admonitory warning that nothing is better or safer in these solemn matters than wise ignorance, because the folly of those who suffer themselves to be, or who wish to be, wise above what is written or permitted of God is worse than the frenzy of madmen.

By this time you must see how sure and certain I hold that will of God concerning which the Scriptures so clearly and fully testify. This same will is, nevertheless, so secret and incomprehensible with reference to the reasons that God wills this or that, or how he wills this or that, that the angelic intellects cannot grasp the comprehension. The fact is that your pride and presumption, and of all like you, so madden all of you that whatever you cannot comprehend but are compelled to relinquish as beyond your capacity, you labor with all your might to make it seem of no importance at all.

As to your continuing to cast in my teeth inconsistencies, contrarieties, and contradictions, I have settled all those a hundred times over. And as to your scurrility, by which you attempt to overwhelm me, all that being insipid and pointless penetrates me not. And as to your charge against me that I am an imitator of God, you, on account of your presumptuous and devil-like imitation of his wisdom, will one day find to your eternal cost what it is to exalt your own wisdom and to make yourself therein equal unto the Most High. The only pain and agony I feel are caused by your frenzied blasphemies, by which you profane the sacred majesty of God, of which profanation he will himself be, in his appointed time, the sure and certain avenger.

As the will of God that he has revealed in his law is good, whatever is contrary to that law and will, I acknowledge to be evil. But when you brawl that the secret and hidden will of God—by which he separates the "vessels of mercy" from the "vessels of wrath" according to his "good pleasure" [Rom. 9:22, 23; Eph. 1:9] and by which he makes use of both vessels as he will—is contrary to his law, you breathe forth from the foul sink of your ignorance a detestable fiction of your brain and a horrible lie.

I freely acknowledge that Christ is speaking of the revealed will of God when he says, "O Jerusalem, Jerusalem, how often would I have gathered thy children together...and ye would not" [Matt. 23:37; Luke 13:34]. He is upbraiding the Jews for the same ingratitude and hardness of heart as he had before done in a song of Moses [Deut. 32:1–43]. And we know full well that God did in reality bestow on the Jewish nation all the blessings that the words of this song express, seeing that by giving them his law, by the ordinances of his worship, and by the many benefits he conferred on that people by which he bound them to himself, he protected them, as it were, by the overshadowing of his wings. He would still have done so had not their indomitable obstinacy and obduracy carried them

away from him. Therefore, after Christ had testified his will so often and in so many different ways, spoken in order to win a perverse nation to obedience, but all in vain, it is with the utmost
justice that he complains of their ingratitude. As to your restricting
all these things to the lifetime of Christ, you do this with your usual
ignorance of these divine things, as if Christ were not the true God
who from the beginning had not ceased to spread the wings of grace
over his own elect people. But here you immediately conclude that
if there were another and secret will in Christ while he thus addressed Jerusalem, the whole life of Christ must have been an inconsistency, as if alluring them by his voice and kindnesses yet
leaving their hearts untouched by the inspiration of his secret Spirit
were in Christ diverse and contrary acts.

In order that the absurdity and futility of your calumny may the
more plainly appear, answer, I ask you, this question: Where does
Christ complain that he was mistaken or deceived by the event that
the vine from which he had expected grapes brought forth wild
grapes? [Isa. 5:2, 4]. What answer have you to give, noble teacher
and skillful rhetorician? Will you impute ignorance to Christ to
avoid making him speak falsely? What? Did the Jews entirely prevent and defeat the purposes of God? According to you, the blessed
God was sitting in doubt all the time as to what the result would
be, and that event quite deceived and surprised him at last. No, nor
will it at all alter the state of the case if you make the saying of
Christ, which he speaks about the state of Jerusalem, refer to the
secret foreknowledge of God. God had elsewhere said, "Surely they
will fear my name" [Zeph. 3:7], but they hastened to corrupt themselves more and more. God had expected some profit from his great
punishments inflicted, but he afterwards complains that he was disappointed. Can you, then, disentangle yourself from this divine set
of truth in no other way than by reducing God to order, and making him depend for the accomplishment of his eternal purposes
upon the free will of men? Surely it is plain and evident to those of
meanest capacity that God, in order to set forth the great wickedness of his people, speaks as in the person and after the manner of

men when they complain that all their labor is lost because they are quite disappointed in their expected success.

It is most certain that those whom God wills to gather unto himself effectually he "draws" by his Spirit [John 6:44], and that what is in his hand and purpose to do, he will, according to his promises, perform. Therefore, when many who are called follow him not, it is openly manifest that the manner of gathering together of which Christ complains as having been unfruitful and inefficacious was not attended with that efficacious influence of his Spirit. He elsewhere makes frequent mention of this, as for instance by the prophet Isaiah: "He shall gather together the dispersed of Judah" [Isa. 11:12]. Again: "The glory of the Lord shall gather thee" [Isa. 58:8]. Again: "I will bring thy seed from the east and gather thee from the west" [Isa. 43:5]. Again: "Your God will be your rereward [or will gather you]" [Isa. 52:12]. For the prophet had just said before this, "The Lord hath made bare his holy arm," that his power might be displayed "before the eyes of all the nations" [v. 10]. Hence it is that the prophet a little afterwards repeats, "For a small moment have I forsaken thee, but with great mercies will I gather thee" [Isa. 54:7]. What I have before advanced concerning the precepts of God is sufficient and abundant, I hope, to stop the mouth of all your blasphemies.

Although God commands nothing feignedly, ambiguously, or fictitiously, but plainly and solemnly declares what he wills and approves, his mind and will are that a different kind of obedience should be rendered to him by his elect, whom he effectually bends and turns to his obedience, from that obedience offered to him by the reprobate, whom he also indeed calls to himself by the outward voice of his word, but whom he determines not "to draw" effectually by his Spirit [John 6:44].

The natural obstinacy and depravity of all men are alike, so that no man will take upon himself the yoke of obedience to God voluntarily and willingly. To some, God promises the Spirit of obedience; others he leaves in their depravity. For notwithstanding all your vain talk about it, the truth is that a "heart of flesh" [Ezek. 11:19] and a "new heart" [Ezek. 36:26] are not promised to all men promiscuously, but to the elect peculiarly, in order that they might walk in the commandments of God. What have you to reply to these things, noble teacher and judge of the truth? And what if God invites the whole mass of mankind to come unto him, and yet knowingly, and of his own will, denies his Spirit to the greater part of them, "drawing" a few only into obedience to himself by his Spirit's secret inspiration and operation? Is the adorable God to be charged, on that account, with inconsistency?

ARTICLE 8

The hardening of Pharaoh, and so his obstinacy of mind and rebellion, was the work of God, even on the testimony of Moses, who ascribes all the rebellion of Pharaoh to God.

ARTICLE 9

The will of God is the supreme cause of all the hardness of heart in men.

Statements and Observations of the Calumniator

Under these eighth and ninth articles, your adversaries ask this question: What, then, does Moses mean when he writes, "And Pharaoh hardened his heart" [Ex. 8:32]? Are we to interpret the words "And Pharaoh hardened his heart" thus: "And God hardened the heart of Pharaoh"? Surely this must be a far more violent manner of speaking than to say, "God hardened the heart of Pharaoh"; that is, God knew Pharaoh as to the natural hardness of his heart, because Pharaoh had refused to obey him. Another like question they ask concerning the words "Today if ye will hear his voice, harden not your hearts" [Heb. 3:15]. If you should interpret this passage by rendering it, "God would not have you harden your hearts," such explanation would involve the greatest absurdity, for it would be making God command men to do what is the prerogative of himself alone. For if the hardening of hearts is the work of God, it is absurd to command men to harden their own hearts or not to harden their own hearts, for they could no more do it than they could add one cubit to their stature or take one cubit from it.

Reply of John Calvin

Here again I beg of my readers, you unholy calumniator of the truth, to give me their confidence and to compare my writings and my whole "line" of teaching with your perverted and mutilated "articles." If they will kindly do this, your slanders will at once be detected, and all the flame of animosity that you thus light up against me will soon go out of itself. Meanwhile, I deny not that I have taught, as Moses and Paul teach, that the heart of Pharaoh "was hardened" of God [Ex. 7:22; Ex. 8:19; Ex. 9:7, 35; Rom. 9:17, 18]. Hereupon, however, despising both Moses and Paul, and considering all that is read in them as nothing, you take upon yourself to expostulate with me and to ask me whether, since we read in one place that "Pharaoh hardened his heart" [Ex. 8:32], there is any necessity for giving a more violent interpretation of the passage and to say that "God hardened the heart of Pharaoh"? Now I need no further reply to this, your question, than that which you furnish in the words of this lying article yourself, which you, pretending to quote from my writings, or corrupting, or not comprehending them, imply that as the will of God is the supreme or remote cause of the hardness, man himself, who hardens his own heart, is and must be the proximate cause of the hardening.

I have everywhere most distinctly shown the difference between the supreme or remote cause, and all mediate and proximate causes. For while a sinner can find the root of every evil affection in himself, what ground can there be for charging God with any fault of such sinner's transgressions? Such an accuser of God acts, as I have elsewhere said, just like the nurse of Medea, as represented by the ancient poet who preposterously exclaims, "O that the planks that formed the ship *Argo* had never been cut down by the axe on Mount Pelion!" For all the while the impure princess, her mistress, was burning with her own depraved lust and felt herself driven head-long by its force to betray and ruin her father's kingdom, this fool-ish nurse blames neither the corrupt passion of her mistress nor the deep enticements of Jason, nor does she see those immediate causes at all; instead, she goes on complaining of the ship that brought Jason to Colchis and laments that such a ship was ever built in Greece. Exactly in the same manner does the man who being con-scious of his own sin and fault, fetches a remote cause of his iniq-uity from afar—even from God himself—utterly and ridiculously forgetting what he himself is.

Surely, then, you must now see that although God does, in his own secret and sovereign way, harden men's hearts, no fault can pos-sibly be imputed to him, because every man hardens his own heart by the essential evil and wickedness of his own nature.

But when God turns the hearts of men to the obedience and worship of himself, that is another form of his working altogether. For as we all are by nature bent on obstinacy and resistance, no man will desire to do good unless he be acted upon of God and led so to do. Although Scripture says, "The preparations of the heart in man are from the Lord" [Prov. 16:1], and the faithful prepare their hearts to seek God and to render him voluntary worship, Scripture by no means contradicts itself herein, but it distinctly shows that all the true worshipers of God render him their service willingly and from an affection and holy freedom of soul. Yet again, this by no means stands in contradiction or in the way of the fact that God all the while performs his part by the operations and influences of his secret Spirit.

But with reference to his hardening men's hearts, that is a dif-ferent way of God's working, as I have just observed, because God does not govern the reprobate by his regenerating Spirit. He gives them over to the devil and leaves them to be the devil's slaves, and he so overrules their depraved wills by his secret judgment and counsel that they can do nothing but what he has decreed. Such is the divine harmony and marvelous consistency of these things that though God hardens whomsoever he will, yet everyone so hardened is the cause and author of his own hardening. But that I may not extend my observations too great a length in replying to this article, let me be permitted to impress on the minds and memories of godly and upright readers the following admonition of Augustine:

> When the apostle says that God "gave" certain persons "over to vile affections" [Rom. 1:26], it is preposterous ignorance to refer this to the longsuffering of God. For the same apostle elsewhere connects the longsuffering of God with his power, as where he says, "What if God, willing to show his wrath, and to make his power known, endured with much longsuffering the vessels of wrath fitted to destruction?" [Rom. 9:22].

Indeed, even if this learned and pious father and teacher had never written or spoken on this great matter, the authority of God alone ought to be enough, and more than sufficient, for our understanding and faith. It is not I who said, "God taketh away the hearts of princes and causeth them to err," or "God held the heart of Pharaoh that he might not incline to humanity and mercy." It is not I that said, "God turned the hearts of the nations and hardened them to hate his people," or "God hissed for the Egyptians and used them as his servants." It was not I that said, "Sennacherib was God's rod in his hand to punish his people." I did not say all these things. They are all the declarations of the Spirit of God himself.

What? When Scripture itself affirms that Saul was carried away from God by an evil spirit, will you ascribe this to the sole patience or mere permission of God? How much nearer the truth is Augustine in his admonitory instruction when he observes,

> The sins that Satan and the wicked commit are their own, but what is accomplished by their sins is effected by the

power of God, who divides the darkness from the light as he will.

Now you charge me with saying what God himself asserts all the while in his own words. In this matter, let the same Augustine reply to you in my stead:

> If Scripture be carefully examined, it shows that God not only directs those good wills of men—wills he has made good out of evil wills—unto good actions and unto eternal life, but that those wills also which remain in their natural corruption are so under the power of God that he turns and inclines them whenever and wherever he will, either to confer blessings or to inflict punishments; and that he does this by judgments the most secret, but at the same time most just.

ARTICLE 10
Satan is a liar at the command of God.

Statements and Observations of the Calumniator

Against this tenth article, Calvin, which is a part of your doctrine, your adversaries argue thus: If Satan is a liar at the command of God, to be a liar is just, and therefore Satan is just. For if it is just to command a lie (and if Calvin speaks the truth, it is), then to obey a lie is also to be considered just from the justice of the precept. And again, as to obey an unjust precept is unjust, so to obey a just precept is just. If Calvin hereupon reply that Satan is not a liar obediently—that is, out of mere obedience to God—we reply, according to Calvin's own sentiments, that Satan's being a liar, but not out of obedience to God, is also at the command of God.

Reply of John Calvin

Only consider what kind of a man it is at whom you hurl your shafts. For that assertion at which you aim your weapon is not mine; it proceeds from the Spirit of God himself. The very words of Scripture are these:"Whom shall I send? and who will go for us?" Immediately God calls Satan and commands him to go and to be a lying spirit in the mouth of all the prophets to deceive Ahab [1 Kings 22:20–22]. Now, then, dog as you are, bark as loud as you will. You will no more obscure the glory of God by your revilings than you can obscure the brightness of the sun by spitting in his blazing face. But here again let me use the words of Augustine rather than my own:

> When God testifies that false prophets are sent by him and that his hand is upon them to cause them to deceive men or kings, this is not an act of his mere patience or permission, but an exercise of his effectual power.

As to your prating that Satan is not a liar by the command of God, out of obedience to that command, it is no marvel that you entangle yourself in knots and nets without number while you refuse to acknowledge that God uses the workings of Satan in an inexplicable manner, according to his sovereign will, so that he may thereby manifest the justice and equity of his supreme dominion. Yet he never liberates the wicked instruments that he uses from the sin and the guilt that are theirs; these instruments his power compels to execute his decrees, and in some sense, even against their own wills. Although your bitter malice may howl an hundred times over, what I utter is not the voice of Calvin but the voice of God, who says, "I have given commandment unto my saints." Therefore, if you imagine that God assumes to himself more than he ought, he will sooner or later find a way to clear and vindicate himself from all such accusations as yours and to take vengeance on all such accusers as you.

ARTICLE II
God gives the will to those who do evil. He also suggests
depraved and dishonest affections, not only permissively, but
also effectively, and that too for his own glory.

Statements and Observations of the Calumniator

Against this eleventh article your opponents argue thus: Calvin
actually attributes to God what evidently belongs to the devil, as is
manifest from the united testimony of the whole of Scripture.
Moreover, if God suggests depraved and dishonest affections and
yet commands us to resist depraved affections, he must positively
command us to resist himself and is therefore inconsistent with
himself. "Every good gift is from above, and cometh down from the
Father of lights," Scripture says [James 1:17]. Are, then, even depraved affections to be considered good gifts? Do they also come
down from the Father of lights? James plainly asserts that "no one
is tempted of God, but every man is tempted by his own heart's
lust" [vv. 13, 14]. And whereas you add that God does this for his
own glory, your opponents maintain that such an idea is absurd.
Nebuchadnezzar did indeed experience the justice and the power
of God when, on account of his own pride, he was changed into the
nature and habits of a brute; and he gave glory to God for the same,
because he judged and plainly saw that God therein was just, as well
as mighty [Dan. 4:25–37].

Reply of John Calvin

Here again you go on, as before, to fabricate monsters out of
your own brain and to slaughter them in your own imagination,
glorying to yourself in a mighty triumph that you vainly think you
have gained over a harmless servant of God. As to the places in my
works wherein I have spoken or taught the doctrines contained in
this article, those places you are, and ever will be, wholly unable to

find. Therefore, without my saying one word, your futility and your impudence also fall to the ground together. As to the murders, the adulteries, the rapines, and the frauds, etc., with which the wicked pollute themselves, my teaching is that all these wickednesses proceed from the desperate evil of their own natures; but I teach that God, who brings light out of darkness, so rules in these wicked men and by them that by his secret, incomprehensible judgment, he executes by the wickedness of these men his own eternal decrees. Now if you will fight against these solemn truths, prepare at once to enter into battle with God himself. He is quite prepared to receive your insane onset.

If there were in you one drop or spark of modesty or docility, the distinction that I ever make and that continually occurs in my writings would at once undoubtedly satisfy your mind. If the wicked who discover the root of all evil in themselves would but ask their own consciences where all the fault lies, those consciences would testify that the whole fault of all their wickedness is found in that root of all iniquity within them. Nor could they fail to see that God, by righteously turning their depraved wills wherever he pleases, uses those evil affections for the working of various good. As to quarreling with this, I tell you again, you are not contending against me but against God himself. O that from your heart you could acknowledge God truly to be the Father of lights. Then you would not, as Paul descriptively expresses it, force yourself by your audacity into "that light which no man can approach unto" [1 Tim. 6:16]. You would not thus turn, by your profane insolence, that light into darkness.

Moreover, you disclose your ignorance and folly when you conclude that because every good thing comes down from the Father of lights, those terrible acts of righteous vengeance at which the wicked fear and tremble do not proceed from the same glorious being. Still greater is your folly and stupidity when you ask me whether I consider depraved and perverse affections to be among the good and perfect gifts that come down from the Father of lights. O yes! You are a solemn proof that there is a wonderful difference between the Spirit of wisdom, judgment, and knowledge, and the spirit of slumber and delusion, although both are sent of God— the one in mercy, the other in judgment. Yes, there is a marvelous difference between the Spirit of regeneration, who creates the faithful anew in the image of God, and an evil spirit from God, who drives the reprobate into madness, as in the case of Saul.

With equal impudence you attack me when I teach that God executes his decrees by means of Satan and the reprobate to the manifestation of his own glory. That Satan is an instrument of his wrath, God plainly testifies both in his word and by universal experience. To what end do we say that God works by the hand of Satan, unless we mean that God works his own glory and its manifestation by means of Satan and his malice and doings? By this clever cavil respecting Satan, you think you have eluded the net of the divine matter. By all your iniquitous contendings against the truth, you cannot hinder God from working his own glory. No! No more than Pharaoh could, by his madness of pride, prevent God from showing forth the brightness of his glory, because God "for that very deed raised him up," that by Pharaoh he might manifest forth the glory of his "power" [Ex. 9:16; Rom. 9:17].

You would meet me by saying that Nebuchadnezzar gave glory to God when he confessed the justice of God in his terrible judgments [Dan. 4:25–37]. But that you might know in what contempt I hold all your pointless and ineffectual shafts, I will myself willingly aid you in your argument and will put into your mind what otherwise never would have entered there. For what end did Joshua call upon Achan to give glory to God? His object was to show that God would be glorified by the detection of Achan's profane theft and lie [Josh. 7:19].

But the essential question now is whether there is only one way in which God can show forth his glory. For if the glory of God did not continually shine forth out of the lies, as well as out of other wickednesses of men, Paul speaks in vain when he says that God alone is true, but all men are liars; he speaks equally in vain when he immediately adds, "But if our unrighteousness commend the

righteousness of God, what shall we say? Is God unrighteous?"
[Rom. 3:4, 5].

When you argue that God's will is that he should be praised by
all nations for the blessings he confers, what you assert is true, provided you grant also that there is a mighty forest of circumstances
out of which God, by his wonderful workings, secures praises and
glory to himself. By your ignorance of this, you bring on yourself
the just punishments of your pride, for professedly laughing at all
sound logic and legitimate reasoning, you perpetually argue nega-
tively from the *species* to the *genus*.

Nor will I deem your profane and blasphemous jest worthy of
any lengthened reply when you intimate that God might as well
punish men for wearing the beards that he himself has created.
Whoever asserted that iniquity was created of God, although it is
true that God, by his secret and incomprehensible purpose, ordains
and overrules the working of that iniquity to righteous, good, and
glorious ends? Away, therefore, with your stupid and insipid insolence when you ignorantly confound the beards of men, which grow
naturally and imperceptibly even while they are asleep, with their
acts of wickedness, which are voluntary, perceptible, and conscious.
Rage against me as rabidly as you will, this I nevertheless hold fast
and maintain: Although God does indeed decree and overrule the
depraved affections of men to the accomplishment of his own eternal purposes; nevertheless, he righteously punishes the depraved
agents and instruments themselves and makes them stand condemned in their own consciences.

Only observe how you again entangle yourself in a net of your
own creation when you pretend to confess that the secrets of God
are unknown to us, and yet would maintain that his justice, like the
justice of man, is clearly comprehensible by us. Suppose anyone
should ask you whether there is any justice contained in the secrets
of God. Would you deny that there is? Would you, then, pretend
or assert that the justice of God in his secret acts, which David and
Paul contemplate with wonder and adoration, is easily intelligible
and plainly known when it surpasses the utmost stretch of their

mental comprehension? Do not the profundity of the depth and the riches of the height of the wisdom of God in his marvelous judgments contain in them justice? Why, then, do you deny that God is just whenever the reason of his works surpasses your comprehension? There is in the Book of Job a divine and remarkable distinction made between the wisdom of God that is unsearchable and holds all human nature at an immeasurable distance by its brightness and that wisdom made manifest to us in his revealed and written law. In the same manner, if you did not thus confound all things, you ought to have made a distinction between the wonderful and profound justice of God that no human capacity can comprehend and the rule of justice that God has prescribed for the regulation of the lives of men in his revealed law. I at once confess that it is by the openly revealed doctrine of the gospel that God will assuredly judge the world. But he will as assuredly vindicate, at the same time, the righteousness of his secret providence against all profane brawlers.

Indeed, were you but acquainted, even in the least degree, with that gospel concerning which you thus vainly prate, you would easily understand how it is that God richly rewards the righteousness that he sets forth in his glorious law, not depriving of their promised crown those who from the heart obey his commandments, and yet righteously punishing all those who refuse their obedience. These latter, nevertheless, he calls his servants, because he holds their hearts in his hands for the accomplishment of his eternal purposes. Hence Nebuchadnezzar, that furious plunderer of nations and slave of Satan, is called by Jeremiah—and with peculiar significance—the "servant" of God [Jer. 25:9; Jer. 27:6].

If I have taught that God, as is manifest by his judgments on every side, inclines the hearts of men hither and thither for the execution of his purposes and decrees, when the prophets of God declare these same things in the same words, and when I cite their own words, why impute you such citations as awful crimes committed by me? Are not these the very words of the divine history? "And again the anger of the Lord was kindled against Israel, and he moved David against them to say, Go, number Israel and Judah" [2 Sam. 24:1].

ARTICLE 12
The wicked, by their acts of wickedness, do God's work rather
than their own.

Statements and Observations of the Calumniator

With reference to this twelfth article, Calvin, which is your doctrine, your opponents argue thus: If this really be the case, then God is often angry at that which is good. For if wickedness is the work of God, wickedness itself is good, for all the works of God are good. And again, if wickedness is good, it follows of necessity that godliness is evil, because it is the direct contrary to wickedness. Hence it will again follow that when the Holy Scriptures command us to hate evil and love that which is good, they command us to love wickedness and hate godliness. Your opponents, moreover, affirm that this article of your doctrine really savors of libertinism, and they consequently marvel that you should be so determined a foe to the libertines.

Reply of John Calvin

Before God, the angels, and the whole world, I again testify that what I did truly teach upon this subject, you, by the basest and most wicked calumny, have utterly perverted. If it really seems to you an absurdity to teach that the wicked do the work of God, enter the battle at once with Jeremiah, the prophet of God, whose words are these: "Cursed is he that doeth the work of the Lord deceitfully, and cursed be he that keepeth back his sword from blood" [Jer. 48:10].

By "the work of the Lord," the prophet evidently and undeniably means hostile slaughters and desolations, which you surely must call wickedness, seeing that they proceed from pure avarice, cruelty, and pride. The Chaldeans were urged on to make war upon Moab by their own ambition and thirst for plunder, so that regardless of all justice, they forced their way by rapine and slaughter to accomplish their inhuman purposes. But since it pleased God to punish, by their hands, the idolatry and defiance of the Moabites, their depravity did not alter the fact of their executing the judgments of God upon the Moabites by their wicked hands. What, then, does your barking and growling avail? What does your profane logic and argument avail that says "Wickedness is good," as if wickedness could be imputed to God because by his wonderful working he turns the wickednesses of men to an end and a purpose entirely different from those that the wicked themselves designed. Indeed, you would even class me with the libertines, the mad delusions of which sect I have labored to expose and confute beyond all other men, so that I need no new defense of myself on the present occasion.

ARTICLE 13
We sin of necessity, with respect to God, whether we sin of our own purpose or accidentally.

ARTICLE 14
Whatever wickednesses men commit of their own will, those wickednesses proceed also from the will of God.

Statements and Observations of the Calumniator

Against these two articles your opponents urge the following arguments: If we sin of necessity, all admonitions are evidently vain, and the prophet Jeremiah therefore speaks these words to the people in vain: "Thus saith the Lord, Behold, I set before you the way of life and the way of death. He that abideth in the city shall die by the sword and by the famine and by the pestilence, but he that goeth out and falleth to the Chaldeans that besiege you, he shall live, and his life shall be unto him for a prey" [Jer. 21:8, 9]. All this warning and admonition is utterly vain, I repeat, if, from the state and necessity of things, to flee unto the Chaldeans was as great an impossibility as to swallow a mountain.

If Calvin here reply that the commandments of God are set before men to render them inexcusable, we rejoin that this also is positively vain. For if any father should command his son to eat up a mountain and the son did it not, the son would be no more inexcusable after such commandment of his father than he was before. In just the same manner, if God should command me not to steal, and yet I must steal of necessity imposed on me by him; and if I can no more abstain from stealing, on account of that necessity, than I can eat up a mountain, I am no more inexcusable after such a commandment than I was before, nor am I more excusable before such commandment than I was afterwards. In a word, the opponents of Calvin argue that if this doctrine of his be really true, a man is inexcusable even before the commandment of God is set before him. From this it will follow that all commandment given with the intent to produce this inexcusableness in man is altogether needless and vain.

Moreover, if the wicked is reprobated of God before he becomes wicked—that is, before he is born, even from all eternity—and if, therefore, he sins of necessity, he is already inexcusable and condemned, even before any precept is given to him. And he is so condemned before he has done any evil act at all, whereas all laws—human and divine—condemn a man after the act and for the act.

Reply of John Calvin

What you really mean or propose to yourself in this thirteenth article I cannot possibly catch or comprehend. You seem to me like one endeavoring to spellbind the senses of men by a buzz of magic whispers. For what are "accidental sins"? Who besides yourself ever fabricated such unheard of creatures as these in the workshop of the human brain? Elsewhere in my writings I have ever taught that all those things which seem to happen accidentally are ruled and

overruled by the secret providence of God. Who gave you the license to gather from thence the idea of an "accidental sin"? And was
the doctrine that I have taught my own and of my own creation?
No! It has God himself for its author. If when a man is cutting the
boughs of a tree, the axe slips from his hand and falls upon the head
of one passing by, is this, do you think, an accident? Not so, thought
Moses, the servant of God. The Holy Spirit declares by him that
the man thus stricken was killed of God. And will you dare to say
that God hurls his weapons and deals his blows on this side and on
that as a man would do who was intoxicated or insane? If, as you
imagine, men sin without the purpose, understanding, or mind of
God, how shall God be judge of the world? And if the things that
are done in the world are done without God's purpose, understanding, mind, and will, in what way does God exceed mortal man?
In what is the adorable God higher and greater than man?

Hence when I affirm that God knows and has his mind concerned in every sin of man, are you driven thereby into such madness
and hatred of the doctrine as to pronounce me the maker of a false
god? Suppose I were to concede to you that men sinned without
God's knowledge and without his mind being at all concerned about
it. What God would be left in heaven or in earth at all by such a concession? Yet you imagine and boast yourself to be a great popular
teacher, whereas by thus depriving God of concerned mind in all
things that men do—whether sins or not—and by merely dignify-
ing him with the title of God, as Lucretius did his dreams, you make
the adorable God nothing more than a lifeless, unconcerned idol.

As to your arguments that if men sin of necessity, all doctrine
is superfluous, all precepts useless, all admonitions vain, and all rebukes and threats absurd—if Augustine's book to Valentinus, *Concerning Compulsion and Grace*, does not suffice to wash these frivolous
objections out of your brain (to the discussion of which subject Augustine was especially appointed of God), you are not worth the
hearing of one word further from me on this sacred matter. Moreover, I have so beaten off Pighius and your favorite master Servetus from their hold of this calumny that teachable and candid

readers require not another word of defense from me on this point of my testimony.

I will offer only this one brief word to your boasting calumnies directed against me on the momentous doctrine of truth now in question. If you will not permit God to command anything that is beyond the natural comprehension of men, when God shall bring you to stand before his tribunal, he will make you see with awful plainness what he has declared, and not in vain, by the mouth of his apostle: He has accomplished by his grace what was impossible by the law [Rom. 8:3]. It is plain and certain that in the law is set forth the perfect righteousness that God required in order that it might be ready at hand and plainly presented before the eyes of all men if men had but strength to do what God commands. But the apostle openly declares that to attain unto the righteousness commanded in the law is, on our part, impossible. What ground have you, then, for contending with and reviling Calvin respecting his doctrine on this divine point?

If you steal of necessity (according to your own argument), are you less excusable after the law has been given than you were before it was given? How widely different is the apostle Paul's opinion of himself where he confesses that he was "sold under sin" [Rom. 7:14], but at the same time he freely and loudly testifies that the law "worketh wrath" [Rom. 4:15]. He thereby shows that it is in vain to stretch forth in our defense the shield of necessity when every man's own conscience condemns him of voluntary and willful wickedness.

I would ask you just this question: A year ago when you had your own hook in your hand by which you might have pulled down firewood to warm your house, was it not your will that drove you to steal wood from your neighbor? If, then, this one act suffices for your righteous condemnation—that you willingly made a base and wicked gain to your neighbor's loss—whatever noise you may make about necessity, necessity did not acquit you on that occasion. And as to your additional noisy argument that no one can be justly condemned except on account of his crime and after his crime, concerning the former there exists no strife nor cause of strife (or none ought to exist) between me and you, because I everywhere teach that no one perishes except by the just judgment of God. But I cannot withhold my testimony that there lies concealed under your words a great depth of poison. For if your statement of the divine matter and your figure of speech are to be received, God will appear unjust who righteously includes the whole race of Abraham under the guilt of original sin.

You deny that it is lawful and right in God to condemn any mortal unless it be on account of sin committed. Numberless mortals are taken out of life while they are still perfect infants. You had better, then, commence your virulent war with God himself, who casts innocent babes, just taken from the wombs of their mothers, under the guilt of original sin and subjects them to his wrath and the just desert of eternal death. Who, I ask you, must not detest the blasphemy of thus contending against God when it is exposed to view, either by the voice or by pen of truth? Curse me as long as you will, but blaspheme not the adorable God, for as to myself, I can never expect to be free or exempt from the reproaches of those who spare not the ever blessed God.

With respect to the second part of your argument, that no one can justly be condemned until after his crime, just weigh in your own balance the lightness and emptiness of your loquacity in this. Your own masters—Pighius, Servetus, and all like barking unclean dogs—will at least confess that all those whom God foreknew to be worthy of eternal destruction were condemned by him before the foundation of the world; whereas you will not grant to God the right to condemn any to eternal death but those who have first been brought before earthly judges for their actually perpetrated crimes. From such arguments as these, readers may at once gather the marvelous extent of your insanity, since you hesitate not to root out, in absolute sport or jest, all solemn order of the divine justice.

Calumniator's False Description of Calvin's God

The false God is slow to mercy and swift to anger. He has created the greatest part of the world to perdition and has predestinated them not only to damnation, but also to the cause of their damnation, and he has therefore decreed from all eternity, and he wills and causes their sins. These sins are consequently of necessity so that neither thefts nor adulteries nor murders are committed except by God's will and instigation, for he suggests depraved and evil affections in men, not only permissively but effectively, and he hardens men's hearts. Therefore, while men are living wickedly, they are doing the work of God rather than their own work, and they cannot do otherwise. This God makes Satan a liar, so that Satan is not the cause of his own lies, but Calvin's God is.

Calumniator's False Conception of the True God

But the God that nature, reason, and the Holy Scriptures teach is plainly the contrary to this God of Calvin, for he is inclined to mercy and slow to anger. And he created the first man, from whom all men arose in his own image, so that he might place him in paradise and bestow upon him eternal life. This God wills that all men should be saved and that no man should perish. For this very end he sent his Son into the world, so that his righteousness might abound wherever the sin of man had abounded. The light of this righteousness "lighteth every man that cometh into the world" [John 1:9], and this Son of God, the Savior of the world, calls aloud to all: "Come unto me, all ye that labor and are heavy laden, and I will give you rest" [Matt. 11:28]. This God suggests good and honorable affections, and he delivers men from the necessity of sinning (into which they precipitate themselves by their disobedience); and he heals all manner of sickness and disease among the people. Indeed, so merciful is he that he never denies his mercy and help unto anyone who prays to him for them. In fact, this true God comes for the very purpose of destroying the works of that God of Calvin and thrusting him out-of-doors.

These two Gods, as they are by nature contrary to each other, beget children directly contrary to each other. The children of that false, merciless God are ever proud, unmerciful, envious, bloodthirsty, calumnious, feigned, carrying one thing on their countenance and another in their heart, impatient, rash, malicious, seditious, contentious, ambitious, avaricious, and lovers of pleasure more than lovers of God. In a word, they are filled with depraved and evil affections with which their God himself had inspired them. But the other God begets men merciful, modest, gentle, benevolent, beneficent, abhorring the shedding of blood, open, candid, speaking the truth out of the abundance of the heart, benign, quiet, peaceful, detesting broils and strifes, despising honors, liberal, lovers of God more than lovers of pleasure. In a word, they are full of all pure and honest affections with which they are inspired by their Father.

These are the views and arguments that your adversaries entertain concerning your doctrine, Calvin, and they advise all men to judge of your doctrine by its fruits. Moreover, they affirm that both you and your disciples bear abundant fruits of your God; that they are, for the most part, contentious, thirsty after revenge, ever tenacious and mindful of an injury received, and filled with numberless other vices that your God begets in them.

If anyone replies to these assertions of your adversaries and alleges that these are not faults caused by your doctrine, your opponents rejoin that your doctrine does evidently beget such men, and that such is the case is manifest from the fact that many, after they have embraced and followed your doctrine, become the kind of persons who before were far from being persons of that evil description; while those who have believed the doctrine of Christ have always been rendered better men, but they affirm that men ever become manifestly worse by your doctrine. They also assert that when you and your followers profess that you hold a sound doctrine, you are not to be believed.

The truth is that I once favored your doctrine and even defended it, although I really did not clearly understand it. For I thought so much of the weight of your authority that I considered the mere entertaining of one thought contrary to it was quite a crime. But now, having heard the arguments of your opponents, I have nothing to say in reply to their conclusions and proofs. Your disciples indeed do attempt a reply in your defense, and among those whom they can find to be favorers of your doctrine they boldly boast of having the truth on their side. But when they come to deal with your opponents, they vacillate and run to your books for protection. What they find there is too weak to support them, for your reasonings are so weak and, for the most part, so unsound that as soon as your book drops from their hands, your reasonings drop from their memories, and therefore they fail to convince your adversaries. However, the arguments of your opponents are manifest, powerful, and easily committed to memory; therefore, they are at once understood by the illiterate, of which description were most of those who followed Christ. Whence it results that the majority of your disciples depend more upon your authority than upon sound reason; and finding that they cannot vanquish their adversaries by argument, they hold them as heretics and bigots, shun their society, and warn all on every side to do the same. On the contrary, I who am always of the opinion that what is said, and not the person who speaks, ought to be the subject of consideration, judge that all men ought to be heard, all things that are said duly proved, and what is good ought to be received and retained.

Therefore, Calvin, if you have any arguments to produce that are true, plain, and sound, and by which your adversaries can be refuted, I ask you to bring them forth before us all and thus prove yourself, in reality, a defender of the truth. You know what is written: "I will give you a mouth and wisdom that none of your adversaries shall be able to gainsay or resist" [Luke 21:15]. As to myself, wherever I can find the truth, I am prepared to follow it and to exhort others to adopt the same course. If you have, perchance, erred (for we are all men), I entreat you, Calvin, give glory to God by a full confession. Your so doing will be more noble and will bring you more fame than the persevering in error. But be not, I pray you, angry with me on account of this my letter. If you are just and true, you have nothing to fear from it—first, because it is to your own advantage to be admonished by its arguments, and second, since you believe that all things are done of necessity, as you say, you must believe that this letter also was written by me of necessity.

Farewell!

Conclusion

It now only remains that I vindicate the glory of the true and eternal God from your profane maledictions and blasphemies.

You boastingly assert that I place the devil before men in place of the true God. My defense needs only to be brief and comprehensive, because all my writings openly testify that I never had before me any other end or purpose or prayer than that the whole world should dedicate itself to God with all fear, reverence, and holiness; also that all men should cultivate equity with a good conscience among and towards each other, and that my own life might not be inconsistent with my doctrine. I will not so disregard and dishonor the grace of God as to compare myself with you or your fellows, whose professed blamelessness of life consists in a mere fawning external appearance. I will only observe that if any unprejudiced and upright arbitrator should sit to judge between us, he would at once acknowledge that holy reverence of God was conspicuous both in my speech and in the actions of my life; and he would, with equal readiness, confess that whatever proceeded from you breathed fear and dread, which all the godly despise and laugh at.

But in order that I may examine as briefly as possible your base calumnies, who or what can be more profane than yourself when you contend that God proves himself to be slow to mercy and quick to anger in predestinating the greater part of the world to eternal death? One thing is certain: Whatever kind of God you might fabricate or imagine for yourself, that one adorable God—who for more than two thousand years left the whole human race, except the one family of Abraham, to wander in total darkness to the destruction of their souls—is to be worshiped and is worshiped by all the godly. If you are prepared to charge God with cruelty because he condescended to bless only one family of the earth with the light of life, while he willed that numberless nations should lie for the same two thousand years sunk in the darkness of their souls' death, one question will furnish a solemn reply to every inquiry into the deep mystery of how it was that whole nations were not utterly destroyed daily until no more peoples existed. How was it that the whole world was not destroyed, if such a thing were possible, a hundred times a year? How was it that during those same two thousand years, so many glorious proofs of God's patience and mercy towards men were manifested? Even Paul the apostle, after having asserted that the "vessels of wrath" were "fitted to destruction" by God's secret and eternal decree [Rom. 9:22], does not forget or hesitate to praise God's patience and longsuffering therein. If, then, the testimony of the apostle does not content you, I think that such a humble one as I may without hesitation despise all your growlings at my doctrine.

God, however, needs not my feeble defense. He is now, and in the last day will be, a mighty avenger of his own righteousness, even though all the foul tongues of the whole world should combine their efforts to becloud that righteousness with obscurity and confusion. Therefore, go on with your band of like spirits to hurl your blasphemies up to the very heavens. They shall all assuredly fall back on your own heads. As to your base revilings, I can bear them with patience and without trouble, provided they touch not the ever blessed God, whose servant I am. I challenge you to stand (where you must one day stand) before his tribunal, that he may show himself, as he one day will show himself, the righteous avenger of his own doctrine, which you thus furiously assail in my feeble person.

As to your description of the nature of the true God, let readers judge how appropriately you argue concerning his divine being from the absurd fact that you make the beginning of all true knowledge of him to proceed from common sense. That there is a God is a truth received by the one consent of all nations and all ages, because the seed and principle of this knowledge is imparted by nature in every human mind. But how shall reason define what God is, when by its own power of sight, it can do nothing but turn the truth into a lie and adulterate whatever of light and understanding true religion and faith possess. The Holy Spirit commands us to become fools, if we would be the true learners of heavenly doctrine, because the natural man himself can neither receive nor taste anything of divine wisdom. On the contrary, you would have human reason and common sense to form a judgment of the great and adorable God. And you would not only set up reason, which by its blindness ever extinguishes God's glory as a leader and guide, but you would also exalt that blind reason above Scripture itself. What marvel is it, then, if you should permit, without hesitation, religions of all kinds to be confounded together and should consider the Turk—who is enveloped in the deliriums of Mohammed and who adores as his deity no one knows what—as much a worshiper of God as he who calls upon the Father of Christ our redeemer, instructed by the sure word and faith of the everlasting gospel? Although you do not patronize infidels seriously is a fact proclaimed aloud by those sarcastic grins of yours, which show your teeth gnashing at every plainest and holiest article of our faith while the excuses that you make for the superstitions of all nations prove your malicious purpose to be to root out of the earth every doctrine of that holy religion that the sacred oracles of God reveal and teach.

Out of that very human reason that is the mother of all errors, you form that God of yours, who wills, without any election or predestination of his own, that all men should be saved. Has, then, the word *election*, which occurs so frequently in Scripture, no meaning whatever? Is it altogether a vain and empty term? Have the law, the prophets, and the gospel no meaning whatever when they everywhere proclaim aloud that all those who were chosen by the eternal counsel of God before the foundation of the world are called and illuminated unto salvation? We repeat, is the united and harmonious testimony of the law, the prophets, and the gospel an utter vanity when they pronounce, free from all ambiguity, that the source and cause of eternal life is the free love of God by which he has loved and embraced not all mankind, but those out of mankind whom he pleased?

What will you gain after all, I ask you, by thus roaring against this truth a hundred times over? You dazzle the sight of the ignorant and the inexperienced by setting before their eyes as a shining cloud your doctrine that God will have all men to be saved. But if these words of the apostle are not in perfect harmony with that election whereby God predestinated his own children unto eternal life, let me ask you this question: How is it that if God willed all men to be saved, he did not show unto all nations and all men the way of salvation? Universally and well known is that remarkable word of God in the law: "Behold, I set before thee this day the way of life and of death" [Deut. 30:19; Jer. 21:8]. If, therefore, God willed to gather together unto salvation all men without distinction, why did he not set before all men in common the way of life and of salvation? Instead, the fact is that he deemed only one family or nation worthy of this high privilege. Nor did he confer this great blessing upon that one family for any other reason than because he loved them (if the testimony of Moses is to be believed), and because he would "choose them for a peculiar people" [Deut. 14:2; Deut. 26:18]

You affirm that Christ was sent down from heaven in order that his righteousness might super-abound wherever sin had abounded [Rom. 5:20], but this one sentence of yours evidences that you have come forth, furnished by the devil out of the very bowels of hell itself, with this spirit and doctrine so that it might conceal every possible religious lie under the show of godliness and truth, and thus you might hold up Christ himself and his true religion to derision. For if wherever sin abounded, the righteousness of Christ was designed of God to super-abound, the condition of Pilate was just as good and as safe as that of Peter or of Paul. But to say nothing of Pilate, Paul declares that the righteousness of Christ and the faith of the gospel can never be separated. And what gospel, I ask you, was there in France and in other distant heathen nations at the time when Christ was upon earth? What? Was not God the same before the coming of his Son as he was when his Son did come, and as he now is and ever will be? Why, then, was it that he withheld the treasure of salvation from the nations of the earth except from the family of Abraham until the "fulness of the time was come" [Gal. 4:4]?

Therefore, swell yourself with rage to the utmost and burst into derision, if you will and must, at the apostle Paul himself, for he declares that "this mystery was made known by the preaching of the gospel, which was before hidden in God" [Eph. 3:9]. And now that the voice of the gospel has sounded forth, the righteousness of Christ comes unto none except those who receive it by faith. And whence comes this faith? If you reply, "By hearing," your answer is true. But remember that it comes not by hearing without the special revelation of the Holy Spirit. Isaiah himself expresses aloud his wonder at the small number of those to whom "the arm of the Lord is revealed" [Isa. 53:1]. And Paul uses the very words of the prophet Isaiah when he confines the gift of faith to the elect alone [Rom. 10:16]. And will you permit and admit no distinction to be made of God in the salvation of men? Christ does indeed say aloud, "Come unto me, all ye that are heavy laden" [Matt. 11:28]. But the same redeemer of men elsewhere also exclaims, "No one can come unto me except my Father which hath sent me draw him" [John 6:44]. Nor is there any want of harmony or oneness of truth when the same Savior who invites all men without exception unto him by his external voice also declares, "A man can receive nothing, except it were given him from above," and "No one can come unto me but those to whom it is given of the Father" [John 3:27; John 6:65].

There is also another Scripture that you smear and defile by your swine-like pollution when you say, "The light of the righteousness of Christ lighteth every man that cometh into the world" [John 1:9]. But had not John, I ask you, just before said "The light shineth in darkness, but the darkness comprehendeth it not" [v. 5]? By these words John signifies that whatever of human reason or understanding had been given to men at the beginning was all stifled and extinguished by sin, and that no other remedy now remains than the enlightening of the blind eyes by the Spirit of Christ. It is indeed quite true that Christ never refused his grace to anyone who asked for it. But you forget all the while that all true prayers and entreaties are dictated and directed by the Spirit of God. You are equally ignorant that faith, which is the fruit and consequence of free election, is the key that opens the ears of God and unlocks the door of the kingdom of heaven. As you are thus evidently ignorant of these first principles of the doctrines of Christ (which if you take away, you bring down the gospel of Christ at once to a level with the dark heathen mysteries of Proserpine or of Bacchus), it is really a marvel that persons ensnared by such enormous errors and delusions should ever find their way at all into the company of Christian men.

As to your foul assertion that my disciples are made of my God like unto myself—cruel, envious, proud, slanderers, carrying one thing on their tongue and another in their heart—I will come forward and refute your impudent reviling. I am prepared to do so, not so much by words as by facts. For as I have no inclination to revile in return, let all your base calumnies, as far as I am concerned, remain dead and buried by my hands, except that I assume the permission (as in sacred duty bound) to make one solemn declaration, calling God to witness, that during the time I fed you at my house, I never saw a man more proud, more perfidious, or more devoid of human kindness. And I am sure that those who do not confess that you are an impostor, a fellow of impudent audacity, a religious buffoon, professedly set to brawl down all godliness—those, I say, who do not confess these to be your real principles have no right judgment of your character. For what particular act of mine you accuse me of cruelty I am anxious to know. I myself know not that act, unless it be with reference to the death of your great master Servetus. But that I myself earnestly entreated that he might not be put to death, his judges themselves are witnesses, in the number of whom at that time were two of his staunch favorers and defenders. But I have said quite enough about myself.

I leave to the consideration and reflection of all men what are the real fruits produced by my doctrine, both in this city and far

and wide throughout many nations. Out of this very school that
you so atrociously attack and unceasingly rend in pieces, God daily
chooses to himself men of the highest principles and of the sweetest fragrance of his truth to illustrate the doctrine of his gospel and
to be the victims of malice and cruelty. All those who really grow
and make any advancement in the doctrine of the gospel (of the
number of whom neither the world nor the church needs to repent
or be ashamed) live a life supported by the slenderest means, with
difficulty indeed but with the greatest patience and with the greatest kindness towards all men; or else, bidding a spontaneous farewell to luxury of every kind, they give themselves up to frugality
peacefully and freely; they all, as one man, resigning the world and
self-enjoyment, aspire to the hope of a blessed immortality. Being
averse to glorying in myself or boasting of myself, I have called to
witness these bright examples of his grace, which God thus sets before the world to prove the truth of and to defend the doctrine that
you vainly endeavor to rend asunder by your foul revilings.

But do tell me what you were at the time that you favored my
doctrine. What was your state of mind at that time? You affirm that
you could never clearly understand it because the weight of my authority stood in your way, inducing you to consider it a perfect
crime to entertain any judgment whatever in the least contrary to
mine. This is a marvelous matter! You must have been a brainless
fellow indeed if you could not comprehend, after so many years'
trial, what I had taught you in the most familiar manner in my own
house and had so often expounded in your hearing in the public
congregation. There are, however, many credible witnesses to the
fact that although I labored long, but in vain, to correct and heal by
every possible means the depravity of your nature, yet during the
time you did profess to be one of my followers, you were restrained
by a somewhat effectual bridle from your evil ways. The real cause
of your alienation from me evidently appears to be a longing desire
to throw off the rein, so that you might break forth with unbridled
license into this your present impious course, which is your true delight and boast.

You affirm that it is a principle with you to regard not *who* it is that speaks, but *what* is spoken. I wish this had been a real principle with you long ago, so that you might have profited by the labors of others and thus accustomed yourself to a teachable spirit. Now, however, since audacity and loquacity are your only powers, all the favor you can procure to yourself from the evil-minded is gotten from your base despising of others. I would arrogate nothing to myself. But I really seem to myself to have so far deserved well of the church that if a place among the faithful servants of God be given to me by her, no man has a right to labor to bring my authority into contempt. Had you asserted that a few unlearned men looked to my nod or hung upon my judgment or were influenced by my fame and authority, you might have had some color of covering for your calumny. But now, since you magnify it into a notorious disgrace to me that my doctrine does not satisfy or please illiterate men, whom do you think will believe you if you assert that learned and talented men alone have a taste for my books and that they derive their wisdom from them—indeed, that they are so overawed by my authority as not to attempt any judgment of their own? If things be so, we shall prove upon your own authority that nothing can be judged to be true or right but that which seems to the ignorant multitude to be plausible.

Yes, you would drive away all men from the liberal and useful arts and sciences and would boast among your fellows that all study and learning are useless and all the time spent in vain that is devoted to philosophy, to grammar, to logic, and even to divinity itself. You would thus cry down all useful learning for the very reason that you might procure to yourself ignorant disciples and make yourself great among them. And you say that those who followed Christ were such, just as if the Christian faith were a matter standing contrary to and inconsistent with learning. But let Christian readers mark the difference between you and me. I ever affirm that the wisest among men, until they become fools and bid farewell to all their own wisdom, giving themselves up humbly and meekly to the obedience of Christ, are blinded by their own pride and remain utterly unable to taste one drop of heavenly doctrine; for all human reason is tasteless in the mysteries of God, and all human perspicacity is blind. I maintain, therefore, that the beginning and essence of all divine wisdom is humility. This strips us of all the wisdom of the flesh and prepares us to enter upon the mysteries of God with reverence and faith. You, on the contrary, bid ignorant and untaught men to come forth publicly—men who, despising all learning and inflated with pride alone, rashly attempt to pass their judgment on divine things. Nor will you acknowledge any to be legitimate judges in divine matters except those who, content with the opinion of reason and common sense, unceremoniously reject all that does not just suit their own mind and taste.

Respecting the other reproach with which you load my humble followers—that of being heretics—the testimony of the apostle Paul quite satisfies them on that point, upon whose authority they would rather turn away from such real heretics as yourself and your followers than knowingly pollute their ears by listening to their blasphemies. You maintain, however, that such is not your principle of action. You hold that all men ought to be heard. Do you think, then, that the apostle says in vain, "A man that is an heretic, after the first and second admonition, reject" [Titus 3:10]? If anyone had denied to you the right of being heard, you would have had some cause for complaint. But when there was always granted you the liberty of prating as you liked in the public assembly of the people; indeed, when after having been called and almost dragged there, you have often sat down vanquished with nothing to say! What greater liberty of speech would you have if the ears of the godly are ever open to you until they are satiated and nauseated to disgust at your blasphemies against the adorable God? As to yourself, you can find gratification and delight in holding up all the first great principles of godliness to derision. But would you therefore have all the children of God be such fools as to laugh at your audacious impudence or to endure your profane reproaches without a word or an emotion?

With regard to the sacred cause in question, I feel confident that

I have hereby given you a sufficient answer. All readers of a sound mind can easily perceive that I am not altogether destitute of that blessed Spirit who gives a mouth and wisdom, which if you are still determined to resist, you can do nothing more than sustain a disgrace and a confusion corresponding with your obstinacy. Nevertheless, I will not cease to wish and to pray that you may yet bow to the manifest truth of God, though such a thing I scarcely dare to hope.

One final word upon your remaining, profane jeer: I have no ground for being angry at your reproaches because, according to my own doctrine, they were written of necessity. I am here furnished by the Scriptures with a solemn and effectual exhortation to forbearance. Nothing can be more instructive and appropriate in my case, nor better adapted to appease my indignation, than this admonition of David: "Let him curse, for God hath bidden him" [2 Sam. 16:11]. David knew that Shimei on that occasion was driven on by the same rage of cursing as that with which you boil now. But those curses that Shimei thought he was hurling at David under the fortuitous occurrence (to him) of the then present circumstances, David knew by reflection to be directed by the overruling and secret providence of God, and therefore he restrained himself by the utterance of these memorable words. Surely no man will ever bear the assaults of the devil and of wicked men with a composure and moderation but the man who can turn away his mind and thoughts from those assaults to God alone, who ordained them and can say, using the words of God himself, "The Lord rebuke thee, Satan" [Zech. 3:2].

Amen.

INDEX OF
SCRIPTURE REFERENCES